Special educational needs in the primary school

A practical guide

THIRD EDITION

Jean Gross

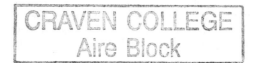
Open University Press
Buckingham • Philadelphia

Open University Press
Celtic Court
22 Ballmoor
Buckingham
MK18 1XW

email: enquiries@openup.co.uk
world wide web: www.openup.co.uk

and
325 Chestnut Street
Philadelphia, PA 19106, USA

First edition published 1993
Reprinted 1995

Second edition published 1996
Reprinted 1998, 2000

First published in this third edition 2002

A catalogue record of this book is available from the British Library

ISBN   0 335 21217 4 (pb)

Library of Congress Cataloging-in-Publication Data
Gross, Jean.
   Special educational needs in the primary school:a practical guide / Jean Gross.
– 3rd ed.
      p. cm.
   Includes bibliographical references (p.) and index.
   ISBN 0-335-21217-4 (pbk.)
   1. Special education – Great Britain.   2. Special education – Great
Britain – Curricula.   3. Education, Elementary – Great Britain.   4. Classroom
management – Great Britain.   I. Title.

LC3986.G7 G76   2002
371.9′0472′0941–dc21   2001054509

Typeset by Graphicraft Limited, Hong Kong
Printed in Great Britain by Biddles Limited, Guildford and King's Lynn

Special educational needs in the primary school

THIRD EDITION

Contents

Acknowledgements

I am grateful to colleagues in support services in Bristol and Bath and North-East Somerset local education authorities, and to the teachers, parents and children there with whom I have been privileged to work, for the many ideas and examples of good practice which they have contributed to this volume. In particular, thanks go to Tonia Palmer for her help in updating the maths chapter, Jack Humphreys for his behaviour plan format, Graham Davies for his schematic conceptualization of levels of support for pupils, and to the Bath area speech and language therapists for permission to use an extract from their guide for teachers.

The author and publishers are grateful to Thomas Nelson & Sons for permission to quote from Westmacott and Cameron's *Behaviour Can Change* (1981).

1

Current perspectives on special educational needs

Introduction

Teachers have always taught children with a wide range of abilities and achievements. From time to time, a statistic will surface which highlights the extent of this range – for example, the Cockcroft Report's (Cockcroft 1982) estimate of a seven-year range in maths attainment in an average class of 11-year-olds. At one time, those at the bottom of this wide range were called 'educationally subnormal', 'retarded' or 'backward', and placed at the margins of the class teacher's responsibility by their perceived inbuilt blocks and barriers to learning. Later, they became children with 'special educational needs' (SEN), whose learning difficulties were perceived to be less inbuilt and more a product of the context in which they were educated. Meeting their needs was seen as an integral part of all teachers' responsibilities; they were promised a brave new future of support in integrated classrooms, only to slip back to threatened marginalization again in more recent times, in a climate where children can all too easily be considered cheap or costly according to the amount of support they require, the probability that they will help the school to meet its rigorous targets, and the gloss they add (or fail to add) to the school's image.

There are however, many steps that can be taken to reduce the risk of marginalization of vulnerable children. The first is to foster confidence, in all teachers, that they themselves can take effective steps to manage the whole range of abilities and needs within their classes. We must never forget how easily work with children who don't learn or behave well can sap adult confidence: their difficulty in learning makes teachers feel like failures too, and try to allay those uncomfortable feelings by perceiving the child's problems as intractable, intrinsic and best dealt with by someone else with appropriate expertise. Teachers who feel confident that they have enough expertise of their own to make plans that will move the child on in learning, even in very small steps, don't need to pass the buck or suggest they should be elsewhere. Fostering that personal and professional confidence is vital to ensuring a welcome for all children in all classrooms.

The second element in reducing the risk of marginalization is a collective will among school staff, born out of collaborative school development work on inclusion, that their school will be a school for all, and that the things that make for good practice – and popularity with the school's prospective parent clientele – are the same right across the ability range.

In this book we will look at how such a collective will can be achieved, and seek to give straightforward, practical information that will enable all primary teachers to feel confident in planning within-school supportive action for pupils who, for whatever reason, are not learning as well as they might. To begin with, we will focus on terminology, and the ways in which the words used to describe the hard-to-teach encapsulate our concepts about learning. We will also look at the current legislative and administrative framework which defines the respective roles of teachers, parents, schools and local authorities in meeting special needs, and which provides the backdrop against which the individual struggle of each teacher to get the best for each child in the class must be set.

Who has special needs?

Most primary teachers find it easy to jot down the names of children they teach whom they consider to have SEN. The term 'special needs' has an implicit meaning for most of us, but that meaning is hard to put into words and even harder to agree on. The legislation that introduced the term, the 1981 and 1996 Education Acts (DES 1981; DfEE 1996) is of little help, providing only that a child has special needs if 'he has a learning difficulty which calls for special educational provision to be made for him', and adding that a child has a learning difficulty if they have 'a significantly greater difficulty in learning than the majority of children the same age', or 'a disability which either prevents or hinders him from making use of educational facilities of a kind generally provided for children of the same age in schools within the area of the local education authority'. Disabled children are in turn defined as those who 'have a physical or mental impairment which has a substantial and long term adverse effect on the ability to carry out normal day to day activities' (DfES 2001a).

Since the way that attainments are distributed means that roughly half of any group of children will have significantly greater difficulty than the other half in learning any new concept or skill, and since the facilities generally available in schools vary enormously from one area to another, it can be seen that the legal definition could embrace anything from a tiny handful to huge numbers of children. Numbers in fact identified have steadily risen over time: Croll and Moses (2000) report a 40 per cent increase between 1981 and 1998, with over a quarter of children in mainstream Key Stage 2 classes now identified by their schools as having SEN – most of them with learning difficulties. Between 1997 and 2001 alone, there has been a 22 per cent increase in the number of children on primary schools' SEN registers (DfEE 2001).

The term SEN has increasingly become synonymous with judgements about pupils' abilities – or lack of them. Teachers have come to talk of 'my special needs children', or 'my special needs group'. In the same way, and in the same tones, with which they once spoke of 'my remedials' or 'my slow learners'. As originally envisaged, special needs were something a child might have in certain circumstances, with certain learning tasks. The concept was fluid, implying that any child might experience difficulties at some point, rather than that such difficulties were owned by a fixed group who were in some way different from the majority. Current usage, however, has subtly shifted from the notion of special needs as something we may have from time to time towards the notion that they are something some children *are* – forever and a day.

The difference is subtle, but important to grasp. It can best be understood in relation to our own 'special needs' as teachers. All of us find it fairly easy to acknowledge that these exist: that we have teaching skills that are under-developed, areas of the curriculum where we lack confidence. Most would welcome some support in these areas – opportunities to work alongside someone with good practice to share, the chance to spend some extra time catching up on new developments and practices. How many, however, would welcome the headteacher calling us 'one of my special needs teachers'? We may find it helpful to have our learning needs identified, but we do not find permanent labels, attached to ourselves as people rather than to our performance in certain contexts, either helpful or acceptable. Children cannot be expected to feel differently.

Nevertheless, the tendency to label children rather than needs persists, and because of this many writers in the special needs field would prefer to do away with the special needs terminology altogether. Jonathan Solity (1991), for example, argues that the term actively encourages discriminatory practices, such as seating children separately, withdrawing them from the mainstream classroom and giving them work that is obviously different from that of others in the class. A focus on special provision for one in five children with special needs, he feels, distracts our attention from the fact that teachers are not always very good at individualizing instruction for a much larger group. He quotes research by Neville Bennett and his colleagues (1984) (research we will return to in Chapter 3) which showed that 60 per cent of Year 2 children and 70 per cent of Year 3 children in a range of classrooms were observed to be working on tasks that were either much too easy or much too hard for them. Given these figures, Solity sees the task for teachers as meeting *all* children's individual needs not the special needs of a few.

A similar argument derives from the research on school effectiveness, which has in many cases shown that schools tend to be effective or ineffective for all their pupils, irrespective of factors such as social disadvantage which are associated with the incidence of SEN (Slavin 1996). If this is so, and what is good for some pupils is good for all, it again becomes less important to identify a special group requiring a different kind of teaching, and more important to identify the features of high quality education that will mean better achievement for all. From this perspective, pupils who are failing to learn can be seen 'as indicators of the need for reform. They point to the need to improve schooling in a way that will enable them to achieve success' (Ainscow 1991: 3). Instead of offering extra help and support to identified individuals, the focus will be on work with teachers to increase the range of strategies they are able to use effectively in the classroom. Such school improvement programmes can produce dramatic results: for example, a recent

British study (Solity *et al.* 2000) has shown that by introducing a research-based methodology for teaching reading to Reception and Year 1 classes, it was possible to reduce the number of children falling into a defined low achieving band from 65 per cent to 2 per cent. In one American school (Joyce *et al.* 1991) a whole-school improvement programme succeeded in reducing the proportion of students who failed their end of grade assessment from 70 per cent to 6 per cent in two years. Outcomes like this fundamentally challenge the whole concept of SEN – at least as applied to pupils. It is clearly impossible to describe the 70 per cent who previously failed as having special needs: the special needs lay with the school and its staff rather than the children. If this is so in an extreme case like this one, it is likely to apply in other less extreme situations. Hence the view that we should dispense altogether with the special needs terminology.

The main drawback of the term 'special needs' remains that it still, however well intentioned we are in using it, implies that there is necessarily something *intrinsic* about a child's learning difficulty. It reinforces an out of date 'medical' model of disability, rather than the social model which is at the heart of most recent educational thinking in this area (see Figure 1.1). It implies that the special needs characterize the learner rather than the learning situation. This too is an idea so easily challenged that the special needs concept can seem ludicrous: would a child who uses a wheelchair have special needs if the local school had a few ramps rather than steps, or will children with dyslexia have special needs when technology that can translate speech to print and vice versa becomes universally available? Whether something presents a difficulty or not depends entirely on whether the situation or the environment are enabling or disabling. Yet by describing children as 'special needs' we can absolve ourselves from the responsibility to enable, and reinforce the notions of purely within-child or within-family explanations of learning difficulty. It may have been shown that school factors can be much more influential than home background factors on the amount of progress made by pupils (four times more important for reading and ten times more important for maths and writing), but teachers still find it very hard to get away from the idea that learning problems reside primarily in children's individual characteristics and those of their families.

The reasons for this are not hard to find. Again, it comes back to teacher confidence. If teachers do not feel confident and supported by colleagues and resources in planning for children who are not learning, it is entirely natural for them to seek relief from inner discomfort by attributing the failure to learn to factors that are outside their control. What is happening is this:

> Teachers see themselves as significant, or not, in the school and classroom according to whether they are faced with acceptable/satisfactory pupil reactions to school and academic work, or problematic/troublesome ones. That is, when pupils behave and achieve well, teachers tend to see themselves as important influences. When the opposite occurs, teachers see themselves as not influential. In the latter situation, pupil reactions are construed in terms of pupil 'pathologies' or of social determinants beyond the control of the teacher.
>
> (Phillips 1989)

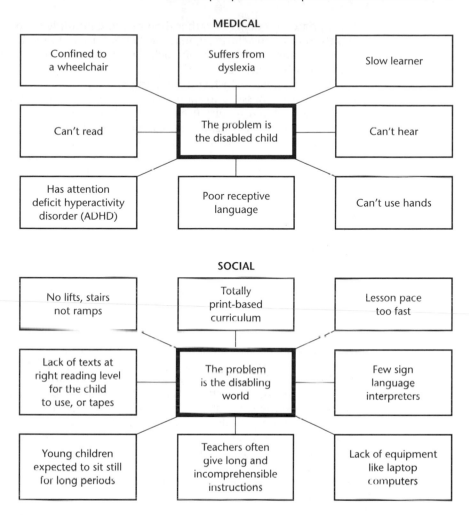

MEDICAL

Confined to a wheelchair	Suffers from dyslexia	Slow learner
Can't read	**The problem is the disabled child**	Can't hear
Has attention deficit hyperactivity disorder (ADHD)	Poor receptive language	Can't use hands

SOCIAL

No lifts, stairs not ramps	Totally print-based curriculum	Lesson pace too fast
Lack of texts at right reading level for the child to use, or tapes	**The problem is the disabling world**	Few sign language interpreters
Young children expected to sit still for long periods	Teachers often give long and incomprehensible instructions	Lack of equipment like laptop computers

Figure 1.1   The medical and social models of disability.

Given all these arguments against the term 'special needs', with all its risks of labelling and its implied focus on 'pupil pathology', some would maintain that a book like this one, with a title concerned with meeting special needs in the primary classroom, should not be written at all. Instead, we should be writing only about meeting individual needs and making schools more effective.

This too has risks, however. Raising every child's achievement will still leave the gaps between high and low achievers that are vastly hurtful to individual children and their parents. Sharing expertise in meeting special needs may be a better way of promoting the truly inclusive classroom than denying that such expertise exists at all. Asking teachers to focus on individualizing programme planning and instruction for all 20 to 30 (or more) children in their class may be asking more than is humanly possible. Since the majority will be able to learn incidentally – that is, from brief, loosely focused exposure to appropriate experiences – rather than needing multiple exposures and direct, tightly focused teaching, it may be better to use limited time in making detailed plans for this kind of teaching for three or four children in a class rather than for them all.

Further arguments in favour of using special needs terminology could be found if it were possible to show that there are some special sorts of teaching that some children require from time to time while others do not. This is a tricky and disputed issue, but on balance the evidence from research is that there are such special requirements – though not nearly so many of them as were once thought (Lewis and Norwich 2000). All children require some things once seen as the particular province of special education – for example, systematic procedures for monitoring progress, parental involvement in their learning, differentiated tasks and the 'climate of warmth and support in which they feel valued and able to risk making mistakes as they learn, without fear of criticism' (NCC 1989). Nevertheless, it is possible to identify some special approaches which some children require more than others. These include:

- The provision of special means of access to the curriculum – for example, the use of a specialist communication system such as Braille or sign language.
- The use of bypass strategies to ensure that difficulties in one area of the curriculum do not hold a child back in other areas – for example, oral presentation of material for a pupil with reading difficulties.
- More explicit teaching of learning strategies – learning *how* to learn.
- A bias towards somewhat more structured teaching methods, especially in specifying the small steps within the broad ladder of learning objectives outlined for all children in the National Curriculum.
- Providing more examples to help pupils learn concepts, and making explicit links between one piece of learning and its generalization to other settings.
- More practice to achieve mastery, rather than the teacher moving on prematurely.
- A focus on increasing the time the child spends 'on task', which research has shown to be particularly low in children with learning or behavioural difficulties, and which correlates highly with academic success.
- A focus on increasing the child's self-confidence and self-esteem, which again features prominently in research on the characteristics of children who are not learning or behaving well, and which teachers are uniquely able to influence as a route to enhancing achievement.

These, then, are the arguments for continuing to think in terms of some children's special needs, rather than simply all children's individual needs. How can the debate be resolved? The answer is probably to continue to identify situations where some children will have special requirements, but to locate the special needs in ourselves as teachers, and in schools as organizations, more readily than we locate them in children. Seen this way, children with special needs are, as Solity (1991) describes them, children that teachers experience difficulty in teaching. This is the best meaning for the term 'special educational need', and the one that is implied throughout this book.

Roles and responsibilities: the legislative framework

Chris is 10. His speech is not always clear, because of articulation difficulties; he uses short, sometimes ungrammatical sentences and finds it hard to process and remember classroom instructions. His reading and written work are poor (he is working towards Level 2 in these areas of the National Curriculum), but with support in writing things down he can do as well as most others his age in science and technology. He has infrequent speech therapy at a local clinic: his speech therapist is keen to devise a programme of language work for Chris to do in school. A special support teacher visits once a week to help Chris with his reading. The class teacher is relieved that he is having extra help from a specialist outside the school, so that she can concentrate on the needs of others in the class. She wonders, though, how Chris will manage in the forthcoming Standard Assessment Tasks (SATs). The headteacher feels concern about whether a child with such a low level of literacy skill should be expected to undertake SATs at all, and would like Chris to be disapplied from the tasks and tests if possible.

Up to the end of the last financial year, Chris also had help from the school's own special needs support teacher, who worked with him for a short period each day, in class, on reading and written work. Now this has become more difficult to arrange, as the school has had to reduce the hours attached to her post. Some parents have complained to the school governors about this, but the governors feel it is not their responsibility and that they have done all they can within the locally managed budget.

Chris is making very slow progress. The educational psychologist is consulted, and at a meeting involving Chris's parents and teachers it is agreed that his needs should be assessed to determine whether the local education authority (LEA) should provide for him through a Statement of SEN. The subsequent multiprofessional assessment makes clear Chris's needs for increased access to specialist language programmes, intensive literacy support and equipment such as a hand-held tape recorder and electronic spellchecker. The LEA, however, is overwhelmed with requests for extra support and technology for children in mainstream schools, which they must meet from the limited funds left over from an educational budget mostly delegated to locally managed schools. They do not employ their own speech therapists, nor is there a language unit available in the area. In their view, Chris's needs should be met locally from the school's own resources.

Where should the responsibility for providing extra resources for Chris lie? And equally, who should be responsible for managing the provision made for him, and monitoring its effectiveness? To find their way through in situations like this, all concerned need a very clear picture of their respective responsibilities. Schools need to know what can legitimately be expected from them, and where the boundaries of their role should lie.

The role of the class teacher

The class teacher's role in relation to special needs is spelled out in the Department for Education and Science (DfES) SEN *Code of Practice* (DfES 2001b). All teachers should be involved in the development of the school's SEN policy and be fully aware of the school's procedures for identifying, assessing and making provision for pupils with SEN. In the classroom, the teacher should make proper provision for curriculum differentiation, following the principles of the National Curriculum inclusion statement, so as to:

- set suitable learning challenges;
- respond to pupils' diverse needs;
- overcome potential barriers to learning and assessment.

The teacher is responsible for contributing to the early identification of children who may have SEN, monitoring performance through ongoing classroom observation and assessment. If this observation of the progress of individual children leads the teacher, in discussion with the parents, to feel that the strategies they are currently using are not resulting in the child learning effectively, they will need to consult the special needs coordinator (SENCO) to review the strategies, and the ways in which they might be developed. The review could lead to the conclusion that the child needs help over and above that which is normally available in the class. Consideration should then be given to helping the child through 'School Action'.

Together the class teacher and the SENCO should collect all the available information about the child and seek additional information from parents. While the SENCO takes the lead in further assessment of the child's strengths and weaknesses, planning support and monitoring/reviewing the action taken, the class teacher remains responsible for working with the child on a daily basis, and for planning and delivering an individualized programme. Either the teacher or the SENCO should record planned strategies to support the child on an Individual Education Plan (IEP), along with three or four targets for the child's progress. The IEP should be reviewed at least twice a year, in consultation with parents and the child. Strategies on the IEP may include different learning materials or specialist equipment, extra adult support either directly or in a planning/staff training role or, if progress remains slow and the child moves on to 'School Action Plus', extra support or advice from an outside agency. The class teacher's role, however, does not cease when outside agencies become involved, as it seems to have done with Chris; the teacher, as the person in most regular contact with the child in school, retains a pivotal role in implementing and evaluating support strategies.

The role of the SENCO

The SENCO, according to the SEN *Code of Practice*, helps to determine the strategic development of the SEN policy and of provision in school, in collaboration with the headteacher and governing body. They also have day-to-day responsibility for the operation of the policy and the coordination of provision. This may involve providing advice and training to colleagues, monitoring the quality of teaching and outcomes for pupils and setting targets for improvement. The SENCO will oversee all the records on children with SEN and may manage a team of learning support assistants (LSAs). Liaison with parents and with external agencies (health, social services, LEA SEN and educational psychology services) is another important part of the role.

The nature of the SENCO role, and the skills and knowledge needed to carry it out effectively, are further described in the *National Standards* for SENCOs, produced by the Teacher Training Agency (TTA 1999). The standards group the SENCO's responsibilities into four broad areas:

- Strategic direction – for example, ensuring that SEN is reflected in the school development plan, and analysing data so as to inform practice.
- Teaching and learning – disseminating the most effective teaching approaches for children with SEN, monitoring what is happening in classrooms for these children, collecting and interpreting assessment data on children so as to inform planning, developing ways of monitoring and recording children's progress, making sure that there is good liaison when children transfer to other schools, liaising with outside agencies and with parents.
- Leading and managing staff – for example, coordinating professional development opportunities for staff.
- Deploying resources – advising on priorities for expenditure, deploying staff and organizing resources.

The role is a broad one, involving large amounts of administration and work related to individual pupils, in addition to the work on developing practice across the school which has emerged as a key focus in recent guidance. Because of this, it is a role that is difficult to fulfil, especially in a context where most primary SENCOs are also class teachers with limited non-contact time. In the right conditions, however, the SENCO will be able to be the person who is central in pulling together provision for children like Chris, linking the systems that exist outside the school with what happens to support him in the classroom.

The role of the school governors

School governors are required under the 1996 Education Act to:

- Do their best to ensure that the necessary provision is made for any pupil who has SEN.
- Make sure that the needs of such children are made known to those that teach them.
- Make sure that parents are always told about a decision by the school that their child has SEN.
- Make sure that all the teachers in the school are aware of the importance of identifying and providing for children with SEN.
- Make sure that children with SEN can join in with other children in school activities.
- Determine the school policy for SEN (in conjunction with the headteacher and the school as a whole).

- Publicize the policy, and report annually to parents on its implementation and effectiveness.
- Report annually to parents on details of steps taken to prevent pupils with disabilities from being treated less favourably than other pupils, on facilities provided to assist access to the school by pupils with disabilities and on arrangements for the admission of pupils with disabilities.
- Prepare and review regularly a plan for improving access for disabled pupils to the school's premises and to its curriculum, and a plan for the provision of information (for example, written information) in a range of accessible formats for disabled pupils. This accessibility plan should be included in the annual governors' report to parents.

The *Code of Practice* also indicates that governors should, in conjunction with the headteacher, establish appropriate staffing and funding arrangements for SEN. Governors are encouraged to appoint a governor or a sub-committee to have specific oversight of the school's arrangements and provision for meeting SEN. Finally, in setting performance objectives for the headteacher, governors must include SEN – for example, as a leadership and management issue, and in relation to pupil outcomes.

The role of the school as a whole

Through their SEN policy, schools are required to publish information for parents on the allocation of resources to and among pupils with SEN. They must identify and name a teacher or teachers responsible for supporting these children (the SENCO or SENCO team), and for advising and supporting colleagues.

They must be open and responsive to expressions of concern by parents, and take account of any information that parents provide about their child. They should be alert to any particular patterns in the school's identification and recording of children's SEN or parents' expressions of concern, and should examine the school's general practices and policies in the light of such patterns. They should not, according to the *Code of Practice*, assume that learning difficulties always result solely, or even mainly, from problems within the child.

As well as ensuring parental involvement in all aspects of planning for their children, schools must make sure that pupils themselves are very actively involved in assessment and decision making.

Schools should adopt a graduated response to SEN which ensures early identification and, where necessary, brings increasing specialist expertise to bear on the difficulties the child is experiencing. They must without fail inform parents where they are making special educational provision for their child. There should be full records of the actions taken and of the outcomes. For children with SEN, the regular school pupil record or profile should include information about the child's progress over time, an overall picture of their strengths and weaknesses, and relevant information from those who are involved with the child – for example, health or social services. The record or profile should include the child's own perception of their difficulties, and how these might be addressed. As well as these regular records, pupils on School Action, School Action Plus or who are Statemented will have IEPs setting short-term targets and outlining the strategies which will be used in providing support.

Schools will need to provide evidence of their planning for a graduated response to a child's needs in school, evidence of regular reviews involving parents, and evidence of the involvement of outside agencies before asking for additional support from the LEA through a Statement of SEN.

Schools are responsible for coordinating and recording the work that has to be done before any part of the National Curriculum (programmes of study and assessment arrangements) can be temporarily modified or disapplied for any pupil who has special needs but no Statement. This can only be done where children are being assessed for a Statement or are likely to be assessed, or if the child has temporary needs (such as temporary severe emotional problems) which make it inappropriate to continue offering the National Curriculum. Generally, however, the need for any such formal procedures is expected to be small, given the provisions for children to work on National Curriculum programmes of study outside their Key Stage. Additional flexibility is provided by the special arrangements for assessment at the end of Key Stage tasks and tests.

Schools are obliged to contribute their professional written advice to the LEA when a pupil is assessed for a possible Statement. If a Statement is issued, they must prepare reports for the annual review of the Statement and co-ordinate the annual review meeting to which parents and relevant agencies must be invited.

Schools must not discriminate against disabled children. For example, in their admission arrangements, by failing to take reasonable steps to include them in the curriculum, failing to take action to stop bullying, or excluding them from school trips or after-school clubs. They do not have to make major alterations to their school building, but they should be prepared to take steps such as switching rooms in which classes are taught where a child who uses a wheelchair cannot access an upper floor, or relocating a school library so that it is accessible.

The roles and rights of parents

Parents' views must be taken into account in planning appropriate provision for children with special needs. Anyone with parental responsibility for a child (not just the people the child lives with) should be actively involved in planning the best ways to meet their child's SEN, and have a real say in the way their child is educated. They should have access, via a local Parent Partnership Scheme, to an independent parent supporter (IPS), to help and guide them in getting the best for their child.

Those with parental responsibility must be formally notified if the school considers their child has SEN; it is at this point that they must be told about the local Parent Partnership Scheme. They must be formally notified of any proposal to assess a child's needs for a possible Statement, or of any proposal to disapply any aspect of the National Curriculum. Parents can request the LEA to assess their child's needs, and the LEA must comply with the request unless they have already made a statutory assessment in the last six months or unless, after examining all the available evidence, it is their opinion that such an assessment is unnecessary. Parents are entitled to be present at any examination related to the assessment procedures, and to receive copies of all the professional advice given in the course of the assessment. They can specify which school they would like to see named on the Statement; the LEA is obliged to comply with that preference, unless the school is unsuitable, or the placement would be incompatible with the efficient education of other children or with the efficient use of resources. They can choose an inclusive placement rather than a special school for their child: if they do, the LEA must in general comply.

Parents can appeal against refusal by an LEA to make a formal assessment or reassessment of a child's special needs, or to issue or maintain a Statement. They can appeal against the content of the Statement, or the school named by the LEA. Appeals are to the Special Educational Needs and Disability Tribunal, a national agency which hears the case put by parents and by the LEA. Parents of disabled children can also appeal to the Tribunal in cases where they believe a school has without justification treated their child less favourably than children who are not disabled. The Tribunal can order remedies such as training for school staff in disability issues, a review or alteration of a school's policy, relocation of facilities or additional tuition to compensate for missed curriculum opportunities.

For all children with special needs, parents are entitled to information – in a range of community languages and on tape – on:

- the school's special needs policy;
- the support available in school and from the LEA;
- procedures for acting on parental concerns;
- the involvement they can expect in assessment and decision making, emphasizing the importance of their contributions;
- how to complain if they are not satisfied with the arrangements made by the school for their child;
- services provided by the local authority for children 'in need';
- local and national voluntary organizations which may be able to give advice, information or counselling.

The role of the LEA

The LEA has a responsibility to assess children's needs under the 1981 and 1996 Education Acts. If it is shown that a child has a learning difficulty (as defined in the Acts) that cannot be met from normally available resources (which are taken to include outreach and peripatetic support and advisory services), the LEA has a responsibility to determine the additional special educational provision for the child. It is placed under a duty to educate the child in an ordinary rather than a special school, unless this would be incompatible with parents' wishes, or the school or LEA cannot take reasonable steps to adapt the mainstream provision without prejudicing the efficient education of other children. In practice, this would only be in cases of challenging behaviour that would significantly disrupt the learning of other pupils or place their safety at risk.

When the 1981 Act came into force it was anticipated that the numbers of children with Statements would be similar to the numbers who had hitherto been placed mainly in special schools and units – about 2 per cent of the school population. Statements would be required, said guidance accompanying the Act, for pupils still placed in special schools and units, and also for some pupils with 'severe and complex' difficulties requiring extra provision in mainstream. In practice, 'severe and complex' has proved hard to interpret. Many LEAs have greatly exceeded the anticipated 2 per cent numbers, and find themselves under increasing pressure to guarantee, via Statements, ever more central resources to children in locally managed mainstream schools. In response, many have sought to develop tighter guidelines on the types of need that schools should expect to meet locally, and those which might require central resources. The SEN *Code of Practice*, and its accompanying good practice guidance, provides a framework (albeit a loose one) for such criteria. In the past, a child's Statement would specify only those additional, central resources provided by the LEA to meet the child's needs. Since a 1990 appeal ruling, this position has become more complicated. The Statement now has to specify all the provision required to meet a child's needs, even if some of that provision is provided by the school. This means that the school as well as the LEA might be in breach of the law if they cease to be able to provide what the Statement specifies.

In making a statutory assessment of a child's special needs, the LEA must, as a minimum, seek advice from the child's parents and school, from the health service and social services and from an educational psychologist. They should try to establish what the child's own views are. The timespan between notifying parents of a decision to assess and the issue of a proposed Statement should not exceed 12 weeks, with a further 8 weeks to issue a final Statement. The LEA has a duty to keep the Statement under annual review.

With regard to the provision of services, such as speech therapy, which have in the past been seen as falling outside the LEA's responsibility, recent guidance makes it clear that addressing speech and language impairment should normally be regarded as educational provision. Prime responsibility for providing speech and language therapy still lies with the health service, but where they do not provide it and it is specified on the Statement as educational provision, the LEA may have to take responsibility.

Once an LEA has assessed a child's needs, decided to issue a Statement and asked the parents to indicate the school they would like their child to attend, it must consult the governing body of the school it proposes to name in the Statement. It must give consideration to the views of those consulted, but has the right to direct admission if a place is available. A governing body cannot refuse to admit a child because of their SEN.

LEAs have responsibilities for providing a wide range of information material for parents, for commissioning or running a local Parent Partnership Scheme and for making sure that where there are disputes about children's SEN, parents and the LEA can access independent arrangements for resolving disagreements.

LEAs are responsible for local funding arrangements for SEN; they can devise a set of weightings for pupils with special needs, with or without Statements, in order to allocate moneys to schools to meet special needs from their own resources via the delegated budget. They must, however, monitor the effectiveness of such provision (DfE 1994). These weightings have most commonly been based on the numbers of pupils in each school taking up free school meals – a crude measure of social disadvantage, but one that never-theless seems to work as well as many more complex measures. In some areas, however, an internal audit by each school of the number of pupils with learning difficulties, and the level of support they require, is moderated by the LEA and used as the basis for allocating funds. Pupils' actual attainment levels on baseline assessment or SATs are also increasingly being used in funding formulae. But whatever the mechanism for allocating funds, the LEA has to make it clear to schools the amounts delegated in respect of SEN and the provision that such funds are expected to cover. They also have to publish information on the support services they make available to schools to help them meet SEN, particularly through School Action Plus.

Finally, local authorities as a whole (not just their education departments) have a range of duties under the 1989 Children Act (DoH 1989). They must provide services such as advice, guidance, counselling, day and after school care, home helps, family centres and assistance with holidays to the families of children defined as 'in need'. The definition of 'need' is as unclear as the 'special need' in education legislation, but will encompass children who are living in situations where their health (physical or mental) or development (physical, intellectual, social or emotional) is likely to be significantly impaired for reasons of disability, neglect or acute family difficulties. Many children with Statements of 'special need' may also be entitled to services as children 'in need' under the Children Act, but not all. The two concepts differ in intent: while 'special needs' are linked to educational provision, the term 'in need' is intended to lead to a wider range of support services to enable families facing troubles of different kinds to look after their children themselves. The main overlap of the two concepts is in their provision for children with disabilities. Here, the Children Act introduced the important new principle that local authorities should provide services to disabled children in their area that will minimize the effects of disability and allow them to lead lives which are as normal as possible – a principle now echoed in the *Special Educational Needs and Disability Act* (DfES 2001a).

School inspection and special needs

Local authority inspection is the main way in which LEAs are held to account for the extent to which they fulfil their statutory duties towards children with SEN. At school level, the accountability is via LEA monitoring, and via the Office for Standards in Education (Ofsted). Judgements about the way in which the school deals with special needs will be made in the context of evaluating educational inclusion as a whole: how far the school 'strives to overcome barriers to learning, rather than avoiding the challenge, or expecting others to take responsibility' (Ofsted 2000).

The main focus will be on the extent to which pupils with SEN are making good progress. Inspectors will analyse (both in short and full inspections) how well different groups of pupils are performing, starting from the school's own assessment data, but also through observing and talking to pupils in lessons and looking at pupils' work (Ofsted 2001). Effective schools are expected to have already analysed the attainment of different groups – boys and girls, for example, or pupils from different ethnic backgrounds, and pupils with SEN. They should have set clear targets or goals based on their analysis. Inspectors will want to see how the school uses baseline assessment data, test or other assessment data, and information from IEPs or Statements to set appropriately challenging targets for groups of pupils with SEN. They will look carefully at how the school tracks, measures and monitors the progress made by pupils with SEN over time.

In teachers' planning and in classroom observations, inspectors will look for evidence that teachers are clear about what they want different groups of pupils to learn in each lesson (and what they actually learn), that the whole range of inclusive teaching strategies set out in National Curriculum guidance are being used, and that teachers use support staff and other resources (especially information and communication technology – ICT) effectively. They may look for evidence of the SENCO's role in supporting and developing colleagues' classroom practice in relation to SEN.

In relation to IEPs, they will check that they contain clear targets and that they are practical documents which classroom teachers can use in their practice. Classroom teachers need to be able to show that they take pupils' learning targets into account in the way they plan and the way they adapt and modify tasks to match the overall objectives of their lessons. IEPs need to be effective in ensuring that individual needs are met (for example, through extra help in literacy or numeracy, or in promoting independence skills, or via counselling). They also, however, need to enable the child to have full access to the curriculum: arrangements for extra help need to be seen to be organized so as to achieve the right balance between full participation in class and support provided on a withdrawal basis.

Inspectors will look at pupils' Statements and will check that the provision on the Statement is being made; they are likely also to ask to see samples of pupils' work over time, so as to assess progress. Inclusion into all aspects of the life of the school will be monitored, particularly for Statemented pupils who attend resource bases or designated units.

At a broader level, the inspection framework asks for judgements to be made on how effective and consistent the school's procedures are for identifying SEN and deciding where help is needed. They will want to know whether parents of children with SEN are actively involved in their education, and how well the school communicates with parents who themselves may have learning difficulties. In a full inspection, they may talk to visiting specialists from outside the school.

Finally, at an organizational and managerial level, inspectors will look at the school's policies and plans, and talk to the headteacher and governors to make sure the school is meeting the statutory responsibilities described earlier in this chapter. Crucially, they will want to establish how far the school's allocation of resources and responsibilities is effective in promoting the achievement of pupils with SEN.

Conclusion

Definitions are difficult. It is hard to pin down just who has needs, and even harder to determine whose responsibility it is to meet them. The legislative framework attempts this; its intention (to safeguard the rights of children) is admirable, even if by its focus on identifying and providing for certain children with 'needs' that others don't have, it runs the risk of distracting attention from equally pressing questions addressed in this introductory chapter: how schools and society can adapt themselves better to individuals so that ultimately no one needs the stigma of being special. In the next two chapters, we will return squarely to this alternative, as we focus on the school and the curriculum rather than the individual child in need.

Developing and reviewing a whole-school policy

Whole school policies and school management

Writing and reviewing whole-school curricular and policy statements is a familiar exercise for most teachers these days, and, since schools are legally required to have a policy on special needs, most teachers will have had some involvement with their school's SEN policy over the past few years.

Often, however, those who contribute to the development and review of a whole-school policy do so because of perceived external demands (the LEA has asked to see our policy, and Ofsted are coming soon . . .), rather than the kinds of internal process which make the need for a coherent, shared policy clear to all. In these circumstances, there are great temptations to adopt an off-the-peg policy from another school or published source, adapted slightly to meet local needs. Such policies, however good they look on paper, may never make the leap from paper to classroom practice. If they are to affect practice, and meet the real needs of children, parents and staff, it will be necessary to focus on the *process* of policy development and review, rather than the outcome, and to start the process with a real awareness of the reasons why whole-school policies are needed and the benefits they can bring.

Without this attention to the process of policy development, policies (of any kind) can simply end up confirming the status quo – becoming, as Joan Dalton (1997) writes, 'useful little documents, committing us all to carrying on much as before'. Reviewing a policy provides an ideal opportunity to do something different: to examine what is happening in the school for children with SEN, to see if what is happening is good enough and to plan together to make changes where they are needed.

Whole school policies: the rationale

In one school, a recently appointed teacher of Year 5 has several children in her class whose reading skills have not yet developed beyond Level 1 in National Curriculum terms, and whose written recording is usually restricted to a few short sentences. The children go out once a week for extra help with their work, but their teacher feels this is not enough, and wants to do more. When she asks in school about appropriate material for her guided reading sessions with the children, she finds there is a shortage of anything other than simple stories with an infant interest level. There is no one who can advise her on how to overcome the children's dislike of writing. The children all say they would like to improve their handwriting and spelling; there are resources for the combined practice of handwriting and spelling patterns in school, but each teacher keeps their own favourites in their own classroom.

In another school nearby, the same problem meets a different response. Here the SENCO meets with the class teacher to plan time when the children with literacy difficulties will be included in mixed ability groups to write (on the word processor) and publish personalized story books for each member of the Reception class. There is a central resource bank of spelling and handwriting materials, coded against the National Literacy Strategy (NLS) framework objectives. The problem of shortage of books at appropriate reading and interest levels has been identified by all staff and is being tackled: a budget has been allocated for next year and the literacy coordinator and SENCO are researching good materials. Meanwhile, when the class teacher raises at a staff meeting the problem of developing these children's reading, colleagues suggest that each child is linked with a reading partner from a Year 6 class for regular paired reading of books that would be too difficult for the younger children to manage alone, but possible given the older child's support. Finally, the new teacher meets with the support teacher who has been withdrawing the children for extra help. The support teacher explains that her role in the school is to work with identified children to help them reach learning targets they have set with their class teacher; there will be regular review meetings to monitor progress.

The difference between these two schools is one of individual versus collective responsibility. In one, we can imagine each teacher withdrawing to their own room and closing the door: what happens to any children inside who have special needs will be determined by the knowledge, skills and resources available to that classroom teacher, perhaps supplemented by the separately held knowledge, skills and resources of a support teacher. In the other, responsibility is shared, advice is available, resources are commonly held, lines of responsibility are clearly outlined and systematic procedures are in place for monitoring and recording pupils' progress.

The benefits of such a whole-school response to special needs are obvious. What is also clear, however, is that the benefits for the school in the second example did not come about without a good deal of hard work: these were staff who had together committed time and energy to the process of policy development.

Whole-school policy: development and review

Step 1: looking at practice – where we are now

The overt purposes of looking at current practice in a school are twofold: to define any problems that the school is experiencing in providing for special needs (so that key areas can be highlighted for development and actions planned), and to identify the things that are already going well (so as to check that these have been incorporated into the school policy document). There can also be a third, less obvious, purpose which is to promote changes in attitudes through the feedback on current practices that is gathered – particularly from pupils and parents – in the course of the review.

The 'Where we are now' phase of SEN policy review can most usefully be seen as a sub-set of questions schools will want to ask themselves about how far they have succeeded in establishing an inclusive ethos in the school as a whole – how good they are at responding to diversity and difference of all kinds, and reaching out to their communities to make their school genuinely a 'school for all'. Self-review tools like the Centre for Studies in Inclusive Education's (CSIE) *Index for Inclusion* (Booth *et al.* 2000), or Birmingham City Council's *Success for Everyone* (Bonathan *et al.* 2000), will be helpful here.

Moving on from these to focus on the particular SEN issues such a review will have highlighted, an audit of current practice will include:

- Gathering information and perceptions from as wide a group as possible – staff, parents, pupils, governors and external agencies who visit the school.
- Asking staff for their perceptions of the school's strengths and weaknesses in meeting special needs: if a questionnaire is to be used, it should include questions on the availability of information on pupils' special needs and appropriate teaching approaches, availability of materials and resources, the role of the SENCO, the use of additional adults in or out of the classroom to help individuals or groups, the role of outside agencies and the links made with parents.
- Gathering information on current staff levels of confidence and professional development needs in key areas. One way of doing this is to ask each member of staff to sort cards (see Table 2.1) into three piles: 'Things I feel very confident about'; 'Things I feel moderately confident about'; and 'Things I do not feel confident about'. An exercise like this will make it possible to identify patterns in staff development needs, and also to identify strengths in collective expertise – areas where colleagues can act as a support for one another.
- Considering the perspective of children in the school who have been identified as having special needs. For example, by discussing with them things that they enjoy and look forward to in school and things they do not, who they sit and work with in the classroom and how they feel about that, how they feel about any extra support provided to them, how they feel about themselves as learners and anything they would really like to achieve or change about themselves in school.
- Meeting with parents and carers of children with special needs to ask about their perception of positives and negatives in the ways in which

Table 2.1 A card sort to assess staff levels of confidence and professional development needs

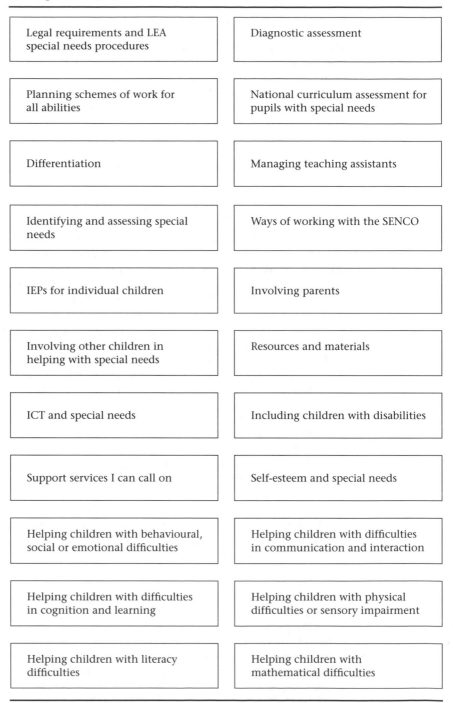

Legal requirements and LEA special needs procedures	Diagnostic assessment
Planning schemes of work for all abilities	National curriculum assessment for pupils with special needs
Differentiation	Managing teaching assistants
Identifying and assessing special needs	Ways of working with the SENCO
IEPs for individual children	Involving parents
Involving other children in helping with special needs	Resources and materials
ICT and special needs	Including children with disabilities
Support services I can call on	Self-esteem and special needs
Helping children with behavioural, social or emotional difficulties	Helping children with difficulties in communication and interaction
Helping children with difficulties in cognition and learning	Helping children with physical difficulties or sensory impairment
Helping children with literacy difficulties	Helping children with mathematical difficulties

their children's difficulties have been discussed with them, the ways in which information has been shared and the ways in which they have been involved in forward planning.

- Examining existing curricular policy documents, schemes of work and teachers' planning, to see how they address the issues of SEN.
- Gathering and looking together at examples of current records of assessment and action for children with special needs.
- Looking at the way children with special needs currently spend their time in school, by recording their activities in the form of running diaries, pupil logs or blocked-in timetables. Asking about their opportunities to receive awards and commendations, and about any opportunities they have to help others as well as to be helped.
- Looking at samples of children's work.
- Classroom observation, focusing on whether there are links between IEPs and what happens in classrooms, whether support staff are deployed effectively, whether pupils are developing independence and whether teachers are able to use a range of inclusive teaching strategies.
- Analysing data on outcomes for pupils with SEN in different year groups, in terms of attainment, exclusions or other behavioural measures.

The outcomes of this information gathering phase need then to be shared (again, as widely as possible) with all staff and governors, through displays, presentations and written reports

Step 2: developing a vision – where we would like to be

Having gathered and shared information on the school's existing response to SEN, the next step is to establish the broad vision which the school holds for meeting children's individual or special needs: the values and principles it would wish to adhere to, and its view on the entitlements of children and parents.

It will be useful to consult policy guidelines developed by others – for example, the LEA – but the vision *must* be personal to each particular school, and owned by those who work there. For this reason all staff and governors should share the discussion and activities which will develop the vision.

Activities should focus attention on the needs of children who have difficulty in learning, but can usefully draw on adults' own experience as learners. For example, staff and governors might discuss in pairs an experience of a time when they were trying to learn something new which they found difficult. Points to talk about include how this made them feel and behave, and what kind of help they wanted and did not want. Alternatively, they might try out some difficult tasks (like writing at speed to dictation using the non-preferred hand, or reading aloud from a text which is partly obscured, or working in small groups on a task where some groups are given only part of the information they will need to complete the task), then discuss any negative feelings or behaviours that result, and ways in which these might have been avoided. They could be asked to work together to define what would be a good classroom experience for children with SEN. Put together with information from the review phase on the perceptions and experiences of children and their parents, activities of this kind will help the group to formulate their ideas on the general principles for the school in delivering the curriculum and offering support to children with special needs.

Step 3: comparing vision and practice

It should now be possible for staff to consider together the information from the review of current practice in the light of the agreed, general principles for meeting children's individual needs in school: to compare 'where we are now' with 'where we would like to be'. One way of doing this is to list individually and as a group the strengths in current practice, which should be incorporated into the whole-school policy document under relevant headings (see below); then to list the major gaps or problem areas. The group can work to agree several key problem areas which should be prioritized in the policy document for action and development, and then work on these one by one using a four-stage problem solving process:

● What exactly is the problem? (getting it clear)
● How would we like things to be instead?
● How can we get there? (generating solutions)
● Which is the best solution? (evaluating possible solutions)

The conclusions from these problem solving groups will feed into the final policy.

Step 4: drafting the policy

The minimum content of a special needs policy should include, under government regulations:

Basic information

● The objectives of the SEN policy.
● The name of the SENCO or teacher responsible for day-to-day implementation.
● The arrangements for coordinating provision, including strategic management and target setting.
● Information on any SEN specialism or special unit the school might have, on special facilities increasing access to the school for pupils with SEN, and on relevant admission arrangements.

Identification, assessment and provision

● How resources are allocated to and among pupils with SEN.
● Arrangements for identification, assessment and review.
● How pupils with SEN will be enabled to access a broad, balanced curriculum including the National Curriculum.
● Integration arrangements.
● How any complaints about provision can be made.
● Criteria for evaluating the success of the policy.

School staffing and outside links

- SEN in-service education and training (INSET) arrangements.
- Use made of support services and other teachers and facilities from outside the school.
- Links with special schools and other mainstream schools; transition arrangements.
- Partnership with parents.
- Links with other agencies – health, social services, voluntary organizations.

Additionally, many schools will want to include their own working definition of special needs, the vision and values they hold and details of the roles and responsibilities held by school staff and governors.

It is important to check that the school's policy does actually cover all of the prescribed content. Several studies (Thomas and Tarr 1996; Ofsted 1997) have shown that this is not the case in the majority of schools. Typically, policies do not cover strategic management, include little detail about funding, do not offer specific information on how available resources are allocated and are weak on describing the actual strategies the school uses to promote inclusion.

Step 5: evaluating the policy

Since schools have been asked to report on the effectiveness of their special needs policy each year, they have begun to give thought to the difficult question of evaluation. Many are setting themselves targets against which they can measure the success of the school as a whole in meeting SEN. Targets might include:

- An annual reduction in the percentage of children who have not attained Level 1 in the core subjects at the end of Key Stage 1, and an annual reduction in the percentage of children not attaining Level 2 or 3 at the end of Key Stage 2.
- Value-added outcomes for lower attaining pupils between the end of Key Stage 1 and the end of Key Stage 2 which are as good as, or exceed, the national average.
- An annual increase in the percentage of children with complex SEN making at least a one level jump in the core subjects over a Key Stage.
- A reduction in permanent and fixed-term exclusions.
- An increase in the number of children moving within the *Code of Practice* framework from School Action Plus to School Action, or from School Action to ordinary differentiated learning opportunities.

Other possible performance indicators could be:

- Measures of pupil self-esteem.
- Parental participation in developing and reviewing IEPs.
- Parental and pupil views as assessed by repeat survey.
- An increase in the number of pupils reintegrating to the school from local special schools.

- A decrease in the number of children leaving the school to go to special schools.
- Evidence of increased accessibility for disabled pupils.
- Teacher planning showing evidence of differentiation.
- Measures of staff confidence in meeting the special needs of pupils.

What makes a good SEN policy?

A good whole-school policy for SEN will have a number of key characteristics (Reeves and Berger 1999).

First, it will reflect a shared vision of what the school really wants to achieve, expressed in the form of clear objectives. Box 2.1 gives an example of what these objectives might look like.

A good SEN policy will be accessible to all members of the school community (written in plain English, and summarized in a leaflet for parents which is also available on tape and in a range of community languages).

It will be a *live* document, with key aspects embodied in the school prospectus, in job descriptions and in induction arrangements for new staff. The core vision and objectives will be written into other curriculum policy documents and the success criteria and evaluation arrangements will be built into the cycle of reports to governors and governors' meetings. Its description of how strategic planning for SEN is managed will be linked into the school's overall planning cycles and mechanisms.

It will tell people exactly what provision the school makes for SEN. One way of doing this is via a 'provision map' (see Table 2.2), which not only shows what is provided, at what cost, but also acts as a check that there is progression in the provision and that pupils are not getting the same 'diet' year on year.

Box 2.1 Extract from a school SEN policy

Objectives of our policy

- We will be able to meet the needs of as wide a range of children as possible who live in our catchment area.
- All children will move on from our school well equipped in the basic skills of literacy, numeracy, social interaction and personal organization.
- The progress of pupils will be continuously monitored to identify needs as they arise; needs will be identified and support provided as early as possible in children's time with us.
- Parents/carers will be fully involved at every stage in plans to meet their child's special needs.
- Children themselves will be involved, wherever possible, in planning.
- Full access to the curriculum will be provided through differentiated planning by class teachers, SENCOs and support staff as appropriate.
- All staff will see meeting special needs as part of their job, and will be confident in the skills they need in order to discharge their responsibilities.

Table 2.2 Provision map

Year	Provision/resource	Cost (per week)
Nursery	• Daily language support, based around regular nursery activities • Teaching to individual targets, based on Portage model of assessment and intervention • Home/school book bags; suggested activities around sharing a book • Parenting group	5 hours nursery nurse
Reception	• Daily speaking and listening programme with nursery nurse using, for example, appropriate section of the Teaching Talking handbook • Small-group phonological awareness programme (Sound Beginnings) • Nurture group placement	2.5 hours nursery nurse 2.5 hours teaching assistant Full-time teacher
Years 1/2	• ICT, for example, Animated Alphabet • Spring term Year 1, early literacy support programme • Individual reward system • School meals supervisory assistant support during lunchtime	5 hours teaching assistant
Years 3/4	• ICT, for example, Talking Pen Down, Wordshark • Phonographix group • Additional literacy support catch-up programme • Social skills group	1 hour SENCO 2.5 hours teaching assistant 1 hour SENCO 2.5 hours teaching assistant 1 hour deputy head
Years 5/6	• Lunchtime library group • Homework club and family literacy project • Precision teaching, maths • Play reading group using, for example, Penguin plays • Phonographix group • Paired reading with older mentors (Year 10 from local secondary schools) • Behaviour log and reward system • Circle of friends • Individual counselling	5 hours library assistant External funding 3 hours teaching assistant Volunteer helper 1 hour SENCO 1 hour SENCO 20 minutes per day teaching assistant 1 hour SENCO 1 hour per week from LEA support service

It will describe the criteria used to identify children who will be placed on the SEN register, and the criteria used to determine how school SEN funding is allocated – which groups of children will receive what form of support. Any parent picking up the policy should be in no doubt about what the level of need has to be for a child to be entitled to additional help.

It will give clear guidance on how SEN is coordinated and managed within the school, what everybody's responsibilities are, and when the school would expect to draw on outside expertise. It will be specific about when things

---

Box 2.2   Extract from a school SEN policy

Arrangements for partnership with parents/carers

Parents/carers will be involved at all stages of the education planning process for children with SEN.

Parental concerns will be acted on promptly, initially via a meeting with the class teacher. Children will be the subject of School Action to meet their needs if parents have a concern which is not resolved by discussions with the class teacher and subsequent discussion with the SENCO.

An appointment will be made for the class teacher to meet with parents/carers where the school has concerns and has identified the child as having SEN, to make sure that they are in agreement.

All IEP meetings and reviews should draw equally on the views of parents, school and, where appropriate, the child him/herself. At such meetings we will make sure that the child's strengths as well as weaknesses are discussed, that we listen to parents' suggestions about how to make things better in school for their child, that where we make suggestions as to how parents can help at home, these are specific and achievable, and that all parents go away from the meeting clear about the action that will be taken, and the way in which outcomes will be monitored and reviewed.

Ideas and materials for supporting learning at home will be discussed with parents and distributed on request. Parents/carers will also be invited to work alongside pupils in the classroom where this is appropriate.

We regularly offer workshops for parents on using paired reading to support their child. A maths games loans library is also available to support numeracy work at home.

A range of information on special needs, including contacts for local and national support groups, is available in our parents room.

Regular communication between home and school will ensure that all concerns are promptly acted on. Where issues remain unresolved, however, parents/carers are able to make a complaint by contacting the headteacher or, as a next step, the governing body. Our complaints procedure, available from the school office, sets out the steps we take to respond to complaints in more detail.

---

are done – for example, 'the SENCO will meet with each class teacher half-termly to review issues related to pupils on school-based support, and will meet to discuss and review children on School Action Plus support or Statements through six-weekly IEP meetings. All pupils are reviewed at least termly. The SENCO monitors curriculum planning for SEN and is able to support class teachers with their planning on request'.

The policy will be equally specific in relation to parental involvement (see Box 2.2). It will show that the school has thought hard about describing its access arrangements for disabled children and adults – for example:

We have made sure that there is good lighting and safety
arrangements (for example, markings on steps) for children and adults
with visual impairments. Our classrooms provide good acoustic

Box 2.3   Extract from a school SEN policy

Evaluating the success of our policy

Individual targets for SEN will be reviewed through IEP meetings; outcomes will be summarized in the annual governors' report.

Target setting for all pupils takes place half-termly and within each Key Stage. Percentage targets are set for children to achieve Level 2 in the National Curriculum at the end of Key Stage 1, and Level 4 at the end of Key Stage 2. Targets are also set, within the Basic Skills Policy, for children identified as having SEN. These targets aim towards increasing the number of children with SEN achieving either Level 2 or Level 4 at the appropriate Key Stage, and become more ambitious from year to year. We aim to ensure that all pupils leaving the end of Key Stage 2 achieve at least Level 2. We also aim never to permanently exclude any child with identified special needs, and to achieve an annual reduction in the number of fixed-term exclusions used overall in the school. Our success in all these areas is evaluated annually and reported to parents in the governors' annual report.

We undertake a regular 'stocktake' of how we are doing in SEN using the school self-evaluation framework set out by Ofsted.

Every four years – or more often if our evaluation shows we are not meeting our SEN targets – we take a more in-depth look at how our SEN policy is working. This involves classroom observation and sampling IEPs and other SEN records.

The SENCO provides information to the governing body as to the number of pupils identified as having SEN, twice a year in March and October. The number of pupils moving from one type of School Action to another will also be noted.

SEN is a standing item at all curriculum and finance sub-committee meetings and will be reported at full governing body meetings through sub-committee reports which are then discussed as necessary. Once a year, in October, the full governing body will discuss SEN outcomes and issues.

The SENCO will meet regularly with the SEN governor to discuss current SEN progress and issues. The SEN governor will lead governor monitoring of the SEN policy through sampling, observations and other procedures to be agreed annually.

conditions so that the effects of hearing impairment are minimized (part-carpeting, curtains, quiet areas). Our personal, social and health education programme helps children be aware of and positively value the differences between people as well as the similarities, and to be sensitive to one another's needs.

The policy will embody the arrangements for evaluating its success by setting out whole-school targets for improvement and identifying the responsibilities of the governing body in evaluation. Box 2.3, another extract from a school's policy, provides a model of how this might be done.

An example: Reviewing the whole-school policy at Glendown Primary School

Glendown is a seven-class, 210-pupil primary school in a small town. It serves a mixed area with both owner-occupied houses and a small council estate. Many of the children take free school meals. The school has a (part-time) SENCO whose role includes collating special needs records and discussing with class teachers whether/when to refer on to outside agencies. She also does some withdrawal groups for reading in Key Stage 1 and teaches the Literacy Hour to bottom sets of children in Key Stage 2.

Information from the review of special needs provision came from a survey of staff opinion, an interview with individual pupils undertaken by the SENCO, discussion with outside agencies, a survey of resources in school suitable for children with special needs, a check on existing curricular policy documents and on programmes of study, and finally a log completed by all teachers of the tasks set to a pupil with special needs, and a pupil of average ability with no special needs, at fixed points in the day over a two-week period.

The log of tasks revealed that in many classrooms children with special needs were spending more time completing written tasks than were other children, and correspondingly less time on such activities as individual reading, using the computer to input and print out work, and group discussion. They were often engaged in relatively routine individual tasks rather than investigative or group projects.

The staff questionnaire indicated that most teachers felt the school was good at helping children with literacy problems. They also felt that parental involvement for parents of children with special needs was high, with parents being drawn in early to discuss their child's difficulties through the school's system of regularly recording and reviewing plans for individual children, and through the paired reading home programme set up by the SENCO. Staff felt that children with special needs were generally identified at an early stage. Several staff mentioned as a strength the initiative by the school's ICT coordinator, who had invited the advisory teacher for ICT to come to a staff meeting and demonstrate useful software for children with special needs; they felt that the software was now well used in several classrooms and that the children enjoyed it.

As for weaknesses, staff felt that they lacked knowledge of other resources that might be useful for children with special needs, and of general strategies for teaching slow learners. Helping children with behaviour problems was another area where staff felt they needed more advice and training. Several teachers said that they felt there should be more sharing of expertise and resources in school, rather than just expecting the SENCO to do everything. Others (possibly as a result of logging children's activities) felt that the school should look at the curriculum offered to children with special needs, and try to make it more interesting and relevant.

Current school policy documents and programmes of study included few references to meeting special learning needs, with the exception of the science documents, where the science coordinator had produced guidelines on ways in which materials and tasks could be adapted to meet the needs of children with a wide range of difficulties.

When the SENCO interviewed groups of children, they mentioned not enjoying or looking forward to tasks involving a lot of writing, spelling tests, being kept in to finish work and (for junior aged children) having to use reading books 'from the infants'. All the children said they sat and worked in class with the same group all day. They were not unhappy about this, regarding these children as their friends, but they did not like being referred to as 'Mrs Thorne's group': one child said 'the others . . . 'cos we have to have help, they say we're Mrs Thorne's thickies'. Most of them said they felt they were not as clever as others, and that they did not often feel proud of their work.

External support agencies said that they felt the school was very strong in parental involvement and in the quality of its individual education plans for children. Also mentioned were its structured approaches to literacy for children who had difficulties, and the fact that the school had chosen to spend money on a non-class based SENCO and given her an important role. Areas where the school was perhaps not doing so well were highlighted as the low self-esteem and lack of opportunities for success for many children with special needs in what was basically quite an 'academic' school. Support staff also reported feeling isolated from the class teachers, whom they rarely seemed able to talk to on visits.

The survey of resources brought to light a cupboard full of materials for language and listening skills ordered by a teacher who had left, and a very unequal provision between classes of games and worksheets to support basic skills. A local special school kept a permanent display of materials for children with special needs, but no one from Glendown except the SENCO had yet visited or borrowed equipment.

In reviewing the general principles for their special needs policy, the Glendown staff found some aspects easy to agree on. These included full access to the whole range of curricular experiences for all children in the school, a curriculum that offered opportunities for success to all and an acceptance by the class teacher of ultimate responsibility for coordinating systems to meet the special needs of individuals in the class.

There was considerable debate on whether support should be offered to children in Key Stage 1 on a withdrawal basis or in class, and on whether priority should be given to supporting children still experiencing difficulties at the upper end of the school, or to younger classes. The impact of the school's setting policy for the Literacy and Numeracy Hours in Key Stage 2 was also the subject of much discussion. Eventually it was agreed that priority for support in English and maths should be given to younger children, but that there should still be provision for particular children's ongoing and individual needs in older groups wherever possible. It was agreed that the SENCO should work differently in Key Stage 1, spending more time in helping class teachers to plan differentiated Literacy and Numeracy Hours, and working with groups within the lesson rather than withdrawing them. In Key Stage 2, the school decided to carry on with setting, but to have different sets for English and maths, and to make sure that in the afternoons, for other subjects, children worked in mixed ability pairs and groups.

There was also debate over the principle of inclusion. Some staff felt strongly that for some children special schools and units were the only answer; other felt that all children should have a right to be educated in their own local schools. There was a general concern that the requirement for schools to publish the results of National Curriculum assessments was putting pressure on the school and could make it less willing to include children with special needs. Glendown staff and governors decided that, despite this pressure, they would hold to a clear policy of basing decisions on inclusion on the needs of individual children and of others in their class, and not on considerations about overall achievement levels within the school.

In their policy document, staff went on to record and expand on existing good practice under headings of parental involvement, record keeping and differentiation of the curriculum (using the work that had been done in science as a model).

They made a long list of areas that were seen as problems: over-reliance on the SENCO at the expense of sharing expertise, inadequate and unevenly distributed resources, support limited to children with literacy problems, an often unstimulating curriculum for children with special needs, low self-esteem and lack of opportunities for success for some children, policies for pupil groupings, assessment and provision of materials that singled out children with special needs in unhelpful ways.

It was felt that by redefining the role of the SENCO to include working alongside the class teacher and helping to adapt materials and schemes of work, many of these problems would be tackled. Three other key areas were identified as priorities for further development work in the school over the next six months.

For the first area, the problem of pupil groupings, staff decided that the best strategy would be a plan to develop staff skills in managing mixed ability group work, using the expertise of two members of staff who regularly worked with their classes to help the children learn the skills of working effectively together on problem-solving activities and other shared tasks.

For the second, that of the low self-esteem of children with special needs in the school, staff listed together all the ways they could think of to celebrate children's successes in and out of school, and their progress in work or in behaviour. This led to several developments, including a board on which photographs of children were pinned next to positive things which other children and teachers had written about them, and records of special talents or successes.

For the third problem area, that of resources in school, it was decided first to ask teachers from the resource base at the local special school to bring a selection of materials to a staff meeting and talk about their use. Eventually, staff planned to develop their own resource bank of materials, centrally held and indexed according to National Curriculum programmes of study.

In the light of their work in these three areas, they later added further detail to their whole-school policy. The final version was then used as a basis of a leaflet for parents explaining what the school could offer to children with special needs, and as a tool for self-evaluation at the next agreed review date for the policy – two years from its inception.

Conclusion

The example of Glendown highlights many of the important issues in developing a whole-school policy for SEN. The school might have chosen to base their policy on an off-the-peg model, and probably agreed an elegant, comprehensive and clear document in half the time. That they did not take this route reflects the relative importance they placed on process rather than product, on ensuring maximum commitment to the policy from all those involved. Finding the 'points of pain' for children and staff through the review of practice, negotiating priorities together and allowing time for further development all meant that this particular policy was more than just another piece of paper; instead it represented the staff's real efforts to work collectively rather than individually to meet the whole range of needs in the children they taught.

Special needs and the National Curriculum

Introduction

The National Curriculum has brought many benefits to children with SEN. It has enriched the range of curricular experiences available to children in special schools and mainstream resource bases. It has made it easier for children to move between such special provisions and mainstream classes because of the increased continuity of learning experiences across different settings. It has sharpened assessment and definition of need, by providing a shared vocabulary, and has helped teachers to see more clearly how a child may have special needs in one area or subject but not in others. Teachers' enhanced expertise in assessment of all children's progress through detailed observation within the classroom has been particularly helpful for children with difficulties in learning – for whom detailed observation of this kind is an essential precondition to offering timely and appropriate forms of support.

The most important contribution the National Curriculum has made to the development of good special needs practice, however, is not in continuity or assessment, or the shared vocabulary: it is in the emphasis it has brought on how to adapt tasks, and teaching and learning styles, to make the *same* overall programmes of study, specified for each Key Stage, accessible and meaningful to all children in a class. The word for this is *differentiation*, and differentiation within the National Curriculum is the main focus of this chapter.

Differentiation

Research has shown that on the whole, primary teachers find differentiation very difficult. The studies of British classrooms by Neville Bennett (1991) provide the evidence. In observations of maths and language work among 6- to 8-year-old children, Bennett found that on average only around four out of ten tasks given to children were matched to their level of ability. Nearly half the tasks given to low attainers were too hard for them; 40 per cent of tasks given to high attainers were too easy for them. In classes of 8- to

11-year-olds, nearly two-thirds of all tasks given to the lowest attainers were too difficult. This applied particularly to written work: the children found practical tasks very much easier.

The National Curriculum, when introduced, initially had the effect of decreasing rather than increasing teachers' confidence in their ability to adapt tasks and teaching and learning styles to meet the very wide range of ability in their classes. Over three-quarters of a large group of primary teachers surveyed when the National Curriculum was introduced (Wragg *et al.* 1989) felt that including children with special needs in the prescribed curriculum would be difficult.

The difficulty many teachers have with differentiation was brought even more sharply into focus with the introduction of the prescribed termly objectives and whole-class interactive teaching models of the Literacy Hour and daily maths lesson. Faced with the challenges of these new ways of working, an increasing number of schools, initially at least, opted for setting in the belief that this would obviate the need to plan for differentiation.

Yet in principle the ladder of learning steps prescribed by the National Curriculum and the National Literacy and Numeracy Strategy (NLS/NNS) frameworks offers a great deal of practical support to teachers, helping them to plan in a differentiated way. At their best, these frameworks enable teachers to accommodate in their planning an awareness of the things some children lower down on the ladder may still need to be learning, and of the steps further up the ladder that some very able children may be ready to take. Here is an example:

> In planning work in her Year 5 class, one teacher recorded the range of levels of attainment which the work in each subject area could involve. She planned to cover work on water in geography, linked to work on changes of state in science. The investigations she planned on evaporation and condensation would provide scope for children with learning difficulties to make the kinds of simple observations and deductions required at Levels 1 and 2 of the attainment target (AT) on scientific enquiry. At the same time she would also ensure opportunities for other pupils to demonstrate attainment at Level 5 by identifying key factors they thought might affect rates of evaporation, when designing a fair test to investigate a prediction based on these factors. Some pupils would be able to succeed on AT3 at Level 3, describing ways in which materials are changed by heating or cooling; others would be expected to use the appropriate scientific terms to describe changes (Level 4). Mathematical work arising from the experiments on evaporation would provide work on the need to use standard measures, from Level 2 of the shape, space and measures AT, right up to Level 6/7 for a child in the class with particular mathematical gifts, who would need to be challenged to devise a compound measure of evaporation rate using volume and time.
>
> Work on water in geography would be aimed for the majority of the class at Level 4, with pupils being helped to recognize and describe geographical patterns related to water distribution using maps and atlases. Some children would, however, be asked to extend their work by looking at the issues of who owns and pays for water, and

examining issues around water provision in less economically developed countries. These children could be challenged to demonstrate the kind of awareness of different perspectives expected at Level 5. For other children, working at Level 2, investigation would focus mainly on water in the local environment and how their own families used, accessed and paid for it.

One child in the class with severe learning difficulties and a Statement of SEN would, with the help of his parents, compile a picture and symbol record of the ways in which his family used water day by day.

In their literacy work, pupils followed the theme through with a study of traditional folk-tales, legends and myths about water. The repetitive, rhyming structure of tales like *Bringing the Rain to Kapiti Plain* (Aardema 1997) enabled all children, even those with limited reading skills, to join in during shared text work, and to access Year 5, Term 2 work on performing narrative poems in a range of ways. The rhymes in the story provided a useful opportunity for a small group of children still working at Level 2 to identify the different spelling patterns for the phoneme 'ow'; others found examples of soft and hard 'cs' and tried to deduce the spelling rule. Some more able children were asked to translate the theme of one of the folk-tales or myths they had read into a present-day context; the less able children, with help from a teaching assistant, reviewed the styles of traditional story language and the words used in openings and endings.

This teacher used the National Curriculum documentation as a framework to help her identify opportunities for broadening what might have been fairly mundane work, so as to stretch some children in particular directions and to include work properly matched to the needs of children with learning difficulties. We will return to her planning later in the chapter, but first we need to consider in more detail what differentiation actually involves, and how it can be planned for.

A model for differentiation

As well as its detailed ladder of learning steps, the National Curriculum has provided all teachers with a model on which to base their thinking about differentiation. Every subject document incorporates a statutory inclusion statement. The inclusion statement outlines how teachers can modify the National Curriculum programmes of study to provide all pupils with relevant and challenging work at each Key Stage, and sets out three principles for a more inclusive curriculum:

- setting suitable learning challenges;
- responding to pupils' diverse learning needs;
- overcoming potential barriers to learning.

The NLS, in its training materials on including pupils with SEN within the Literacy Hour (NLS 2000), has translated these principles into a schematic

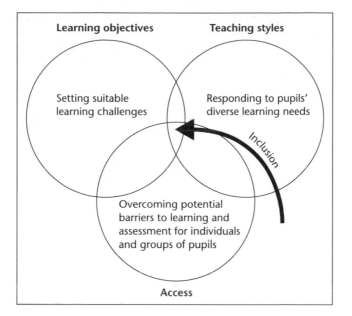

Figure 3.1 Differentiation and inclusion: the three circle model.

way of thinking about differentiation. This is based on three circles (see Figure 3.1). Let us look at each of these circles in turn.

Learning objectives means that the teacher decides on outcomes for particular individuals or groups which are different from those pertaining to the broad band of children in the class as a whole. These may be taken from steps further up the ladder of learning (for more able pupils) or from steps lower down (for children with SEN). The teacher then gears their explanations, modelling and questioning in whole-class teaching, and the tasks they set up for individuals or groups who are working independently, so that children will achieve these objectives.

Teaching styles means the teacher planning the way they will vary their methods so as to match the unique needs of individuals or groups, and secure motivation and concentration. It might mean presenting information visually – as 'mind maps' or spider diagrams – for children who are visual learners, as well as in sequential explanatory text for children who are verbal learners. It might mean setting some children a series of short tasks which can each be completed in five minutes, to match their current span of concentration, while other children are set extended tasks which will take half an hour or more.

Access means finding ways of 'bypassing' impairments which children may have, so that they can access the curriculum. Here, what is taught (the learning objectives) remain the same for all, but the child requires a way around whatever obstacles are in the way of their learning: widened doorways into the classroom for a child who uses a wheelchair, the use of a radio aid for a child who is hearing impaired, texts put on tape or read aloud by a peer for a child who cannot read, a support assistant to go over the teacher's instructions one to one for a child with a receptive language impairment.

Teachers can use the three circle model to look at the kinds of differentiation they are currently using in their classrooms. If differentiation is going well and children are genuinely being included, they will probably be using strategies from all three circles. Alternatively, they may find that children are struggling because they are targeting the right learning objectives but not changing their teaching style to match the needs of a particular group, or that access is being provided (by a teaching assistant supporting the child in class, for example), but the child is accessing an inappropriate set of learning objectives which have not been differentiated.

It is the balance between the three circles which we need to achieve: those rare but satisfying moments when all three come together, and the child finds that they are in the space where the circles overlap. This is the space we can call real inclusion.

Choosing the right learning objective

The most basic strategy for differentiation of the curriculum is *differentiation by outcome* – that is, aiming for different outcomes for children according to what assessment has indicated are the next steps in their learning. The National Curriculum ATs and associated programmes of study, and the NLS and NNS frameworks, as we have seen, support this approach in that they break down curricular areas into a series of roughly hierarchical steps, with ideas for appropriate tasks at each level.

The difficulty, however, is that the gaps between the steps of the ladder can sometimes be very wide, and there is little information on intermediate steps and associated tasks.

As an example, we can look at the measurement work that would be involved in the science experiments for the work on water. It is a large leap for any child between ordering objects using direct comparison (maths AT3, Level 1) and using everyday standard units to measure length and mass (Level 2). Bridging steps are needed, and for the child with learning difficulties these may need to be very small and tightly documented.

In order to be able to differentiate by outcome, then, the teacher needs to know how to work out the bridging steps that will lead up to a particular skill or concept. Let us see how this might be done for one aspect of measurement work: telling the time (AT3, Level 3).

The teacher's first step is to consider the range of sub-skills necessary to be able to tell the time. They will recognize that the child must be able to understand and use certain language concepts, such as long and short (for the hands of the clock), and near and nearest (for when the short hand is nearest to . . .). The child must be able to name written numerals to twelve, to count in fives, and have some understanding of simple fractions (half and quarter). The teacher's next step is to put these sub-skills into roughly hierarchical order of difficulty. They will end up with something like the steps in Box 3.1 – though not necessarily exactly like this, since there are always several equally valid ways of breaking down a task. Now it will be possible to locate the point at which tasks should be pitched for each child in the class: sorting objects into long and short piles for one child, perhaps, while another group work on the counting in fives sequence, and in another corner children

---

Box 3.1   Small steps to target. Maths AT3 Level 3: telling the time

Associates regularly occurring events with particular times:
at 1 o'clock we eat lunch etc. ☐

Understands vocabulary 'long and short' ☐

Understands vocabulary 'near and nearest' ☐

Recognizes and names numbers 1–12 ☐

Tells time by the hour ☐

Understands concept of 'half' ☐

Tells time by half hour ☐

Understands concept of 'quarter' ☐

Understands language of 'past and to the hour' ☐

Tells time by quarter past and to ☐

Counts aloud in fives ☐

Writes number sequence in fives ☐

Tells time to nearest five minutes past the hour by counting
round in fives ☐

Matches appropriate digital times to analogue clock face ☐

Tells time to nearest five minutes to the hour by counting
back in fives ☐

Automatically associates clock positions with times past and to the
hour without needing to count round or back in fives ☐

---

take turns to set times on an analogue clock for the rest of the group to reproduce on a digital one.

Most teachers are very familiar with the idea of sub-skills and small steps for concepts as clearly defined as many in the maths curriculum. The same approach, however, can be applied in other less clearly defined areas. Take, for example, a Year 4 class where all the children have been given a worksheet involving putting key words for the topic they are studying into alphabetical order, and looking up their meaning in the dictionary. For a third of the class the task is just about manageable. Another third find it easy and finish quickly. Quite a few children, however, do not really know where to start. Among them are children who don't know the sequence of letters of the alphabet, and children at an even earlier stage who are not sure of all their letter sounds. For them, the task they have been given is widely adrift from the prior knowledge and skills they bring to it. This teacher urgently needs a mental map of the small steps that lead up to the ability to 'use a dictionary to learn or check the spellings of words' (NLS framework, Year 3, Term 2 objectives), in order to plan differentiated tasks for the class. Using such a mental map (see Box 3.2), they will be able to offer a range of activities from

Box 3.2 Small steps to target. English AT3: using a dictionary

Understands concepts of print: front/back, page, word, letter ☐

Identifies the first phoneme of a word on an auditory basis: 'bag' begins with the phoneme 'buh' ☐

Matches auditory to written sounds (buh-b) using picture cues (e.g. picture of a ball next to b) ☐

Uses alphabetically ordered word bank, with picture cues for each letter ☐

Can point to the right written letter for each letter sound, without picture cues ☐

Can sound and name each letter of the alphabet in lower case ☐

Can sound and name each letter of the alphabet in upper case ☐

Uses alphabetically ordered word bank without picture cues ☐

Uses simple alphabetical picture dictionary ☐

Matches sound-written letter-letter names (buh-b-bee) ☐

Recites alphabet in order ☐

Orders first quartile (a–g) of the alphabet on an alphabet arc, using plastic or wooden letters ☐

Orders second quartile (h–m) ☐

Orders third quartile (n–t) ☐

Orders last quartile (u–z) ☐

Orders whole alphabet ☐

Writes alphabet in order from memory ☐

Quickly finds a named plastic or wooden letter from the arc in front of them ☐

Can tell the name of a missing letter or letters on the arc ☐

Can recognize mixed-up letters on the arc and replace in the correct order ☐

Inserts missing letters into written alphabet ☐

Can arrange a selection of letters (e.g. r, k, f) in alphabetical order ☐

Can organize words into alphabetical order using the first letter ☐

Understands the purpose and organization of a dictionary ☐

Says whether a letter falls into the first, second, third or fourth quartile of a dictionary and can open dictionary to this quartile ☐

Orders words alphabetically on the basis of second letter when first is the same ☐

Orders words on the basis of third letter when first and second are the same ☐

Quickly locates such words in children's dictionary ☐

sorting the words on the worksheet by initial sound, to entering them into personal alphabetical word books, to looking them up in simple children's dictionaries or in adult versions.

Learning how to break down skills and concepts into small steps takes practice. It is, however, an essential competency for special needs work. It is also an immediate confidence builder for both teachers and pupils, shifting as it does the emphasis from what the child *can't* do to what in the earlier small steps they *can* do, and what the next learning step might be.

It is not, however, necessary for every teacher or group of teachers to reinvent the wheel by working out for themselves the small steps for every core skill and concept in the National Curriculum. The Qualifications and Curriculum Authority (QCA) (2001a, 2001b) have done some of this work through their guidance on target setting for pupils with SEN, which introduced the 'p' levels (small steps within Level 1 and between Levels 1 and 2), and through related guidance on planning, teaching and assessing the curriculum for pupils with learning difficulties. Commercially published materials are also readily available – for example, in Learning Development Aids' (LDA) *Assessment for the NLS Framework* materials, and the Special Needs Individualized Programme Planning (SNIPP) materials produced by Northumberland LEA: sources are listed at the end of this book. The school special needs resource area should include some of these materials, alongside the home-grown versions which individual teachers in the school may have produced in relation to particular schemes of work.

Choosing the right teaching style

Differentiation is not just a matter of providing children with tasks aimed at learning objectives matched to their status on a hypothetical learning ladder. Were it so, we might as well return wholesale to the practice of streaming, with children pursuing largely separate curricula and with status accorded mainly to high-fliers. Fortunately, however, the National Curriculum is open to other forms of differentiation as well: to situations where the task and the learning objective stay the same for all children, including those with special needs, and where the differentiation strategies are applied within the shared task by varying the way in which the task is presented to the children, or the way they are asked to approach it, or the ways in which they record their learning.

Teaching styles can be varied in a number of ways:

- Using teaching approaches matched to children's preferred learning styles – visual, verbal, kinaesthetic, fast paced, slower paced, etc.
- Taking 'time out' from whole-class teaching for children to talk in pairs, so as to sustain concentration and link inputs to the child's own language/experience.
- Using interactive strategies during whole-class teaching – children having cards to hold up, or their own small whiteboards, or coming to the front to take a role.
- Simplifying/extending tasks – for example, by providing a long, abstract piece of text for one group to work on and a short, concrete piece for another group.

- Choosing more motivating activities by linking tasks to children's individual interests.
- Dividing longer pieces of classroom work into shorter tasks, each with its own endpoint.
- Increasing the use of active learning approaches (wordstorming, drama, role play, card sorts, making posters or a display, group discussion, group problem-solving activities).
- Providing opportunities for repetition and reinforcement – the same type of activity presented in different ways, reviewing earlier learning regularly, giving the child the opportunity to teach something newly-learned to others.
- Using a variety of pupil groupings so that children are able to draw on each other's strengths and skills to achieve genuinely collaborative learning.
- Using praise/reward to help some children stay on task.
- Making tasks more open ('Devise your own experiment to explore friction . . .'), or more closed ('Follow the step-by-step instructions on the card').
- Making questions more open ('What do you think about . . . ?'), or more closed ('Do you think x . . . or y . . . ?).

Using access strategies

Access (or bypass) strategies are used when a child can work at the same level, on the same learning objectives, using the same teaching styles as other children, but needs to be able to bypass an impairment or difficulty in order to access the work. A child with a visual impairment, for example, is provided with texts that have been enlarged on the photocopier; a child with language difficulties is given the instructions for a task one by one instead of all at once; a group of children who can't yet tell the time but need to be able to read a clock face for a science experiment use a clock on which the teacher has stuck peel-off labels saying 'five past', 'ten past' next to the relevant numbers; a child who finds writing difficult works with a more fluent writer who acts as a scribe.

The 'menu' of bypass strategies needs to cover the inputs to the child's learning (the teacher's input, the instructions and texts used, the resources/materials used by the child for the task) and the outputs required (written or other responses).

Inputs can be made more accessible by:

- Simplifying verbal instructions (short sentences, simpler vocabulary).
- Demonstration.
- Using visual and concrete aids – real objects, signs/symbols, photo cards.
- Making sure that the teacher can be seen and heard – background noise avoided where possible, light source in front of teacher not behind.
- Carefully planning pupils' seating.
- Varying content so as to ensure a mixture of concrete examples, directly related to pupils' direct experience, and some more abstract/remote examples.
- Clarifying new or difficult vocabulary.
- Checking for understanding of instructions – for example, by asking a child to repeat them.
- Providing reminders of instructions – for example, task boards or cards.

- Writing down and leaving on view instructions after saying them.
- Reading aloud key text or instructions before the children read them.
- Putting up a glossary of word meanings for difficult vocabulary.
- Simplifying written worksheets and texts (short sentences, active not passive verbs, making instructions stand out boldly).
- Supplementing information in books with tapes, video, pictures, charts and diagrams.
- Providing texts with speech-supported computer access.

Outputs can be differentiated by:

- Using alternatives to written recording: oral presentation, tape recordings, video recordings, models, photos, posters, drama, key word lists, drawings, dictation to a helper, dramatic presentation, pictures/diagrams/flowcharts, computer aided recording.
- Providing prompt sheets for writing: questions to answer, key words to build each section or paragraph around, sentences or paragraphs to put in the correct order, paragraph openings.
- Providing clue cards.
- Using cloze procedure, where the pupil fills in missing words from the text rather than writing up from scratch.
- Using cooperative writing in groups or pairs.
- Providing 'scaffolding' – for example, writing frames, word lists, word mats.
- Using tasks where the response involves sorting/categorizing objects, pictures or cards with words or letters on them, instead of writing – for example, sorting statements into biography versus autobiography.
- Using tasks involving matching – for example, matching labels to objects, or labels to parts of diagrams, sentences or pictures.
- Using tasks where the response is highlighting – for example, highlighting nouns in one colour, verbs in another.
- Using word-processing with speech feedback and on-screen word banks.

Differentiation in practice: an example

The three circles of differentiation need to be built into the teacher's planning at an early stage, in relation to the particular needs of children in the class. This was the approach taken by the teacher we met earlier in the chapter for her work on water, and these were some of the ideas she came up with:

> For work in English on the 'water' folk-tales and legends, she asked her teaching assistant to read the shared texts ahead of time with a group of children so that they were prepared for them when it came to class shared reading. The group also made a glossary of word meanings for new or difficult words. For the task of preparing to perform the *Bringing the Rain to Kapiti Plain* narrative poem she had children work in mixed ability groups and made sure that the roles of children with literacy difficulties included making picture props and taking easier 'parts' – lines that were repeated cumulatively throughout the text, and were hence familiar. For another day's independent

work, while some children were writing their modern-day versions of legends, those with special needs did a labelling activity, matching words to pictures in the text with Blu-Tack.

As part of their geography work, the teacher wanted to extend pupils' speaking and listening skills. She organized a short debate on whether it is right to flood rural communities in the process of building dams, in order to bring water to newly industrialized areas. She knew that several children would find this difficult; she planned to give each of them a set of cards on which were written statements about the issue which they could sort into two piles – those they agreed with and those they disagreed with. They would then discuss with a friend their reasons for agreeing or disagreeing with each statement, and use all this as a basis for their contribution when it came to discussion in larger groups.

Throughout the geographical work on water across the world the teacher made sure that the books available included several with large, clear print and plenty of illustrations. A display of the processes involved in water purification was interesting, but involved a lot of reading: the teacher asked a group of moderately good readers to make a tape of the text and captions, so that other children could listen to it while using the display. Before they watched a video on the water cycle, she planned to give some children with difficulties in picking out key features of inputs a card specifying key things to look out for.

The main need in science, the teacher felt, was to provide a step-by-step description (for some children) of how to go about the experiments on evaporation, condensation and filtration, and make sure that the children could understand her science work cards. She rewrote sentences like 'In this experiment you will be comparing the rate of evaporation in large and small containers' to say 'You are going to find out whether water evaporates faster in small containers, or in big ones'. During the practical sessions, less able children worked with a partner of higher ability, with the simplified instructions (accompanied by diagrams) to refer to. Afterwards, they could choose to record their work on a pre-prepared sheet. Sometimes this supplied a framework of headings (of the 'what we used', 'what we did' type); sometimes it took the form of a cloze passage – a piece of text in which the teacher had Tipp-exed out key words and written them at the bottom so that the child could choose which one should go in each space.

Mathematics and ICT opportunities arising from the science and geography work included homework activities to record the use of water in the home on a spreadsheet. To help everyone participate, the teacher decided that the initial work of planning the spreadsheet and deciding how to record the data would be done in mixed ability groups. Later, however, a group of more able mathematicians would be given an open-ended opportunity to extract comparisons from their data.

All this differentiation took a considerable amount of prior organization from the teacher. Classrooms offering an undifferentiated curriculum require relatively little prior organization: the teacher has to plan one scheme of work, make one master of each worksheet, order one set of materials. The demands on the teacher are likely to be of a reactive rather than proactive kind, as they grapple with the insistent demands for help and the behavioural difficulties that are likely to arise when tasks are not matched to individuals. For the teacher offering a differentiated curriculum, the situation is reversed: far fewer on the spot demands for explanation and help, but a great deal to do before the children arrive. The necessary organization and planning *is* time consuming; the bonus is that once it is done, it can be used again, and the stress on the teacher is likely to be a lot less.

Ideally, the prior planning can be a team effort. Bale (1999) describes how, in her school, all short-term plans have a section on differentiation. Weekly planning meetings for year groups provide staff with the opportunity to plan together for any necessary modifications; there is also a section in the planning format to identify specific tasks for teaching assistants.

Pupil groupings and cooperative learning

One way in which the teacher can reduce the demands on them when teaching in a differentiated way is to make use of the largely untapped resource available in the classroom – other children.

Other children need to be involved whenever one of their peers is struggling with an aspect of learning or behaviour, because of the supreme power of the social world to motivate, challenge and reward: for most children, interaction with the peer group is the most important thing that happens at school, and work with a peer is a more powerful energizer than even the most inspiring teaching.

The main models for liberating this peer energy have been summarized by Charlton (1998), and include collaborative group work and pair work leading to peer and cross-age tutoring.

The return to such cooperative learning is not the traditional answer to differentiation in British classrooms. Croll and Moses (1985), for example, found that children with special needs were given *less* time on work involving cooperating with other pupils than were their classmates without special needs. Even today, giving children with special needs a series of individual and individualized tasks (often in worksheet form) is still the preferred teacher response to special needs in most primary classrooms; the number of schools resorting to rigid setting practices which preclude mixed ability cooperative learning continues to increase.

Such approaches can, however, deny the children who most need it the opportunity to learn from the kind of social dialogue with 'more knowledgeable others' which is fundamental to human learning and development. As Diane Montgomery (1990) argues:

> Children with learning difficulties need classrooms in which there is collaborative learning, negotiation, oral problem solving and discussion between pupils. The individualized programme and remedial tutorial are generally unsuitable as the *main* teaching vehicle for them, for they limit the communication channels which are open for learning, and throw them back on their own limited cognitive resources.

Cooperative group work, then, fosters learning in children with special needs because it increases the resources they can draw on. It is also particularly beneficial for children with special needs because it works on the particular attitudes and behaviours that have been shown to be problematic for them: it enhances self-esteem (Johnson and Johnson 1987) and increases engagement with learning tasks by as much as 20 per cent (Bennett 1991).

What does collaborative group work for pupils with special needs actually mean? First, it does not mean just seating groups of pupils together to do their work. As observational research has repeatedly shown, the kinds of cooperation this leads to are most often chat among the children about what was on television last night, what page they are on, and who has hidden the rubber. The ORACLE study (Galton *et al.* 1980) showed that children spent up to five hours a week interacting with each other in class, but three-quarters of these interactions had nothing to do with the task in hand. In many situations that pass as group work, children sit together but do individual work; the grouping is purely an organizational device allowing for occasional economies of direct teaching input. More recently, McPake *et al.* (1999) have shown that children sitting around tables were on task for less than half their time. Where the teacher taught the whole class, their time on task rose to 74 per cent. The children did best of all, however, on the rare occasions when they worked *together* on a task, when they were on task for an average of 93 per cent of the time.

To achieve genuinely collaborative group work, children need to be given the kinds of challenging tasks with a common goal that are encouraged by the National Curriculum. These can be language based: buzz- and wordstorming groups, collaboration around an adventure game on a computer, group story composition, critical support for each other's writing, providing a forum to share responses to a story or poem, standpoint taking, group prioritizing and ranking of issues and concerns. Or they can be of the practical, problem solving variety: design a home for yourself given information about climate, terrain and tools available, find out how many children in the class are left- and right-handed, make a cart that will roll down a slope, fill three boxes $\square + \square \times \square$ with cards numbered 1, 2 and 3 to make the largest and smallest possible answer.

The next essential for successful collaborative work in a differentiated curriculum is to plan the composition of the groups. Here the message from research is becoming clear: for cooperative learning where the teacher acts as facilitator but not instructor, mixed ability groups work better than single ability groups for children of average and below average ability, and at least as well as single ability groups for children of above average ability. Swing and Peterson (1982), for example, found that both high and low attaining children learned more in mixed ability groups, and hypothesized that the more able children gained a deeper understanding of, and a greater hold on new learning through explaining and justifying their ideas to the less able. Slavin (1996), in a two-year study of schools using cooperative learning found particularly positive effects on the achievement of the very ablest pupils – those in the top 5–10 per cent of their classes. Bennett (1991) analysed the kinds of talk in groups of all high, all average and all low ability children. He found that if grouped together the low attainers tended to use low-quality discourse, with very little sharing of explanations or knowledge. Low attainers in mixed ability groups, however, benefited from the more sophisticated talk and achieved more. High attainers performed well whichever group they happened to be a member of – an important finding that should help to allay the widespread fear that mixed ability group work may hold back the more able children.

Bennett's research also looked at different types of mixed ability group, some with two more able children to one less able, and some with the reverse. He concluded:

> On every criterion it was the two low and one high group which was superior. What appeared to happen in the other combination is that the two high attainers talked together whilst the low attainer was ignored, or opted out, and as a consequence misunderstood the basis on which decisions were being made. In the two low and one high combination, on the other hand, the high attainer took on the role of peer tutor and support.
>
> (Bennett 1991: 586)

Other strategies which will help children with special needs to get the most out of cooperative learning include preparing them ahead of time for their contribution to the group, and allocating tasks and roles within the group. Less confident children can be asked to talk, plan, or research first in a friendship pair, before joining up into fours or sixes to complete the task as a group. Or the teacher can use the jigsaw technique, where small groups of four to five are given a topic, and each student is made responsible for becoming an expert in a particular aspect. The children go off to do their research, coming together at the end to teach each other the information or use it for a task. For example, if the class is going to find out about materials that dissolve in water (Norman 1990), the children start in what are called 'home' groups to discuss the kinds of things they may do and be allocated a number. Then children from across the home groups with the same number join up as an 'expert' group with a particular investigation to do. When the investigations are finished, the children return to their home groups, where they are able to take an expert role in contributing their own findings to the discussion that puts all the pieces of the jigsaw together.

Another group work structure (McNamara and Moreton 1997) has children start in mixed ability groups; each group is given a colour of the rainbow – red, orange, yellow and so on. Each group is then given information about an event or situation from a particular point of view. For example, when studying the Spanish Armada, one group might be given information from the point of view of the Spanish sailors, another from the point of view of Queen Elizabeth, another an English cabin boy, another Drake, and another the Plymouth townspeople. The best reader in the group might read the account to the others, who summarize the key points. Then each member of the group goes off to join others in new 'rainbow' groups, representing all the perspectives. These new groups discuss the similarities and differences in viewpoints and try to arrive at a balanced description.

A further confidence-building system is to set up a carousel or workstation approach in which children work in groups of six at different tables, on tasks which can be closed ('Follow written directions to make a Roman stylus and wax tablet'), or open ('Build a tower of newspaper able to support the weight of a brick'). When it is time to change activity and move on to a new table, three children stay at the workstation and three move on. The three children staying on tutor the new arrivals in how to tackle the task, freeing the teacher to work in a focused way with one group at a time.

Participation within the group can also be encouraged by allocating children to particular roles: materials gatherer, reader, scribe, checker, timekeeper, chairperson. Sometimes these roles will rotate; sometimes they will make use of children's individual strengths on a more permanent basis. Even children with major special needs and abilities very disparate from those of other group members can be successfully integrated if they are provided with a useful group process role. Johnson and Johnson (1987) describe strategies such as asking the pupil to be responsible for explaining the group's decision, checking that everyone in the group has understood the decision, or praising members for their contributions.

Using cooperative group work, then, as a means of increasing access to the curriculum for children with special needs, will involve setting up mixed ability groups in which more able children are in the minority and in which everyone is encouraged to participate by developing prior expertise and taking on clear roles. Incentives are also important: much research (Slavin 1996) has shown that for cooperative learning to work effectively the rewards which children achieve (for example, marks given, or certificates) should be based on the sum of all the group members' individual performances. In this way, the group's task is to make sure that *everyone* in the group has mastered the content or succeeded in completing the task.

Cooperative groups will function best if they have the opportunity to work together on a variety of tasks for a term or more, so that they can profit from the experience of developing effective teamwork over a period of time. One way of encouraging this is to build in time for group members to review, after each task, the way they worked together and organized themselves (see Table 3.1).

Also helpful is having one member of the group in turn to act as observer during the group's work, perhaps focusing on individuals' contributions using a rating sheet based on the ground rules the group has adopted (see Box 3.3). Explicit teaching of the skills of turn-taking, listening and acknowledging others' contributions may be needed; McNamara and Moreton (1997) provide inspiring ideas on how this can be done, and on the essential place of mixed ability paired work as a prelude to work in larger groups.

Just as adults do, children need to learn to work together: for some children with special needs, the opportunity to learn over time, through actual experience and constructive feedback from peers, may be particularly important and worth any amount of adult lecturing on how to behave in groups.

Work with one mixed ability group over an extended period, however, needs to be balanced with opportunities to work in other types of grouping. Flexibility is the key to success: there is no reason to believe that working all day every day in one mixed group will meet all the needs of pupils with learning difficulties, any more than will asking them to work all day every day in one 'slow learners' group. Given the evidence that many children with special needs require a greater structure to their learning, and more opportunities for repetition and reinforcement than their peers, time needs to be

Table 3.1 Reviewing a group task

What helped . . .	What got in the way . . .
When we decided that Alison would be the leader	We kept on chatting
When we split up to do different jobs	We didn't listen to Andrew's idea
	We took too long to do the measuring

Box 3.3 Rating sheet

WORKING WELL TOGETHER

Name _____

Group _____

Activity _____

Date _____

Did this person:

1 Listen to others?
         YES   A LITTLE   NO

2 Praise others' ideas?
         YES   A LITTLE   NO

3 Give some ideas?
         YES   A LITTLE   NO

4 Help sort out arguments?
         YES   A LITTLE   NO

5 Help the group get the job done on time?
         YES   NO

found for direct instruction of groups of children who are all at a similar stage in their learning, and at a similar rung on the National Curriculum ladder. As well as guided reading and writing, bringing together a group of children around a big book which the teacher is using to introduce concepts of print, or teaching a group of children about place value, are examples of this very necessary kind of work. For children with special needs, increasing the amount of time spent on such group work (with the teacher present throughout in an instructional role) is not just economical of teacher time; it can also make a big difference to children's concentration and achievement. Croll and Moses (1985), for example, showed that for slow learning children and children with behaviour problems, whose overall levels of time spent concentrating on the task in hand were below average, a shift to group work with the teacher rather than individual work or class work meant a very big rise in their engagement with learning.

Organizing for differentiation

Mixed ability pair work and cooperative group work are two of the organizational structures which the teacher can use to ensure curriculum access for the whole range of abilities within the classroom. This is not, however, the only answer. Teachers also need to consider how they will ensure differentiation during whole-class teaching, and when pupils are working independently.

What will good differentiation look like at these times – in the Literacy Hour and daily maths lesson, for example? In whole-class work, the teacher will:

● Explain new or difficult vocabulary and be able to refer to wall displays which remind the children of what these words or symbols mean.
● Check for understanding of instructions, often by asking one child to repeat them for the class.
● Give children time to respond to questions, or 'think time' in pairs before coming up with answers.
● Reflect back children's contributions in expanded form, or have one child's contribution expanded on by other pupils.
● Use all the interactive strategies suggested by their training on the literacy and numeracy frameworks, so that children (particularly those with attentional difficulties) have frequent opportunities to show their understanding by holding up cards or objects, writing on an individual whiteboard or coming to the front to take a role.
● Use visual aids – real objects, pictures, photo cards, cut-out symbols, words and numbers on cards – anything that children can see, touch or manipulate.

The teacher needs to plan the questions they ask during whole-class teaching, so as to include all children. They will identify the focus for the class as a whole – for example, in the Literacy Hour for a Year 4 class, 'Identify a range of punctuation (commas, semicolons, dashes etc.) and respond to them appropriately when reading'. Then they will link those whole-class objectives with objectives which appear earlier in the 'learning ladder' and are relevant to particular children in the class with SEN – for example, 'Recognizing and responding appropriately to full stops and capital letters'. The teacher will ask questions about the shared text which are at different levels: asking some children to read (with the right expression) sentences with semicolons and colons, while asking a child with SEN to read sentences demarcated by full stops. The class can then be asked to compare the intonation for each type of punctuation. In maths, the teacher will engage children in a shared activity, but at different levels – when counting round the class, for example, by asking some children to count in ones to five, with others then counting on from five in tens and a third group counting on further in hundreds.

As well as differentiating their questioning, the teacher will want to model (or, even better, ask other children to model) learning objectives at a number of different levels, appropriate to the needs of individual children. An example here might be teaching diagonal joins in handwriting to a Year 3 class; while demonstrating these, the teacher can also model the correct starting point for the single letter 'a' which a particular child needs to work on.

For parts of the whole-class teaching it may be best to differentiate by running a parallel group. In the Literacy Hour this particularly applies to word-level work, when a group of children might, for example, need to work on long vowel phonemes with a support teacher or teaching assistant, while the rest of the class work on suffixes.

Another model is the one suggested for the daily maths lesson, where the teacher teaches the whole class, then some children go off to work on their own while the teacher continues to teach the rest, and then they go off to their tasks while the teacher continues to work with one or two children who are likely to have difficulty. This organizational strategy will be most effective if the pattern is varied, so that sometimes the children who stay behind to work alone or in a pair with the teacher are more able pupils needing extension work: in this way the self-esteem of the children with SEN will not be affected.

Differentiation of work in the independent part of the daily lesson can follow a number of different models:

- Children can work in collaborative pairs or collaborative mixed ability groups.
- A group of children with SEN can work together with an additional adult, following a structured programme matched to their needs – for example, a catch-up programme.
- Children can work independently on set class tasks which have been differentiated by learning objective – for example, where the class are counting vehicles which pass the school for a bar chart, a pupil who is learning to count to three might be asked to count buses (as these are infrequent), while other children learning to count in higher numbers count the more frequent types of vehicle.
- Children can work individually on set class tasks that have been differentiated using strategies from the 'access' and 'teaching styles' menus which we looked at earlier in this chapter.
- Children can work independently on activities structured around their own very individual learning needs – for example, a child in a Year 4 class

who is working towards Level 1 might do a tracing activity linked to a motor skills target on their IEP.

The secret of success if children are working individually will be the adjustment of tasks to reflect the learning objectives appropriate to the child, through the planning process which the NNS characterizes as building in challenge (for some more able pupils), reinforcement (for the broad band of children in the class) and simplification (for children with learning difficulties). Success will also rely on the careful choice of tasks which offer alternatives to conventional written recording. In the Literacy Hour, the child might be:

- matching words or sentences to pictures;
- reordering words to make sentences from the shared text;
- sequencing pictures, sentences, paragraphs or pages from the text;
- matching the beginning and endings of sentences from the text;
- sorting objects according to initial sounds;
- using self-checking materials like LDA's 'Stile';
- rereading a favourite part of a book to a friend;
- listening to a tape of the shared text;
- highlighting parts of the text for a particular purpose.

As an example of this kind of differentiation, consider this teacher's planning:

When teaching her class about verbs, the teacher planned work for a group of children with literacy difficulties which would minimize the amount of writing expected from them. She gave the children photocopied passages of text matched to their independent reading ability. The children had to highlight all the verbs in the passages. After this, each child was given a set of sentences in which they had to identify the verb and experiment with substitute verbs. While more able pupils used a thesaurus for this, the group of children with SEN had alternative verbs to choose from, presented on cards for them to physically place on top of the existing verb. Another day, the group sorted cards into 'verb' and 'non-verb' piles, and had sentences to colour code using highlighter pens (one colour for nouns, one for verbs; other children in the class also colour coded adjectives and pronouns). After colour coding, they cut up their sentences and worked with a partner to arrange the words to make as many sentences as they could. The task was to note the position of the verb in the sentences they had created, and feed back their observations in the plenary session.

It is important in plenary sessions, whatever the subject, to have the whole class together. It is this that gives the right message about the importance of everbody's work and the accountability of all to show how they have used their time in pursuit of shared-class goals. Differentiation needs to apply here too, with careful planning of the plenary so that it reinforces objectives at a number of different levels, and so that all children have an opportunity to contribute.

Conclusion

This chapter has focused on the benefits (some potential, some actual) of the National Curriculum for children with SEN, particularly the encouragement of group work and the emphasis on planning for differentiation within programmes of study that are meant for all. The negatives have not been emphasized, partly because they are already widely understood, and partly because a theoretical discussion of the problems inherent in a curriculum largely geared towards narrow academic success would be out of place in a practical guide of this kind. Nor has this chapter touched on the impact, for good or ill, of assessment arrangements within the National Curriculum, or the impact on pupil progress of the elaborate framework for monitoring and reporting assessment outcomes. It is to this that we turn in the next chapter.

Assessment and special educational needs

Introduction

Assessment of children's progress within the National Curriculum is an area in which most teachers are now highly skilled. Concerns remain, however, about how far the systems put in place for the generality of children meet the needs of children with difficulties in learning. The assessment arrangements may help to identify pupils who are failing to make progress, so that appropriate support can be given at an early stage, and may help pupils and teachers to target more clearly the next steps in teaching and learning. Nevertheless, there are risks that for children with special needs the targets may seem unreachable, and the experience of assessment is an experience of failure. The learning steps within the National Curriculum are, as we have seen, very large, and some children will need to have their achievements monitored in greater detail if progress is to be adequately demonstrated. It will be important to find ways of celebrating progress that is made in small steps, and of recording a wide range of achievement. Most importantly, the focus on assessment of achievement within the National Curriculum should not lead us to lose sight of other kinds of assessment, notably the concept of assessing needs, not children – of not asking the question 'What can this child do and not do?' but rather asking 'What does this child *need* from us in terms of resources, tasks and differentiated teaching approaches in order to make progress?'

Identifying special needs

All schools are required by law to identify SEN, let parents know if they consider a child to have SEN, and keep records of children that they have identified. The risks of labelling and creating negative expectations implicit in all such systems need to be balanced by a clear picture on the part of the school of the purposes to be served in identifying special needs. Staff should discuss for themselves what they see as the intended positive outcomes, and regularly monitor the system used to identify needs to make sure that it is fulfilling agreed purposes. Outcomes might include:

● Ensuring the effective deployment of resources, both from within the school and from external support agencies.
● Ensuring continuity of response when the child moves from one class or school to another.
● Ensuring that parents or carers are involved very early on in discussions about the best ways to support the child.
● Initiating further, more detailed, assessment of the child's needs.
● Providing the school with information about areas where the curriculum or teaching approaches may be creating difficulties for pupils.

A major issue in identifying special needs is whether the teacher's own judgements are sufficient, or whether more objective screening instruments should be used. The evidence we have suggests that subjective teacher assessments are quite discriminating: teachers do not just pick out a fixed proportion of children in their classes (the 'bottom end') as having special needs, but instead nominate numbers that vary widely from class to class (Croll and Moses 1985). Diana Moses (1982), however, has shown that when making judgements about whether a particular child has special needs, teachers are heavily influenced by whether the child shows a particular behaviour pattern – low work rate, fidgeting and restlessness – which they associate with the slow learning child. Children who do not show this behaviour pattern, but who are nevertheless picked out as having difficulties on the basis of SATs, tend to be missed in the teacher judgements of special needs.

The focus on regular teacher assessment and testing within the National Curriculum may help to highlight the needs of such children. It may also highlight another group sometimes missed by teachers – those with specific learning difficulties whose performance, perhaps in reading or written language, may not be very much out of step with that of other children in the class, but where there are significant discrepancies between these literacy attainments and the child's own performance in other areas of the curriculum, such as science or speaking and listening.

National Curriculum assessment and baseline assessment at the end of the foundation stage, however, are unlikely to be sufficient on their own to make sure that all special needs come to the notice of the teacher and the school. In addition, many schools will want to use screening instruments that pick up early indicators of difficulty. These include:

● Behaviour checklists (Goodman 1997; Bristol City Council 2000).
● Language screening instruments, such as the AFASIC checklists published by LDA, or the whole-class screening system in NFER-Nelson's 'Teaching Talking'.
● Literacy screening tools, such as the NLS Early Literacy Support screening pack for Year 1, and maths materials from the NNS.
● Checklists for indicators of minor visual or hearing impairment (see Boxes 4.1 and 4.2).
● Checklists for indicators of specific learning difficulty/dyslexia, or the more labour intensive computerized dyslexia screening systems (see Chapter 11).
● Checklists for indicators of motor difficulties/dyspraxia (see Chapter 12).

Box 4.1 Checklist of indicators of possible visual difficulties

- Slower than expected educational progress and short attention span
- Finds it hard to copy from books or the board
- Handwriting difficulties – unusually large, small or poorly formed letters, poor spacing, inability to stay on the line
- Rubs eyes frequently, frowning or scowling, excessive blinking
- Holds reading material at an unusual distance or angle
- Appears clumsy and uncoordinated; often trips or stumbles
- Often loses place or skips lines, letters or words when reading
- Confuses visually similar letters and words
- Tires easily when looking at print or fine detail
- Takes longer than other children to complete reading assignments
- A rigid body when reading or viewing distant objects

Box 4.2 Checklist of indicators of possible hearing loss

- Slower than expected educational progress and short attention span
- May not respond when spoken to, asks for things to be repeated, or gives answers that seem unrelated to the question
- Tends to ignore, mistake or forget instructions
- Watches the speaker's face for clues; watches teacher over-intently
- Seems in a world of their own; daydreams; switches off
- Shows signs of irritability, frustration, temper
- Behaviour erratic; worse when they have a cold, or in listening situations
- Speaks unusually loudly, or indistinctly, with parts of words missing
- Has difficulty acquiring phonic skills for reading and spelling
- Has a history of repeated ear infections; appears catarrhal

---

Box 4.3 Screening checklist for class teachers at the end of Key Stage 1

All responses should be affirmative. If they are not, further investigation or action by the teacher may be indicated. Action may simply be the setting of a review date to ensure progress is monitored through to the development of clear action plans with parents.

Academic skills

All core subjects reported at Level 2.

Study and attention skills

- Responds to class directions, e.g. pack up, line up
- Follows routine sequence of instructions to class, e.g. 'When you've finished your writing put the book on my desk and get ready for PE'

- Listens and responds contextually, staying to the point, for 5–10 mins, e.g. in circle time
- Can recount an experience in sequence
- Can get out and put away equipment independently
- Asks for help when needed
- Has the confidence to make mistakes
- Has the confidence to make an initial attempt at something new after explanation, without adult support
- Completes a task well within competence, during time given, without nagging
- Given time in another lesson, e.g. after break, can pick up and finish work after reminder about task and content
- After an introduction to work, already some familiarity, knows what to do and can make a start
- Can complete a short task, e.g. construction, with two others

Social and personal control

- Has a friend or group to play with
- Can take part in a group activity, sharing equipment
- Can accept some give and take needed in play
- Approaches adult to ask for help, e.g. 'they've bullied me'
- Can admit when they have done something wrong and accept the consequences
- Can generally behave acceptably and safely in the playground
- Can move around school acceptably and safely
- Can generally conform to rules of the class
- Able to lose in a game without having a tantrum

Independence

- Can see to personal needs, e.g. eating, dressing, toileting and personal hygiene
- Usually arrives in the morning with 'things' for the day, e.g. book bag, dinner money, etc.
- Can convey a written message between home and school
- Looks after belongings and looks for them if they get mislaid
- Knows the routines of the class and school

Self-confidence

- Has the confidence to express an opinion in a group
- Can assert self at times in a small group
- Has the confidence to go somewhere new with a friend
- Feels they are good at something in school and can tell you a little about why they feel this
- Can identify something they would like to improve at and feel able to work on
- Talks positively about self at times, e.g. 'I'm good at swimming/I look nice in my new dress/Jo and Les like me'

Physical/medical

- Has no damaging habits
- Hearing good
- Near and distant vision good or wears glasses if needed
- No new medical problems identified other than those already recorded
- No new medication other than those noted in records
- Speech clear and audible, structure and vocabulary commensurate with peers

A good source of advice for schools seeking to build up a comprehensive set of screening tools is often their own LEA: many LEA support services (for example, Newcastle upon Tyne with their 'Complete Works') have produced their own packages, sometimes linked to sets of IEP targets and strategies. Some schools have also developed their own screening systems, linked to the criteria set out in their SEN policies for identifying children as having SEN: an example is given in Box 4.3.

Further assessment

Having identified children who may have special needs, using informal teacher judgement supplemented or moderated by some of the more formal screening instruments, the next step is further, more detailed assessment:

Mr James had noticed that out of all the children in his Year 2 class, Adam seemed to be making the slowest progress with his maths, particularly numeracy work. Mr James decided to make Adam the focus of classroom observation for a few days. Using a notebook and Post-its, he jotted down things he noticed as they happened; he also made time to sit with Adam while he was working on his maths. The observations showed that Adam worked hard and concentrated well when writing or doing practical work, but appeared to daydream when he had to do any work involving written numerals. Listening to him talking about some addition using a number line, Mr James noticed that he used the number line to count right through the number sequence and arrive at the numeral he needed for the calculation. Thus, for 7 + 2, he would count 1-2-3-4-5-6-7 before saying, 'It's seven add two'. Following a hunch, Mr James wrote down the numbers 1 to 10 in random order and asked Adam to name them. Adam could only name a few. He clearly had a real difficulty in remembering the names for numerals, but had managed to get by without this being noticed because he could recall their names if they were in order or if he referred to a number line and went through the whole number sequence. Mr James wondered if Adam might have some visual difficulties which made it hard for him to tell one number from another, and decided to try him on a test where he had to find the right match for written numerals. For example:

5   2 7 5 3 8

Adam had no trouble at all with this. Mr James was puzzled, but when he shared his observations with Adam's parents, they told him that Adam often seemed to forget the names for things: he sometimes took a long time to get his words out, and would express himself in a roundabout way – 'It's in the place you wash dishes' instead of 'the sink', for example. He had been late in talking and had a period of speech therapy before starting school. Mr James contacted the speech therapist who had worked with Adam. She felt that his difficulties with numbers were a legacy of his earlier language difficulties, and probably part of what she called 'word-finding' problems. She and

Mr James discussed some strategies that would help, such as providing Adam with a ruler clearly marked to at least 30 as an always available reference point, and teaching key points (5, 10, 15, 20, 25) from which he could count to arrive at the number name he needed. She also suggested that Adam practise number naming in relaxed contexts far removed from ordinary number work – playing dice games with numbers rather than dots on the dice, playing dominoes with dots to be matched to numerals, using coins in shopping games with purchases marked in amounts like 12p, playing darts with his dad, or collecting information about car number plates. Mr James recorded a plan of action based on these strategies, and discussed it with Adam and his parents; they agreed to review the plan together in six weeks. If it seemed to be helping, they would know that they and the speech therapist were on the right track in their initial assessment of the reasons for Adam's slow progress in maths.

Sadiq was 7, and his teacher was concerned about his immature behaviour; he found it hard to sit still for any length of time in the classroom and didn't always do as he was told. He had, the teacher felt, poor motor control which caused him to struggle with handwriting and drawing. She discussed her concerns with the headteacher and SENCO. The SENCO asked if she could spend some time in the classroom observing Sadiq, and then free the class teacher to do some work with him on his own. The SENCO was able to feed back to the teacher the contrast she observed between Sadiq's unsettled behaviour in the rather formal atmosphere of the classroom and his behaviour in a PE lesson, where he produced very creative ideas and worked well with a group. She suggested that he might need shorter tasks with a more active learning style, and offered to look at the teacher's lesson planning with her to identify opportunities for this. The class teacher, alone with Sadiq, asked him to finish a piece of work. She noticed that he really seemed to be struggling to get his drawings and writing onto the small paper in his exercise book. His letters were erratic in size, with no clear distinction between ascenders and descenders. She asked Sadiq to tell her how he felt about writing. 'It makes my hand hurt', he said. When she suggested that he tell her the rest of his story so that she could write it down for him, he produced some ideas and vocabulary which really astonished her. They agreed that in future Sadiq would use bigger paper and a larger pencil for some of his work, and would tell her when his hand hurt so they could finish the work together. In addition, the teacher would provide him with special handwriting sheets where he could practise getting his 'monkey', 'turtle' and 'giraffe' letters the right size.

In their assessments, these teachers made use of a number of strategies which can help us to gain a clearer picture of the situation when a child seems to have special needs:

- Classroom observation of strengths as well as weaknesses, and of factors in the learning context that may be helping or hindering the child's progress, as well as of factors within the child.

- Child–adult conferencing, to obtain a 'window into the child's mind'.
- Miscue analysis: looking at the child's apparent mistakes to see what light they shed on the strategies and thought processes they are using.
- Using an analysis of the small steps leading up to mastery of a particular skill, in order to see if there are significant gaps in the child's prior knowledge and understanding that make them unable to cope consistently with the task.
- Assessing underlying skills (in perception, memory, motor coordination) to see if there are weaknesses which might be affecting school learning.
- Gathering information on the child's strengths, weaknesses and interests in other situations, notably the home.
- Assessment through action planning: finding out what works and what does not, through deciding on a strategy to support the child, trying it out, and evaluating it.
- Using standardized tests.

Let us look now at each of these diagnostic assessment methods in turn.

Classroom observation

Classroom observation can include making notes or keeping a diary, making a tape recording of the child reading or talking in a group, making a video recording or using a structured format for observing specific behaviours. A record of a child's contribution to group processes (see Chapter 3) would be one example of a structured format; another might be a sheet on which the teacher notes whether a child is on or off task at set intervals during the day; another a sheet on which the teacher records the antecedents, behaviour, consequences (ABCs) for a particular classroom behaviour problem over the course of a week. In all such classroom observation, it is important to gather information on the types of task or setting where the child succeeds, as well as the areas of weakness: such observations provide vital clues to contextual factors which might be contributing to the child's difficulties – such as the overlong tasks Sadiq's teacher was using.

Child–adult conferencing

Through conferencing, the teacher aims to gain a clearer picture of the child's misunderstandings or misconceptions – for example, that they believe that the amount of water changes when it is poured from a tall narrow container into a shallow wide one, or that hitting people at school is morally acceptable if someone else started it. Through conferencing, the teacher should also be able to discover how the child feels about certain tasks or situations, and about themself as a learner. Direct, closed questions are avoided; instead, the teacher uses openers such as 'Tell me about how you feel when...' ('...you're listening to me reading a story', '...you're writing in your journal'), or invitations to complete sentences ('The trouble with having to sit and listen to stories is...'; 'it would be better if...'; 'I feel happy at school when...'; 'I feel sad/angry/worried/embarrassed in school when...'). The child's self-esteem can be explored, using questions like those in Box 4.4, or a card sort like the one in Box 4.5 can be used to elicit perceptions of the self as a learner.

Box 4.4   Exploring the child's self-concept

1 _____ is very good at sports
　Are you like him/her?

2 _____ is always helpful
　Are you like him/her?

3 _____ is very good at school work
　Are you like him/her?

4 _____ usually behaves well
　Are you like him/her?

5 _____ is very clever
　Are you like him/her?

6 _____ is very good looking
　Are you like him/her?

7 _____ is a very happy person
　Are you like him/her?

8 _____ is very strong
　Are you like him/her?

9 _____ has lots of friends
　Are you like him/her?

10 _____ is a kind person
　Are you like him/her?

11 _____ is good at _____
　Are you like him/her?

Ask the child to choose someone in school who fits each description (the same name can appear more than once) and write the name in the blank spaces. For Question 11, fill in the second space with an activity that you know is currently very important to the child and peer group, e.g. karate, maths, skipping. Then ask the child to mark 'Yes', 'No', or 'Somewhere in between' for each of the questions.

(Adapted from Rogers Personal Adjustment Inventory, revised by P. Jeffery, NFER-Nelson)

Box 4.5   Card sort

The child is asked to sort statements into yes, no, maybe

- I usually do as I'm told at school
- I am interested in learning and finding out about things
- I often daydream or mess about instead of doing my work
- I work well with a group
- I work best on my own
- I usually have a try at things before asking for help
- I am often unkind to other children
- People like me to play with them
- My teacher thinks I do good work
- My teacher likes me

Conferencing is easier to fit into the busy classroom if teachers use the idea of 'magic bubble time': the rest of the class are told that for the moment the teacher and the selected child are talking together inside a magic bubble, which will burst if other children break in to ask for the teacher's attention.

Miscue analysis

Miscue analysis is by now familiar to primary teachers as a window into the child's reading strategies. However, it can also be applied to other areas. Sadiq's teacher, for example, used it when looking at his handwriting, asking herself whether it looked messy because of:

- erratic letter sizing;
- erratic letter spacing;
- no spaces between words;
- letters not aligned to a baseline, with correct ascenders and descenders;
- ascenders and descenders not straight and parallel.

Miscue analysis also works well for spelling. Studying the child's invented spellings (or, from another perspective, spelling mistakes) will yield all the information needed in order to plan a teaching programme for the child: high frequency words and letter strings not yet mastered, a need for practice in listening to the sounds in words, or for help in developing visual recall where a child's approach is totally phonetic. Different spelling miscues indicate different teaching strategies – 'sotr' for 'story', for example, indicating a need for help in developing auditory strategies, while 'store' might lead to teaching the final -y pattern in a word family like 'story', 'baby' and 'lady'.

In maths, miscue analysis (particularly if children are asked to explain how they reached a particular conclusion or answer) can indicate anything from simple misunderstandings about place value to a difficulty in retaining number facts, or a need to learn to estimate before calculating.

Box 4.6   Small steps to correct letter formation

Holds pencil correctly

Traces pre-writing shapes   O I − ∩ ∪ ∧ ∨ S ⌡ ⌠

Copies pre-writing shapes   O I − ∩ ∪ ∧ ∨ S ⌡ ⌠

Has established left to right direction of writing

Forms letter group 'a c d o' correctly

Forms letter group 'g q' correctly

Forms letter group 'b f h l t' correctly

Forms letter group 'j p y' correctly

Forms letter group 'k v w x z' correctly

Forms letter group 'i m n r u' correctly

Forms 'e, s' correctly

Using the small steps approach to identify gaps in prior knowledge or understanding

Adam's teacher used this strategy when he found that Adam could match written numbers and name them when in order, but not manage the next step of naming them when presented out of sequence. Once he had established this, he could easily see why Adam took so long to cope with simple addition and subtraction – tasks for which number naming is an essential prerequisite skill. Sadiq's teacher might have used the strategy to see if Sadiq could correctly form the pre-writing shapes which are the precursor to correct letter formation in handwriting (see Box 4.6).

The ability to analyse task demands to find out where the obstacles may lie for a child is a fundamental tool of diagnostic assessment that needs no special tests or techniques. It is not difficult, but it is not always done. A teacher may wonder why a child cannot seem to start sentences with capital letters even after being told many times, but not think to check whether the child understands what a sentence is, or whether they actually know how to write all the capital letters without a reference model. Or a teacher may feel that a child lacks ideas for story writing when a finer task analysis would show that it is ordering ideas that is the real problem, and that the child cannot yet cope with the very fundamental step of sequencing a set of pictures into chronological order.

It is particularly important to look for gaps in a child's prior knowledge and understanding when their performance seems erratic: good one day, but all to pieces the next. As Ireson *et al.* (1989) aptly observe:

> The child's performance of a complex task is impaired when a component of that task has not been mastered. This is a very common problem in human learning. It is like asking a learner driver to negotiate a roundabout before he has mastered gear changes; he may manage to go safely

round a large roundabout if there is little traffic so he does not need to slow down, but the car will go out of control on a small roundabout where he needs to change gears.

Identifying the gaps in a child's understanding will be easier if the school has access in its resource base to some of the commercially available breakdowns of core attainments into the small steps that lead up to them. Some of these materials were described in Chapter 3 and are referenced in the resources section. The QCA 'p' levels, which provide fine-grained performance descriptions of attainment pre-Level 1, and between Level 1 and 2 in the core subjects, are an example.

Assessing underlying perceptual, memory and motor skills

This was the approach used by Adam's teacher when he wondered whether an underlying difficulty in visual discrimination was making it difficult for him to distinguish similar numerals. It was Sadiq's teacher's approach when she felt that his handwriting difficulties were due to poor motor coordination. Some years ago this was an approach much favoured by remedial specialists, at a time when the prevailing model for special needs was a quasi-medical one of diagnosis and cure. Popular assessment tools such as the Aston Index (from LDA) were based on the idea of identifying underlying difficulties. Covering such areas as auditory and visual discrimination and memory, they aimed to help the teacher devise a programme that would remedy any deficits discovered, while directing the main thrust of teaching towards the child's stronger perceptual channels.

Such approaches, while superficially attractive, have tended to fall out of favour over the past decade. Partly this has been in response to the considerable body of research which failed to show any differential effects of teaching programmes matched to underlying strengths and weaknesses (Kavale and Forness 1985). Partly it has been a consequence of the shift away from locating special needs wholly within the child, towards assessment which focuses on factors in the task, the classroom context or the curriculum, which contribute to difficulties in learning or behaviour.

More recently, the underlying skills model has begun to make a comeback. Some research findings, such as those by Bryant and Bradley (1985) on phonological awareness (children's auditory perception of sound patterns in words), have begun to show that there may be some underlying perceptual skill deficits that can be successfully remedied with long-term positive effects on children's learning. It is also true that while some of the internal processes assessed using tools such as the Aston Index are still unproven as prerequisites of progress in attainments like reading and writing, there may nevertheless be more direct and 'surface value' implications of such assessments which are useful for teachers. For example, finding that a child has poor auditory sequential memory may help to explain why they have such difficulty in following a series of instructions given to the whole class, or sitting quietly in listening situations like assembly or story time. And while an action plan including auditory memory training may not be very useful as part of the child's reading programme, it could be very useful in helping develop listening skills. Some suggestions for diagnostic assessment of underlying skills (particularly memory and phonological awareness) are given in Chapter 10.

For the most part, however, assessing underlying skills does not require expensive tests or special equipment. Auditory sequential memory can be assessed as well through seeing what happens when a child is asked to follow progressively more complex classroom instructions as it can through special tests; visual discrimination through asking the child to match a word on a card with similar ones in their reading book, and so on. This is called curriculum-based assessment, and is the most useful focus for the classroom teacher. The outcomes of such assessment need to be firmly tied in to the child's ordinary, everyday learning. Formerly, if a child was thought to have difficulties in a process like visual discrimination, the remedial teacher might prescribe an elaborate series of activities related only very indirectly to the classroom tasks of learning to read, write, count, measure and so on. For example, the child would be given worksheets where they had to match squiggles in varying orientations. Nowadays, it is recognized that there may be little or no transfer from such activities to regular classroom learning, and that skills are better practised 'on the job' – for example, through activities that make children look very closely at real words rather than geometric shapes or meaningless squiggles, if they have poor visual discrimination. Put another way, this means that even though she felt he had underlying difficulties in motor coordination, Sadiq's teacher did better by helping him directly with his handwriting than she ever would have through a programme of activities in general motor skills.

Gathering information from parents

Parents are the real experts on their own children. Any assessment which fails to take into account their historical understanding of the child's difficulties, their perception of the child's strengths and weaknesses, behaviour and interests outside the confines of school, risks missing the essential elements that will lead to successful action planning. Parents know what their children enjoy doing, and what might motivate them to give of their best in school. They know what teaching styles and classroom contexts have in the past suited their child best. They know, like Adam's parents, about potentially significant factors in the child's pre-school development and experiences which may not have got as far as school records. They know about out-of-school stresses which may be making it hard for the child to concentrate on learning. A semi-structured interview with the child's parents or carers, using some of the starting points in Box 4.7, with the issues of confidentiality discussed and agreed information clearly recorded for long-term reference, should be part of the assessment process early on for every child whose progress causes concern.

Finding out what works and what does not: assessment through action planning

Linked with the parental interview is the approach to assessment which rests on identifying key problem areas causing concern to parents, teachers and

---

Box 4.7 Exploring the parents' point of view

How does _____ feel about school?

What does he/she like and dislike at school?

What sort of teaching do you think works best for him/her?

What is he/she good at?

What is he/she interested in outside school?

Are there any ways you wish he/she would change, were different?

Is he/she fairly independent and socially competent?

How do you think his/her friendships are going?

What are his/her relationships like with other members of the family?

What can you tell us about his/her history: health, hearing and eyesight, separations, major events or stresses in his/her life, school changes?

---

the child alike, planning a strategy to deal with these problems, and meeting again at a predetermined interval to evaluate the effectiveness of what was planned. Assessment here is through action, and is a matter of checking on hypotheses about the nature of the difficulties experienced by child or teacher, and the support required to ensure progress. Adam's teacher and speech therapist, for example, felt that his word-finding difficulties became more acute when he was put on the spot to provide answers; if he coped better in the more relaxed and game-like learning situations they planned for him, their hypothesis would be confirmed. Sadiq's teacher felt that she might be contributing to his apparent motor difficulties by asking him to use inappropriate tools; his response to her intervention strategy would tell her if she was right.

Assessment of this kind focuses much more on the context than on the child. The question it seeks to answer is not so much 'What is wrong here?' as 'What will help?' It is about differentiation: assessing, through trial and error, which particular adaptations to tasks, inputs, teaching and learning styles or pupil response will best ensure curriculum access.

Its outcome is a clearer picture of the strategies that have proved successful, and those which are not so useful; the action plans that do not work well are as important an element in the assessment process as those which do. This is a message that needs to be put across to parents and to the child: we are going to try out a plan, and even if it does not work we will all have learned something that will help us plan better next time.

Assessment through action planning is rarely a one-off process. It forms part of a cycle that can be repeated as many times as is necessary to establish effective support mechanisms. It also does not stand alone: it forms part of a tripartite assessment strategy, drawing on and feeding into the other types of information gathering which we have looked at in this chapter.

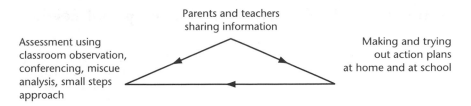

Parents and teachers
sharing information

Assessment using
classroom observation,
conferencing, miscue
analysis, small steps
approach

Making and trying
out action plans
at home and at school

Using standardized tests

Standardized tests are best used as part of the cycle of assessment through action planning, in order to assess the rate of progress brought about by planned interventions. They provide reading, spelling or maths 'ages'. For example, a reading age (RA) of 7 years 6 months in a child with a chronological age (CA) of 10 years 6 months, indicating that the child is reading at a level three years below the average for their age. Standardized tests also provide standardized scores, where a score of 100 is average for the child's age, and a score below 70 indicates performance in the lowest 2 per cent of all children of that age. This information will not of itself help teachers or parents to gain a greater understanding of the child's difficulties, or to plan appropriate interventions. Repeated at intervals over a period of time, however, the tests will show whether the strategies put in place to support the child are helping to narrow the gap between their performance and that of their peers.

Any gain in standardized scores (for example, from 70 to 75) indicates a narrowing of the gap, as do increases over time in reading or spelling or maths ages which are greater than the corresponding increase in the child's chronological age.

Schools can also compare the rate of progress they are achieving for a particular child with benchmarks drawn from research. In relation to literacy, for example, there is evidence (Thomson 1989) that children with literacy difficulties who have only regular classroom teaching and no special help will fall progressively further and further behind their peers, making an average of only five months progress in reading in the space of a year. Those who have help in the form of a structured multisensory teaching programme have been found in some studies (Thomson 1989; Hornsby and Farrer 1990) to make progress in the order of 18 to 24 months per year.

Another idea is to use tools such as the Reading and Spelling Progress Charts (Cook and Cook 1999), which allow teachers to plot successive scores from standardized testing on graphs, and compare progress with an average progress rate for particular tests.

Such methods of assessing progress over time have become particularly important in the light of the revised SEN *Code of Practice* and its associated guidance (DfES 2001b). The guidance suggests that the key test of the need to use School Action, move on to School Action Plus or to Statementing, is evidence that the child's current rate of progress is inadequate. The guidance provides helpful indicators of what could be considered 'adequate' progress for particular types of SEN: the indicators require schools to develop increasingly sophisticated methods for assessing the gains children make over time.

National Curriculum assessment and special needs

How does the tripartite assessment strategy suggested here fit in with National Curriculum assessment? And how can National Curriculum assessment – both teacher assessment and formal assessment through SATs – be made into a useful experience for children with special needs, and their parents? In this section we will try to draw out some common threads from National Curriculum assessments and assessments of special needs, and look at possible ways of reconciling their very different purposes.

The first point to make is that National Curriculum assessment does share at least one purpose with the special needs assessment strategies we have described here: it is in its formative sense intended to help the teacher, child and family establish what their next steps should be in teaching and learning. This is the common ground. Special needs assessment is simply a more fine-grained and frequent application of the same formative process that all children now experience.

Most of the assessment methods suggested here, moreover, are those with which teachers have become increasingly familiar as they have gained experience of National Curriculum assessment: focused classroom observation, child–adult conferencing and miscue analysis. The only real differences between assessment of special needs and teacher assessment for the National Curriculum are the addition of some assessment methodologies – notably the small steps approach – which will not be necessary for the majority of children, and the intimate involvement of parents in information exchange at every step.

If children's progress is recorded against small steps rather than the broad rungs of National Curriculum attainment levels, many of the potentially damaging effects of the summative aspect of National Curriculum assessment can be avoided. Schools should not be satisfied with end of year reports to parents that carry dispiriting messages like 'still working towards Level 2 in English', or 'some progress towards Level 3 has been made'. For children with special needs, schools should employ recording and reporting systems that are a great deal more fine-grained – if possible, managed by the children themselves. An example is shown in Box 4.8. This kind of self-assessment leads naturally into children setting their own targets and enlisting the help of available adults – parents, support teachers, classroom assistants – to work with them towards achieving their goals.

For more general profiling, some children with special needs will benefit from using pre-prepared templates on the word processor, finishing sentences such as 'I can now ... because ...', 'I have most enjoyed ...' and 'I need to improve ...' (Hanson 1991). Combined with a record of achievement in which the child notes all aspects of personal success in and out of school, not just the purely academic, such records of progress towards attainment targets can help to make the National Curriculum assessment process both positive and motivating. Also particularly useful for children with special needs is the now widespread practice of choosing samples of work for individual portfolios and annotating them with the help of the teacher – noting perhaps what the child felt was good about the piece, what they think in general about their work in the area and how it might be improved. The aim of such discussions for children with special needs is to establish

---

**Box 4.8   Example of recording and reporting system:
Level 2 writing targets**

I am a story writer . . .

- I can write a story with an opening ☐
- I can write a story with a setting ☐
- I can write a story with more than one character ☐
- I can write a story with a beginning, middle and end ☐
- I can use 'story' words . . . like 'one day', 'suddenly' ☐
- I use full stops and capital letters correctly in more than half
  my sentences ☐
- I can use joining words like 'and', 'then', 'so' ☐

---

and record together what exactly the pupil will be aiming to achieve next (working faster, listening better, mastering joined writing) and what sorts of experience and teaching will be needed to ensure success.

All these forms of assessment are aimed at preserving the child's self-esteem through following certain fundamental principles:

- self-assessment wherever possible;
- the experience of success through reaching small, achievable targets;
- reporting in a style which demonstrates achievement;
- a focus on the joint responsibility of child and teacher for achieving change.

Use of these principles can be readily observed in properly managed teacher assessment within the National Curriculum.

The one-off forays into children's understandings represented by SATs can sometimes be a different matter. With no opportunity here for breaking the task down into small steps, for self-assessment or for joint forward planning, supporting children with special needs in the SATs can become an exercise in damage limitation. The teacher must seek to preserve self-esteem through making maximum use of the opportunities provided in SATs guidance to enter and leave the tasks at points appropriate to the individual pupil, to intervene and help the child complete the task after the point of failure, and to assess individually or in small groups wherever staffing will allow.

It will also be important to ensure that children with special needs have fair access to the SATs. Here we are looking to make sure that the assessment criteria used relate to the subject and statement of attainment being assessed, and not to any other factors which may disadvantage children with special needs. For example, it means making sure that in science the children's understanding of scientific concepts is being assessed, but not their listening or writing ability; in maths, that the children's understanding of measures or data handling is being assessed, but not their reading ability.

Box 4.9 Differentiation of National Curriculum assessment

Literacy and general learning difficulties
- Extra time
- Rest breaks
- Taped versions of written maths and science tests
- Use of a word processor and spellchecker (with the exception of a spell-checker in spelling assessment or a word processor in handwriting)
- Repetition of parts of questions given orally (or by signing) where questions refer to past and future events or to words and diagrams used earlier in the questions
- Children can dictate written and numerical recording to an adult scribe (except for handwriting assessment)
- Pupil sheets can be read to the children (except in English, other than reading the general instructions) and picture clues added to text

Visual impairment
- Use of Braille, modified print and enlarged versions of the text
- Alternatives to diagrams to enhance visual clarity
- Test papers copied onto coloured paper
- Use of coloured overlays and filter lenses
- Extra time and rest breaks
- Use of mechanical and technological aids

Hearing impairment
- Modified materials for mental arithmetic tests for children who use signing or who lip-read
- Assessment can be on a one-to-one basis in a quiet environment
- Extra time and rest breaks
- Specific objects used as prompts to help recall of questions, repetition of questions
- Use of communicators and signers
- Response by sign, symbols, pointing

Physical impairment and coordination difficulties
- Children can use any aids to mobility or manipulation of objects they normally employ, including a typewriter or word processor
- Children can position concrete objects as an alternative to drawing or mapping
- Adaptations to diagrams to make them clearer for children with spatial perceptual difficulties
- Transcripts of children's written responses
- Enlarged papers
- Extra time, rest breaks

Emotional and behavioural difficulties
- Conducting the activities on a one-to-one basis
- Taking the tests in a separate room
- Giving extra reassurance and encouragement
- Using breaks in the assessment, discontinuing if it is a bad time for a particular child and trying again later

All of the documentation on assessment within the National Curriculum makes it very clear that strategies which bypass particular special needs – for example, modified verbal instructions for children with language difficulties, or oral reporting for children with difficulties in written recording – are legitimate, so long as listening or writing or whatever are not actually being assessed in the activity at issue. Differentiation of the child's mode of response is encouraged. So is differentiation of the input or mode or presentation: outside of reading assessments, all written instructions can be read to pupils, worksheets can be enlarged or cut up or made concrete by replacing pictures with models, verbal instructions can be simplified or repeated. Differentiation of the process between input and response is also to some extent allowable: children who find it hard to work in a group can be assessed individually and breaks in the assessment built in for those with a shorter concentration span.

As for technological and human support, the general principle expressed in the guidance is that if the child normally has the help of a communication assistant, or uses a word processor for recording, or any other aid to mobility or the manipulation of objects, then that support should continue to be available for assessment as well as learning.

In keeping with the spirit of the National Curriculum as a curriculum for all, the recommendations for differentiation of presentation or response, and extra support from adults or technology, are intended to ensure that almost all children can participate in the assessment tasks with some degree of success. It is not envisaged that children with special needs will be exempted in any large numbers from any aspect of the SATs, either through Statements of SEN or through temporary headteacher directions. The references to disapplication of assessments in QCA guidance refer only to obvious areas such as handwriting for children with severe physical disabilities or aspects of speaking and listening for some children with hearing or communication difficulties.

Box 4.9 gives a summary of the guidance on permissible differentiation of assessment tasks, grouped by broad areas of special need, and drawn from the QCA's handbooks on assessment and reporting arrangements. An essential role for SENCOs is to abstract each year the general and specific guidance as it appears in the handbooks, and to plan jointly with class teachers any adaptations that will be necessary for individuals or groups of pupils in the school when they undertake the assessment tasks. The consultative role of the SENCO should also extend to planning for teacher assessment: bypass strategies are equally legitimate here, and equally essential if teachers are to avoid the global perceptions of children's ability, heavily influenced by their written language skills, which have traditionally determined their judgements of pupils in the past.

Conclusion

In this chapter we have looked at some ways in which the potential of assessment for enhancing learning can be realized for children with special needs and their teachers – assessment not just of what children know and can do, but also of factors in the learning environment which will best help them make progress and demonstrate their learning. We have touched on record keeping in the context of self-assessment, and on action planning in the context of finding out what works and what does not for a particular child. In the next chapter we return to these issues in more detail, describing a flexible structure for planning and recording intervention for children with special needs that can be used to ensure efficient transfer of information both within and between schools.

5 Action planning and record keeping

Introduction

The idea of developing and evaluating action plans for children with special needs at different levels, beginning within school and widening progressively if necessary to involve external agencies, is now second nature in most mainstream schools. The process has, however, generated its own problems for teachers, children and parents. In recent years, a number of surveys of schools' arrangements for meeting the national SEN *Code of Practice* (Ofsted 1997, 1999; Bowers *et al.* 1998) have highlighted the oppressive weight of administration and paperwork generated by the well-intentioned aim that every child with significant SEN should have an IEP describing their needs and how those needs will be met.

The difficulty has arisen because of the sheer number of IEPs which many schools are seeking to implement. Funding systems, league tables and an emphasis on IEPs in many Ofsted inspections has encouraged a focus on large numbers of these documents as the main evidence of need in the school, and of the support systems in place to meet need.

As a result, IEPs have increasingly become in many cases 'just bits of paper, recording measurable and sometimes meaningless targets in the absence of ownership or involvement of the person potentially most willing and able to put in the energy needed to achieve them – the child him or herself' (Gross 2000).

Effective IEPs

In the light of this, many schools are now seeking to reduce the number of IEPs that they write, so that the process of planning for children can become more involving and more meaningful. This is possible if we push up the boundaries of what we consider to be an 'individual' need, to encompass only those lower incidence needs which cannot be predicted year on year from the school's catchment area and level of social deprivation. High incidence, predictable needs, relating to groups of children in every class who experience literacy or behaviour difficulties, are tackled though the class teacher's regular medium and short-term planning, supplemented by group provisions drawn from the school's provision 'map'.

IEPs are in this model reserved for those children with less commonly occurring types of difficulty, and perhaps also for those situations where the teacher feels a sense of 'stuckness', and where the combined energies of home, school and the child are going to be needed to move things on – not necessarily for ever, but for long enough to kick-start progress.

In this model, when IEPs are put in place, they are not just a piece of paper written in isolation by the class teacher or SENCO, or pulled off a computerized bank of targets and related strategies: they are instead the written record of a much more important human process. This planning process brings together all the people most concerned about the child's progress (parent, teacher and child) at a meeting whose purpose is to share information, clarify the broad objectives for the child's progress, remind everyone of the child's strengths, and arrive collaboratively at some priority targets to which all present can subscribe and all contribute.

The process rests on the answers given by all parties to a series of questions, never better described than by Westmacott and Cameron (1981), as shown in Figure 5.1.

Figure 5.1 The problem-solving approach (Westmacott and Cameron 1981).

Listing assets

Starting an action planning meeting by listing a child's assets has many advantages. First, it sets a positive note that makes it clear to parents and to the child (if present at the planning meeting, as many older children should be), that they are valued and appreciated. Second, it provides information that will be helpful in developing the action plan – about what the child finds motivating, what strengths they might share with others in order to build self-esteem, what interests the teacher might work through, what classroom (and home) contexts help produce the best learning and behaviour.

Listing and prioritizing problems

Listing problem areas is the easiest part of the problem-solving process for teachers, parents and the child alike. We are all practised in identifying deficiencies in ourselves and others, often much more so than in identifying strengths. What is not so easy is making sure that the language we use to describe problems is precise and accurate, and narrowing down long lists of problems into a manageable few.

Yet the process of prioritizing a few key problems, and working on those, is a real confidence builder. Much of the sense of inadequacy and lack of confidence felt by many classroom teachers working with special needs stems from the simple problem of not knowing where to start. When a child experiences difficulties in many areas of the curriculum, and perhaps in behaviour and relationships as well, it is easy to feel overwhelmed by all that needs to be done. The problem-solving approach prevents this: it enables all concerned to acknowledge that there will be many areas that they cannot tackle for the moment, but one or more on which they will all concentrate. It increases the chance of success because it ensures that energies are not dissipated over too wide an area, and that there is consistency: parents, teachers and the child are all working towards a common goal.

Which problems should be prioritized? It is best to choose:

- Those problems which the child feels are important and wants to work on – that is, those which tie in with their main life concerns at the time. These might, for example, include reading at the point where a child realizes a younger brother or sister is overtaking them, and suddenly begins to care passionately about doing better; or 'neat writing' if that is the one thing that matters to the child about their work at the moment.
- Those problems where there is some chance of success within a reasonably short time scale – for example, tackling an immediate problem of helping the child learn to control their temper, rather than a much more long-term problem in making and maintaining friendships.
- Those problems which underpin others – for example, low self-esteem or inappropriate learning behaviours (concentration, personal organization, willingness to tackle something new), which lead to poor performance in a wide range of social and learning situations.

The language in which the priority problems are expressed should be free from ambiguity. 'Can't concentrate' could mean anything from daydreaming, to wandering the classroom, to talking or interfering with other children's work. 'Aggressive' could mean that the child shouts at other children, or hits them, or swears at the teacher. 'Immature' could mean anything from not being able to do up buttons on a shirt to not being able to tolerate losing in a game. In all of these examples, the action taken to resolve the problem would depend on which of the several interpretations most accurately described it. This is why it is important to use words with only one interpretation wherever possible.

Problems often become clearer if they are described in terms of what the child or teacher *does*, using verbs rather than adjectives: 'Julie talks to her friends when she should be working'; 'Darren often pushes other children over'; 'Paul doesn't make use of meaning or phonic cues when reading'. Such language avoids negative labelling of children's personal qualities, it means that everyone is tackling the same problem, it is non-emotive and comes across as less critical and negative than language like 'lacking in confidence', 'withdrawn', 'disruptive' or 'a poor reader'.

Specifying a desired outcome: setting targets and agreeing strategies

Once three or four priority problems have been agreed, the next step is to establish targets for the action plan that will try to tackle them. The question here is 'What do we want the child to be doing *instead* of what is happening now?' The target is also a yardstick for measuring progress, answering the question 'How will we know if we have succeeded?'

If a child has repeated temper outbursts when teased or when other children will not do as they ask, what might be wanted instead is for them to develop and successfully use a range of other behavioural strategies to cope with provocation. If a child waits to be told what every unfamiliar word says when reading, the target might be that they will regularly try a guess based on initial letter and reading on and back. If they have difficulty in working independently, the target might be that they will start each piece of work unaided and only ask for help after trying alone for at least five minutes.

Once again, targets need to be specific and clearly defined: they must describe an end state that everyone can see and agree on. Sometimes this will mean unpacking a vague description into something observable: 'Develops a love of books', for example, into 'Asks for stories to be read to them at home', 'Chooses to spend some time each day at school in the book corner', 'Handles books without damaging them'.

Behaviour difficulties can be particularly hard to pin down in this way: some examples of positively phrased targets for commonly occurring behavioural, emotional and social difficulties are given in Table 5.1.

Sometimes the process of defining a target is enough in itself to ensure success – just because for the first time, perhaps, everyone has agreed and shared with the child what they actually want them to do, rather than what they are fed up with them not doing. Sometimes, however, plans need to be made and recorded for particular strategies which parents, teachers and the child will use to reach the target – paired reading at home each night, regular praise from the teacher for starting work unaided, practice in deep breathing and relaxation to control temper outbursts, and so on.

Table 5.1 Positively phrased targets for behavioural, emotional or social difficulties

Problem	Example of positive target
Can't concentrate	Stays in seat during lessons unless given permission to move about
Lacks confidence	Tackles new task independently without asking for help for at least ten minutes
Aggressive	Recognizes when getting angry and asks permission for cool-off time
Withdrawn	Takes a specified role in group task, involving speaking to other group members
Disruptive	Keeps hands, feet and objects to themselves during lessons
Low self-esteem	Accepts adult praise without tearing up work/misbehaving
Disorganized	Packs bag for school each night using checklist and timetable

Finally, a review date should be set and recorded when all concerned will meet again to see if the strategies are working and consider whether to discontinue the plan, make a new one, or seek further advice from outside agencies.

An example

Alan Morris was in a Year 6 class. He was having extra help with his reading but was also about a year behind others in his class in maths. He was a very well liked child, popular both with other children and with adults. He was good at all forms of sport, and showed considerable interest and aptitude in work with computers. At a meeting attended by his parents, class teacher, the SENCO and Alan himself these strengths were listed. Everyone began by saying something they valued in Alan or something he was good at. Going on to the problem areas, Alan said he thought that his biggest problem was his writing: though he felt he was quite a good reader now, his written work was no good. His teacher said that from her point of view the main concern was that Alan seemed to be falling further and further behind in all the basic subjects, and that she was not succeeding in getting him to finish things off. His tray was always full of uncompleted bits of work. He was also very disorganized. Often he could not find the things he needed to tackle a piece of work, or would forget to bring things from home that he needed.

Mr and Mrs Morris said that they thought a lot of messages from school never reached them: Alan had always been a one for losing notes he was meant to bring home, and losing everything else, like his reading book. His room was always a mess and he would not make any effort to sort it out. He never seemed to know what day it was or when he had PE or swimming and needed his kit. They did not know how he was going to cope when he went to secondary school; he had a sister there, so they knew how much the children were expected to do in the way of organizing themselves with what they needed each day, and with homework.

The SENCO suggested that they make a list of everyone's concerns, and then try to decide which were the most important ones to tackle. Alan's teacher and Mr and Mrs Morris agreed that though there were problems in specific areas like maths, it would be better to choose a more general priority like helping Alan to get more work finished, since this would help him to do better in all his school subjects. They also felt that because he was coming up to secondary school transfer, it would be extremely important to help him learn to organize himself for learning. The SENCO suggested they add a third priority, Alan's writing, since this was what mattered most to him at the moment. Some further discussion led them to the conclusion that the real problem here was not so much that he could not produce good written work (which he could, from time to time), but that he did not feel he was any good as a writer. He did not like the look of his work, or the fact that his friends wrote loads while he just did half a page or so.

The SENCO summed up the priority problem areas: Alan often does not finish his work, forgets messages and does not have the right equipment at the right time, and is not proud of himself as a writer. From there it was easy to answer the question, 'What do we want to see him doing instead?' Everyone, including Alan, agreed that they wanted to see him finishing more of his written work, relaying messages accurately between home and school, knowing what he was doing each day and organizing the things he would need, and being able to feel he was a good writer.

Alan's teacher thought it would be useful if she helped him to make a checklist of jobs to be done at the start of each day in class. The SENCO suggested that it should have drawings or a keyword for each task to act as prompts. Alan would tick off each job as he finished it. If at the end of the day he had done everything on the checklist, he would be allowed to use the computer to type in the day of the week and colour it, a privilege he much enjoyed.

Mrs Morris wondered whether it would help Alan if he had an in-tray for unfinished work, as do people in offices, as well as his ordinary tray, instead of everything being jumbled up with his bags of crisps and pencils and reading books. The teacher thought that this was a very good idea, and would help to stop his work getting so messy. She asked Alan what he thought he should do if the in-tray began to pile up. He said he thought it would be fair for him to have to stay in at lunchtime to catch up a bit. This was agreed.

It was also planned to use a home–school diary, similar to the one Alan would use at secondary school, to record messages in. Alan would staple letters home into the diary. Mr and Mrs Morris would ask to see the diary every night; they would also make a weekly calendar with him to stick on the inside cover of the diary, showing what activities he had each day at school and what he would need. Alan agreed to check the calendar and organize his equipment before bed every night. To help him get better at remembering things, his teacher would send home a verbal message every Friday and his parents would note in the diary whether he remembered it.

To help Alan feel more positive about his writing, he would do one piece of work a week, from first draft to published version, entirely on the computer, and have this work displayed. He would also be given opportunities to tape-record some longer pieces of work which either a classroom helper or his parents would type on the word processor for him. It was stressed that real, adult writers often have people to type things for them.

Alan's parents agreed to come into school again at the end of term, to discuss with Alan and his teacher whether the planned strategies were working, and what should happen next.

Involving the pupil

Pupil involvement in planning the IEP is essential. This is because of the particular way in which targets operate. Targets *do* work: we have only to look at the increase in the number of children achieving Level 4 at the end of Key Stage 2, or the reduction in exclusions which many schools have achieved, to see this. Most education professionals have by now experienced for themselves the powerful effect of working towards a target for which they felt personally accountable, and which was clear, measurable and time-constrained.

The targets we have all as individuals experienced, however, have one thing in common: for them to work, we needed to know what they were and to be constantly reminded of them, frequently monitored on them and recognized if we achieved them. Yet if we undertake the exercise of asking children with SEN what their IEP targets are, we consistently find that they have no idea: 'the views of the pupils are rarely sought in the preparation of IEPs or in the review process' (Ofsted 1999). The targets may have been made up by the SENCO sitting at home with their paperwork, or they may have been spawned by a computer program. Even if the child was involved originally in agreeing targets, the chances are that no one has reminded them of what the targets are since then.

Involving the pupil in setting targets, and then in monitoring progress towards them, overcomes these problems. For older children, this may mean full involvement in the type of planning meeting described in the previous section. For younger children, it may mean a short session with the teacher and parent, during which they might, for example:

- draw pictures to show things they would like to be able to do better;
- help fill in a child-friendly record like the one in Figure 5.2, designed by the staff of Barrs Court Primary School in Bristol;
- act out how it would look if they met a target – if they were able, say, to really listen at carpet time or concentrate on their work;
- choose a target to work on from a selection on cards.

The format used by the school for its IEPs can reflect the pupil's involvement. Targets should be framed in the language of 'I will be able to . . .', or 'I will . . .'. Child and teacher can discuss and agree a date by which this will happen, and maybe colour in the agreed date on a small calendar imported into the IEP format.

My Point of View.

Things I enjoy doing at home and / or school

I don't enjoy ...

because ...

I am able to do these things well

Name :-

Date :-

Things that worry me (people, events, experiences)

The nicest thing about me is ...

My target is ...

I would like to be better at ...

I need to put more effort into ...

People who can help me achieve my target ...

Figure 5.2 Format for involving child in action planning.

The strategies for achieving the targets can also be written in child-friendly language, under headings like 'How will I do it?' and 'What support will I need?' Alternatively, children can record under the strategies headings the things they will do to help themselves, and then take the IEP to the adults (or peers) who will be involved, so that they can write down what they are going to do to help. This way, the child owns the whole plan, recognizing that they need support but actively seeking it out rather than being a passive recipient.

All those who are going to contribute to the IEP (including the child) should sign it. Each target should have a space against it for a record of when it is achieved – again, signed and dated by the child as well as the teacher or other adult key worker.

Another effective way of involving pupils is described by Pearson (2000). Here, targets are agreed by teacher and child and recorded on an IEP target card. The teacher and child discuss what would help the child achieve each

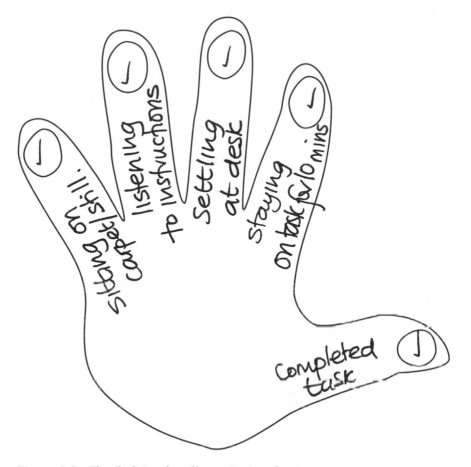

Figure 5.3 The 'helping hand' monitoring sheet.

of the targets, and this is written on the card too. Subsequently, the child actively seeks evidence that they have achieved the target: it is the child's responsibility to collect the evidence in the form of signatures from adults or peers. When there are two signatures against a target, the child takes the card to the teacher, who will validate the evidence and praise the child both for reaching the target and using the system to monitor their own progress.

Simpler monitoring systems for younger children might be visual, like the 'helping hand' in Figure 5.3. Here the child discusses whether they have met behavioural targets on a daily basis, taking the monitoring sheet home each day to share with their parents. Recording progress in a journal or achievement book, and choosing samples of work to show progress, are other ways of keeping targets alive for the child over a period of time.

All children, even the very young, can take part in the review of their IEPs. Figure 5.4 is an example of this, which uses a standard format to gather the views of all those involved. Figure 5.5 shows a format which can be used to involve the child in reflecting on their progress over a longer period – in this case, preparation for an annual review of the pupil's Statement.

INDIVIDUAL EDUCATION PLAN **PLAN NUMBER:** ☐

Name: O. Year group: 3 Date of review:

Parent/carer comments	Pupil's comments	Teacher/support agency comment
What went well? O is taking Pride in his colouring/drawing stays in his seat until the task is completed at Home. Consentration is improving	What went well? ①100% not throwthings ②Ican Stady my Seat Longer	What went well? O has learnt not to throw things in the classroom and he now manages to stay on his seat for longer periods of time.
What needs doing? O needs to consentrate for Longer periods of time. He need to be able to work on his own ✗.	What needs doing? ✗ LISTENING to my Teacher; ②To stop couing out	What needs doing? O still needs to learn not to call/shout out in class. O still needs to improve his consentration span.

Figure 5.4 Format for involving pupils and parents in an IEP review.

Pupil's Name E.

Completed by dictated by E. to Mrs. S

1. Please comment on the progress you think you have made since the last review.

Last year E felt he was angry and kept getting into fights. He was upset because he wasn't growing.
He feels he is less angry. He is now 4ft. 4ins. but would like to be taller.
There are fewer fights.

2. What do you feel that you are good at in school and at home eg. sports, hobbies, interests, particular school subjects?

E said he enjoys play-fighting with his older brother.
He enjoys playing games on the computer at home (Nintendo + Super Nintendo)

He enjoys listening to pop/dance music.
He enjoys swimming and can swim 10 metres.

3. What would you like to achieve in the next year?

E would like to be better at Maths and drawing – he says he is rubbish at Maths but quite good at drawing.
He wants to get more good behaviour certificates.
He does not want to be sent to the Headteacher for bad behaviour

4. What do you feel would help you the most?

E wants his brother to play with him during school play times to help him keep out of trouble.
E wants to carry on his discussions with Mr. G
He has to put his hand up to ask for help in class.

Figure 5.5 Format for a pupil's contribution to an annual Statement review.

Record keeping

The IEP itself, as outlined in this chapter, will be a short document used to write down the three or four targets the child is working on, and the strategies they and others will use to achieve them. Success or exit criteria should also be included: these refine the target in specific, measurable, achievable, realistic and time-constrained (SMART) terms. If the child has written as their target that 'I will control my temper', for example, there could be a further column headed 'How will I know I've reached my target?', saying 'When I've asked to go to the cool-off area in the playground or in class instead of arguing, ten times in a row'.

The school should also attach as part of the IEP a copy of its provision 'map', highlighting on the map any extra provision the child is going to access over the period of the plan. This will not be all the information which is kept about the child. As well as the actual IEPs, the child's personal pupil records will also need, over time, to build up a cumulative picture of the child's strengths and difficulties gleaned from assessment, and a record of any agencies who have been involved with the child. Even more important is a record of how the child can best be helped to access the curriculum – what learning objectives are relevant, what teaching styles work best, and what if any 'bypass' strategies are needed.

One way of doing this, and at the same time making sense of the numerous IEPs and other bits of paper that will accumulate year by year, is to keep a special needs summary card for each child who has been on the SEN register (see Table 5.2). Its purpose is to provide information at a glance, for each incoming teacher and for external agencies, about the child's main areas of difficulty, what has been tried so far and with what result, what external agencies have been involved, and what may need to be done in the next school year.

Conclusion

In this chapter we have considered some formats that schools might want to use to keep track of the response they make to individual children's special needs. Aspects of these might well be incorporated into their whole-school special needs policy: each school will need to design a system, however, that meets its own unique requirements and those of the local authority. Each school will also need to build into its plans a regular review of the chosen system for planning IEPs and keeping pupil records, perhaps by sampling records from time to time to make sure that they meet criteria of orderliness, objectivity and above all, usefulness.

We should never lose sight of the principle that all record keeping is only worthwhile in so far as it provides a guide on what to do next – for parents, teachers and children. The question of how to adapt the curriculum so that it is maximally responsive to the needs of the whole range of children can only be answered if there are records of what has proved successful and unsuccessful in the past. Equally, given the limited financial resources for schools, good record keeping is essential if scant support teaching time or extra equipment is to be targeted where it will do most good. It is to this issue, of managing limited resources, that we turn in the next chapter.

Table 5.2 Special needs summary card

Child's name: Jessica	Date of birth:	
Focus	Reception	Year 1
School action		School action started October 1999, IEP reviewed once. Small group help with LSA twice weekly
School action plus/external agency involvement	Speech therapy, ended December 1998	
Health, hearing, eyesight	Speech difficulty. Hearing loss in right ear. Grommets inserted summer 1992	Hearing OK, speech clear. Missed a lot of school in autumn term because of asthma
Main strengths and interests		Good relationships with peers. Takes in maths ideas quickly
Main concerns		Poor listening skills and concentration
Curriculum access: what has worked		Giving instructions in short chunks, prefaced by her name
IEP strategies: what has worked		Listening skills games in group; use of tapes at listening centre. Parents have successfully read to her each night for longer periods (now up to 15 minutes sustained concentration)
Reminders		Annual hearing check needed. Suggest further school action next year

Telephone:	Address:	Parental responsibility held by:	
Year 2	*Year 3*	*Year 4*	
IEPs reviewed twice daily, 1:1 with LSA for 15 minutes			
Learning Support Service consulted for informal advice, November 2000	Ongoing input to IEP from Learning Support Service, all year. IEPs reviewed twice. Small group help with school literacy support teacher, two hours per week	Educational psychologist involved, September 2002. Direct teaching from LSS, 12-week programme, one hour per week plus 3 × 20 minutes daily back-up from school LSA. IEPs reviewed termly	
Hearing still OK			
Very good at maths Gets on well with others	Nice art work. Works hard. Good progress in maths	Art good. Helpful to adults. Lots of interests outside school: Brownies, first aid course, swimming club	
Very slow progress with reading. Can't remember how to write short words. Concentration erratic	Reading – little progress despite a lot of effort	Reading and written work. Also maths – falling behind because can't read materials? Lots of quarrels with other children	
Using computer with Clicker Plus for writing works well. Still needs instructions in short chunks	Needs to dictate some work to a scribe	Cloze procedure when writing. Needs a peer as reading helper, especially in maths	
A teaching to targets programme with daily practice of writing her name and high-frequency words from memory.	Paired reading at home has helped, and the multisensory programme the support teacher has set up on sight vocabulary and phonics	Strategies to boost self-esteem – she's been helping Year 1 children with their reading, did the art work for school Christmas card etc. Support teacher has started to use Phonographix for word level work – seems to be working	
Next review with parents and support teacher due October	Review with parents and support teacher due November	Review with educational psychologist in autumn term – parents want need for Statement to be discussed	

6 Making provision – finding the time

Introduction

The first question asked by teachers in relation to any special plans for supporting children with special needs is 'Where can I find the time?' While school budgets remain under pressure, there can be no assumption that additional adult support from SEN teachers or teaching assistants is always going to be available to the class teacher.

In this climate, it has become ever more important to look at the best ways of using any limited support teaching or teaching assistant time available, and to look creatively at all the alternatives to the kinds of one-to-one or small group support long held to be the panacea for all special needs. It has become important to consider which elements of this kind of help (careful target setting, immediate feedback, close monitoring, positive input to the child's self-esteem) each child actually needs, and what flexible ways there might be of providing these elements within the classroom, using a mixture of physical resources (ICT, specially designed materials) and accessible human resources (peers, parents, volunteer helpers). It is also important to make sure that provision for children with SEN is conceptualized in terms of increasing levels of intensity (see Figure 6.1), and that the lowest or least adult-intensive levels are in place or have been considered before higher-level support is deployed.

Finding the time

Something most schools will want to do when developing or reviewing a policy on allocating time to special needs support is to think collectively, at a staff meeting, about all the possible times in the school day when teachers could find time to spend short periods with an individual child or group of children who need an extra boost, and all possible ways in which staff could collaborate to free each other for such work. There may be times when classes can be shared – for story or television time, music practice, putting on a performance for each other or showing work they have done. There are rarely

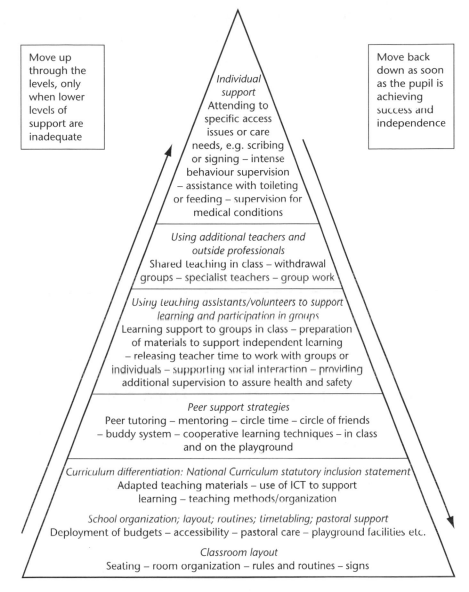

Move up through the levels, only when lower levels of support are inadequate

Move back down as soon as the pupil is achieving success and independence

Individual support
Attending to specific access issues or care needs, e.g. scribing or signing – intense behaviour supervision – assistance with toileting or feeding – supervision for medical conditions

Using additional teachers and outside professionals
Shared teaching in class – withdrawal groups – specialist teachers – group work

Using teaching assistants/volunteers to support learning and participation in groups
Learning support to groups in class – preparation of materials to support independent learning – releasing teacher time to work with groups or individuals – supporting social interaction – providing additional supervision to assure health and safety

Peer support strategies
Peer tutoring – mentoring – circle time – circle of friends – buddy system – cooperative learning techniques – in class and on the playground

Curriculum differentiation: National Curriculum statutory inclusion statement
Adapted teaching materials – use of ICT to support learning – teaching methods/organization

School organization; layout; routines; timetabling; pastoral support
Deployment of budgets – accessibility – pastoral care – playground facilities etc.

Classroom layout
Seating – room organization – rules and routines – signs

Figure 6.1 Levels of support.

any magical solutions, but at least everyone will know that they have looked as creatively as possible at what might be achievable. Whatever is agreed, it is important that it is reliable: it is no good the headteacher promising to come in and free the teacher to work with a group if half the time they will be called away by other more pressing commitments. Many action plans for children with special needs fail because they are founded on something that proves impossible to deliver regularly: more than many other children, they need consistency of input, and in these cases it may be better to make a small-scale plan that can be relied on rather than a more ambitious one that cannot.

Other ways in which it may be possible to create extra time for children with special learning needs include organizing the day so that there are short periods when the rest of the class work with minimum supervision. One teacher, for example, sets useful but low supervision board work (such as handwriting practice or dictionary skills) for the first 15 minutes of each day, while she supervises a small group of children with special needs more intensively on individualized programmes of daily activities.

Time for individualized programmes can also be created by looking at how children spend any spare time in the classroom. Many of the difficulties in learning which have traditionally been ascribed to a failure in the child to take in and remember new ideas actually occur because of the way in which learning has been structured: the teacher has moved on when a new skill or concept has been acquired, but not practised to the point where it becomes fluent and automatic. Without such extra practice in 'fluency' (Haring *et al.* 1978) the learning may not stick. Ann Lewis (1995), in her book on primary special needs and the National Curriculum, suggests that to help pupils reach the stage of fluency, teachers should plan games, quizzes and timed tests to be done in pairs, which children use when they have finished set tasks and have a few minutes to spare in the classroom. One teacher uses this idea regularly with her class: spare time has become known as 'top-up time', and children know where to go for games and ideas cards that will help them top up on acquired skills in maths, handwriting, spelling and reading.

Managing small amounts of teaching time

If, despite teachers collaborating to share classes, and reorganizing the way children work, only a small amount of teacher time can be freed, then the best use of it may be to work out (perhaps with the help of the SENCO) a plan involving short periods of daily tightly focused activities which the child can manage to do independently in class, or manage with the help of a peer or a volunteer helper.

Such programmes require the very clear targeting of exactly what it is hoped the child will achieve, which was described in Chapter 5. Here is an example:

Mrs Castle, a Year 3 teacher, was concerned about Ben's slow progress with reading and the technical aspects of written work. Her 'bypass' strategies for differentiating the curriculum were working well: she was careful about the level of difficulty of anything he had to read in subjects other than English, and he was increasingly managing to record his ideas with support from his friend Sam when editing first drafts. In English, however, he was stuck at a level of very simple texts: he made very good use of context when reading and his miscues invariably made a kind of sense, but he made little or no use of phonic strategies. His sight vocabulary of high frequency words did not seem to be growing. He also seemed to be stuck in spelling; he was not showing spontaneous use of any common spelling patterns for the long vowel phonemes.

Mrs Castle decided to target his knowledge and application of these phonic skills in her action plan. No extra teaching or teaching assistant support was available, and the SENCO warned that Ben might need a lot of repetition and reinforcement: he had already been part of an Additional Literacy Support group with a teaching assistant, but with little success. She used LDA's assessment pack for the NLS to pinpoint exactly which word level objectives Ben had yet to master, and suggested some suitable materials. Mrs Castle decided to arrange for Ben to practise a new spelling pattern each week, with a break every third week when he would review words from lists he had worked on previously. She discussed with Ben some of the ways in which he might work on learning the spelling patterns, and agreed with him a daily sequence of activities as follows:

Monday. Copy list of words into exercise book, using joined writing and look-cover-write-check. Read through the words with Sam.
Tuesday. Work with Sam to make up a silly sentence or rhyme linking as many of the words as you can: write it on a card, illustrate it, and put it on the wall.
Wednesday. Use Wordshark software to practise the pattern.
Thursday. Use phonic worksheets to practise the letter string.
Friday Have Sam ask you to make each word on your list with plastic letters.

Every day, Sam and Ben also tested each other on the word list, and quickly went through a pack of cards that had spelling patterns written on one side and a key clue picture and word for each on the reverse: Ben had to say each sound and record how many he got right.

Mrs Castle wrote what Ben had to do on the first page of a special exercise book and had him add drawings to help him remember each day's instructions. On the next page she put a format he could use independently to record his progress:

	Date		
Target	Working on	Mastered	Checked
I can spell words with the 'ee' pattern			
I can spell words with the 'oa' pattern			

The remainder of the book was used as a weekly diary in which Ben entered the week's word list and his scores on the daily run through the pack of cards.

All this took Mrs Castle about 20 minutes, with an additional 10 minutes each week to sort out a word list and supporting materials, and to monitor Ben's work through the diary from time to time. Ben's parents were asked to help by looking in the diary to see which spelling patterns he had mastered, and praising him for any attempt to apply them when doing shared reading or writing at home.

Another way of managing a small amount of teacher time is to use what are sometimes called *precision teaching* or *teaching to targets* approaches. Here, the teacher chooses a small-scale teaching target, based on an identified gap in the child's knowledge or skills. The target needs to be something that it is important for the child to learn, and to be achievable within a time scale of a few weeks. A useful suggestion is to set targets at the limit of what the child can do *with help* (Ireson *et al.* 1989).

The target – for example, that the child will 'correctly add within 20, count-ing on from the larger number', or 'spell correctly words with the spelling pattern – "le"' – is recorded on a learning chart, as in the example in Box 6.1. Then the teacher records on the learning chart the instructions they or another helper will use when working with the child: for example, 'add these two numbers', or 'write these words as I say them', and the materials needed – a number line, perhaps, or a prepared list of five words. The teacher decides how often it will be possible to work with the child on the learning target: perhaps once a day in school, and once a day at home. Then they set a criterion which will indicate when the child has reached mastery of the learning target: in this case, 'when they have got nine out of ten additions right on four successive days', or 'when they have spelled all five words right on three successive occasions, and can also generalize to a new word with the "-le" spelling pattern'. This criterion is recorded on the chart under 'when to stop'. Teacher and child determine a way of celebrating success: for example, taking the chart and the child's work to show another teacher, or having some extra time on the computer with a friend, or a gold star. The teacher adds any relevant materials that might be useful for the child to work on independently, to back up the work on the learning chart – for example, playing a number game or using spelling worksheets.

Once the learning chart has been filled in, the child spends a few minutes each day working with a helper (the teacher, a teaching assistant, volunteer helper or peer) on the task on the chart, until they reach the mastery cri-terion. The role of the support person is to correct any mistakes straight away, and immediately help the child to the right answer. The helper puts a tick or a star on the learning chart for each correct unaided response, and a dot if help was needed. Box 6.2 gives an example of a learning chart com-pleted in this way.

The advantages of this kind of approach are that it provides a structure which any helper coming into the classroom can easily learn to use, and that it makes sure that teaching goes on until the child has actually mastered the piece of learning, rather than stopping (as is usually the case in classrooms) when some of the class may have got the idea, and some not – or only half learned it, so that it still has to be thought about rather than having become automatic.

The difference between learning something to the point of mastery and other types of learning can be illustrated by an analogy – that of teaching children to cross the road safely. This is something we naturally teach to the point of mastery: we give the child plenty of opportunities to practise the skills of looking right, left and so on with our support, and would not dream of stopping the teaching until the child has fulfilled our own implicit success criterion – getting the whole process right independently several times with-out a slip-up. This can be contrasted with our more hit-and-miss approach to

Box 6.1   Learning chart

Learning Chart	Child's Name:
1 Target for the week:	4 When to stop:
2 Instruction:	5 Rewards:
	6 Backup resources for independent practice:

Materials:
3 How many times each day: Next pupil target:

Mon   Tues   Wed   Thurs   Fri   Mon   Tues   Wed   Thurs   Fri

Key: ✔ if correct ● if help needed

(Adapted from Jewell 1986)

Box 6.2   Completed learning chart

Learning Chart   **Child's Name:** Gemma P.

1 Target for the week:
Gemma will complete addition within 20 calculations correctly, counting from the larger number.

2 Instruction: Add these two numbers.

Materials: Number line.
3 How many times each day:
Once.

4 When to stop: When she gets nine out of ten calculations right for four days in a row.

5 Rewards: Take work and chart to Mrs K.

6 Backup resources for independent practice:
LDA's Stile Maths.

Next pupil target: Addition to 20 without number line.

Mon	Tues	Wed	Thurs	Fri	Mon	Tues	Wed	Thurs	Fri
●	✔	✔	✔	✔	✔	✔	✔	✔	✔
●	✔	✔	●	✔	✔	✔	✔	✔	✔
●	✔	✔	✔	✔	●	✔	✔	✔	✔
●	✔	●	✔	●	✔	✔	✔	✔	✔
●	●	●	✔	✔	●	✔	✔	✔	●
✔	●	●	●	✔	✔	✔	✔	✔	✔
✔	●	✔	●	●	✔	✔	✔	✔	✔
●	✔	●	✔	✔	✔	✔	●	✔	✔
●	●	●	✔	✔	✔	✔	✔	✔	✔
●	●	✔	●	✔	●	●	✔	✔	✔

Key: ✔ if correct ● if help needed

teaching many other skills, when we may show the child how to do something once or twice, hope they have got it, and then move on to something else. For some children, this will work. But for many children with learning difficulties it does not: they have not a sufficiently secure hold on a new skill to remember it for very long, and become easily confused by the introduction of something new.

For some children, then – particularly those who seem to know something one minute and forget in the next – the consistency of precision teaching using a learning chart can be very helpful. Indeed, there is much documentary evidence from the Portage pre-school home teaching scheme, and from work with older children (Miller *et al.* 1985) to show that it is. There are also many objections to the approach – for example, that it is narrow, overly prescriptive and, above all, boring for children. And so it can be, if used without regularly checking with all those involved (helper, parent and child) how they are feeling about it, and if used across the curriculum rather than for just a few key skills which underpin much of what a child will learn subsequently. But given these preconditions, it can be a sensible way of making maximum use of the few minutes a day of individual teaching help which can realistically be expected for many children with special needs in busy classrooms.

Making use of peer tutoring

One readily available source of support for children with special needs is peer tutoring: asking one child (either from the same class or from another age group) to take on a direct teaching role with another. There is a great deal of evidence which demonstrates the effectiveness of peer tutoring: one study (Levin and Glass 1986), for example, compared the effect of an increase in teaching time, reductions in class size, computer assisted learning and peer tutoring, and found that *only* the latter was effective in raising achievement in maths.

Many teachers, however, feel that peer tutoring is somehow unethical – that the child who is the helper is wasting valuable learning time, that they will feel put upon or held back and that their parents will object. Fortunately, the research evidence makes it so abundantly clear that peer tutoring benefits the tutor as much as (and very often more than) it benefits the tutee, that such objections can be easily answered.

Projects in which children tutor others of their own age or younger in reading typically demonstrate that tutors make substantial gains in their own learning – around two-and-a-half times the gains they would normally be expected to make over the project period; tutees make about twice the normal gain (Limbrick *et al.* 1985). There have been similar results reported from studies of peer tutoring in many other curriculum areas: mathematics, spelling, language development, computer skills and problem solving (Charlton 1998; Topping and Ehly 1998). It is thought that the enhanced self-esteem engendered by acting as teacher to another child may be one reason for the powerful positive effects on tutors; other explanations advanced (Slavin 1996; McNamara and Moreton 1997) include the opportunities that tutoring provides for consolidating the tutor's own learning; as any teacher knows, there is no better way of obtaining a sure grasp of a concept than to have to teach it to others.

An example of a project in one primary school illustrates the impact on children of being chosen as peer tutors:

> A teacher of a Year 6 class was very concerned about the extremely poor reading skills of a group of children in her class. She decided to pair each of her poor readers with a child from a Key Stage 1 class. The aim, the older children were told, was 'to help your partner with their reading'. The younger child would choose a book and the older child talk about the pictures and story with them, or the pair would read what they could together. The older group were given a lot of praise from their own teacher and the Key Stage 1 teacher. They were told how well the younger ones' reading was coming on, and of changes in their attitude to books and to learning. After a few months the teacher reassessed the reading skills of her class. The children who had acted as peer tutors had made rapid progress. One boy, for example, had gone from being nearly three years behind in his reading to being only a few months behind.

Low-achieving, poorly-motivated children have most to gain by acting as tutors; schools can make use of this by forming partnerships between Years 5 and 6 children and those in younger groups, as with the teacher in the example, or by setting up a scheme with a neighbouring secondary school involving their older pupils. Maher (1984) reports several highly successful projects on these lines, in which 14–16-year-olds with a history of disruptive behaviour and underachievement tutored 9–11-year-old slow learners. He found that the older pupils made surprisingly good tutors, and showed massive gains in school attendance and performance. The tutees showed improvements of 15 to 20 per cent in task completion and performance on attainment tests over the ten-week tutoring period, with two 30-minute tutoring sessions per week.

While cross-age tutoring has particular benefits for enhancing self-esteem and motivation, same-age tutors can be just as effective in enhancing learning. McNamara and Moreton (1997) provide us with an inspiring model for organizing classrooms based on peer tutoring and pair work across the whole curriculum. Same-age tutoring projects are also easier to organize: there have been many reports of successful schemes that have divided classes or year groups into two, on the basis of reading ability, and established hearer–reader partnerships involving every child (Horner 1990; Leeves 1990). These are described in more detail in Chapters 11 and 12 along with some of the techniques (like cued spelling and paired reading) which lend themselves to peer tutoring projects.

Peer-tutoring components

The essential components of a successful peer tutoring scheme have been described by Topping (1987). On the basis of research evidence he suggests that projects should be time-limited, running initially for about six to ten weeks, after which the teacher seeks the views of tutor and tutee and decides with them whether the tutoring should stop, continue as it is or continue in another form. The tutor and tutee should work together regularly, for 15–30 minutes, at least three times a week in class time, supplemented if they wish by more work in their free time. Careful training of tutors is vital: peer tutoring works best if the tutor has a clear structure to work from, which is demonstrated by the teacher and then practised under guidance. The tutor should also be provided with simple written instructions in the form of a manual or handbook. Tutor and tutee must have some way of recording progress, and the teacher must plan to monitor the tutoring by looking at these records, observing occasional sessions and holding review meetings.

Parental involvement

Peer tutoring is one way of increasing the amount of individual attention available to children with special needs. Another is involving parents more actively in their children's learning. This can have benefits beyond the merely instructional: the opportunities it provides for parents and children to learn more about each other, spend more time together and share both the struggle and the pleasure of learning can lead to changes in the child's self-acceptance that unlock whole areas of hidden potential.

It can only do this, however, if the experience of parental involvement is one which makes the child feel valued and successful. It is the fear that this will not be the case that makes many teachers shy away from setting parents and children tasks to do together: despite the massive amount of evidence on the effectiveness of parental involvement projects, they are aware that in individual cases parents can find getting their child to do a set task a battle that spoils rather than enhances their relationship, can find it hard to tolerate the child's mistakes or remember to praise them for successes, and can, on occasion, push the child too hard to the point where all learning becomes an anxious chore.

In these circumstances, it is all too easy to back off from asking parents to become involved. Parental involvement remains a real challenge for schools; recent research (Rathbone 2001) found that nearly half of the parents surveyed did not feel involved in reviews of their child's progress, and while the majority believed they could contribute vital information about their child's needs, schools did not always seek out or use this information. Ofsted surveys (1997, 1999) of the implementation of the SEN *Code of Practice* have consistently noted schools' concerns about the time it takes to liaise with parents, and that parent partnership tended to be a good intention rather than a description of actual practice.

To leave it at this, however, risks depriving the child of a readily available and often highly motivated source of support. It means leaving parents and carers who on many occasions want very much to do something to help with little guidance about what might be best, so that the field is open for inappropriate teaching methodologies or targets. Instead of forgoing parental involvement, it may be better to negotiate something – however small – which the parent knows they can to without becoming anxious or angry, and which the child will be willing to do without argument. By asking three questions – 'How does it go when you try to work with your child at home?'; 'What helps it go well?'; 'What makes it go badly?' – the teacher can find out which problems might be solved and which sidestepped. If getting the child to work at home is a battle, the answer might be sending home educational games, making the amount of time spent initially very small or using a contract with the child linked to a reward system at home or school. If the parents say the problem is their own impatience, it may be possible to find someone else (grandparent, brother or sister) who can work with the child, use a technique (like paired reading) where the importance of mistakes is minimized or offer the parents training in noticing and praising success.

What about parents who appear not to want to be involved in their child's learning? It is certainly true that on the surface at least some parents of children with special needs seem unwilling to engage in active plans to support the child: their feelings about their child's difficulties in learning or adjustment are often those which cause awkwardness in their relationships with the school and make the establishment of a working partnership a particularly sensitive issue. Before making assumptions about their lack of interest, however, we may need to look at our own practice; we may need to recognize, as Klein (2000) puts it, that 'parents don't exist solely as the receptacles of bad news about their children's problem behaviour or poor attainment. If they are to be won over to the value of their child's education and the important role that they have to play, they must be offered positive overtures and given encouraging glimpses of their children, too'. Where this happens, schools can be unexpectedly successful in involving parents, as this example shows:

> at one school the staff put a lot of effort into involving parents of children with special needs. Even though the school serves an area of high social deprivation, ninety five per cent of its parents attend parents' evenings. This is where initial discussions about a child's special needs take place, and if parents *aren't* there someone will try to catch them later: 'We missed you at parents' evening – how about popping in tomorrow after school?' Positives are stressed: 'Have you seen how well his reading is doing/come in and see his books – you'll be pleased.' Any letter home is preceded by an informal chat with the class teacher and followed up by the SENCO. If parents themselves have literacy difficulties the school will always phone instead of sending a letter. Parents are always welcome in school, helping with all sorts of curricular and extra-curricular activities and working groups; this made it easy for the SENCO to set up a support group for parents, who come in once a week for coffee and activities like watching a video on helping your child at home, learning about paired reading, and swapping books from the library.
>
> Gross (1996)

Schools who are willing to persist in their efforts to involve all parents in particular projects – using evening as well as daytime group meetings, small informal groups with class teachers, home visits from the education welfare officer or teachers – will have the best chance of reaching their parents.

There are certain necessary preconditions for engaging and maintaining high levels of involvement: there needs to be a clear structure in what the parents are being asked to do to help the child that is demonstrated, practised and later on monitored in some way by school staff. There also needs to be an effort to maintain the impetus of any parental involvement scheme by varying and developing the work done at home: one year paired reading, for example (Topping and Wolfendale 1985), another a paired maths scheme (Arora and Bamford 1989), or reading and spelling games (Young and Tyre 1983).

At the level of action plans for the individual child rather than whole-school or class parental involvement projects, success in engaging parents will depend on factors surrounding the way in which invitations to parents to discuss their child's progress are given, and how meetings are handled. Many parents are put off by fears based on their own experiences of school, or by meetings where they have no control of the agenda, no sense of being listened to, no privacy, and where all that comes across is apparent criticisms of their child. Much of this can be avoided if there is a whole-school context where parents are not just called in when there are problems, but can see meetings about their child's special needs as just one aspect of generally close and friendly contact between home and school.

At a recent meeting between a group of parents of children with special needs and a group of teachers and SENCOs in mainstream primary schools, the parents were clear about the factors that help communication between themselves and the school – and those which do not. Top of their list of blocks to communication was a feeling of not being listened to, and of meeting teachers who went on the defensive if they made any comment about how things could be made better in school for the child. They also disliked feeling outnumbered at meetings and having to be the ones making the running in arranging for follow-up and review. What they wanted, they said, was a structure for meetings which:

- involved them early on, when the child's progress first gave cause for concern rather than when problems had escalated;
- had a clear agenda made known to them beforehand, along with an invitation to add issues and concerns they would like discussed;
- included information about the child's strengths as well as difficulties;
- included opportunities for them to put their views on the best ways to help the child give their best in school;
- allowed them to comment on how things could be made better for the child in school without teachers going on the defensive as a result;
- included accurate information on the procedures used by the school and LEA to assess and provide for special needs;
- gave them specific rather than general suggestions on how to help their child at home;
- ended with a clear agreement on the action to be taken, who would take it, and with a plan to meet again to review progress.

These parents valued teachers who were honest and had evidence of the child's work to show; an approach by the teacher that began with, 'I don't feel I'm doing a very good job with . . .' rather than 'He can't . . .' was appreciated.

Table 6.1 Common 'blocks' to listening

Don't say	Do say
I don't know why you're worried, he's doing as well as can be expected	Tell me more about why you are worried
She'll grow out of it	I can see that this is a real concern to you, and we need to do something about it
There's a lot worse than him, so we can't really give him any extra help at this stage	We can help him best at this stage by being clear about the targets we want him to achieve, and making a plan for how we can all work together on them
She tends to be disruptive/lazy/ a chatterbox/a fusspot	I've noticed that at the moment she calls out in class quite a lot/it takes her a while to get started on her work/she tends to chat at times when I'd want to see her get the job done/she seems to need quite a lot of reassurance before getting going
He's not dyslexic, dyspraxic, or ADHD	It's important we look into this; tell me what you've noticed

Parents need to feel listened to; Table 6.1 shows some of the common 'blocks' to listening which parents can encounter and some alternative ways of responding to parental concerns. All are based on the principle of active listening – that is, making a real attempt to understand what the parent is saying and the feelings behind the words, to summarize this understanding and check it out before asking further questions that will help both teacher and parent to arrive at a clear, shared grasp of the problem.

The way in which an initial invitation to a meeting is given can be off-putting: many parents report nights of worry after a casual invitation to 'pop in and discuss Andrew's learning problems', or after a more formal letter expressing concern and setting a date and time for a meeting with the teachers. The best way to give an invitation for a first discussion about a child's special needs is probably orally, if possible at a regular parent–teacher evening, when it will arise naturally from the general overview of progress and where the purposes of such a meeting can be explained and clarified. Some schools like to add to the verbal invitation a short information sheet, taken from the whole-school special needs policy or the school prospectus, which describes the steps that will be taken when a teacher or parent expresses concern about a child's progress, and the ways in which parents will be involved at each stage, along the lines of:

At X primary school there will occasionally be times when a teacher feels the school should try harder to help particular children make better progress. When this happens, we would ask you to come into school for a conference with your child's teacher, and perhaps also the headteacher or the teacher with responsibility for special educational needs.

This kind of conference happens very often in school: we find that many children need a little extra help from time to time.

At the conference, you will be asked to tell us more about your child's strengths and interests outside school. We would also like you to help us with your ideas about ways to get the best from him or her. We will use this information, and the information the teacher has gained from observing the child closely in school, to decide on a plan of action – things the teacher can do, things the child can do, things you can do at home which may help sort out any problems.

We will set a date when everyone concerned will meet again to see whether the plan has succeeded. At this meeting, another plan may be agreed, or we may decide to ask for advice from one of the outside support services available to us, such as the Special Needs Support Service or the psychology service.

For almost all children, this kind of special help will be enough. If not, we may be able to involve the local education authority in making a fuller assessment, jointly with you, of what the child needs in order to ensure progress.

Types of support parents can give include:

- direct help with specific work at home;
- taking a checking and monitoring role (for example, checking that home-work has been done, or agreeing to spend time each evening playing a favourite game with the child if they have not been in trouble at school that day);
- freeing professional time to work with the child by helping in school with the preparation of materials or supervising groups under the direction of the teacher.

If direct teaching at home is to be used, paired reading and maths, or cued spelling (see Chapter 12) are techniques that have all proved helpful in providing a structure to the work. The teaching-to-targets approach using a learning chart also lends itself well to parental involvement:

Box 6.3 gives an example of a chart developed for David, a 5-year-old experiencing great difficulty in assigning numerals to counted sets. Assessment showed that he had not mastered an essential component skill: he was not only unable to match written numbers to oral number names, but also could not reliably distinguish numerals from each other. He could, however, count sets accurately with one-to-one correspondence. For a week or two he worked intensively on matching plastic numerals and numerals on cards with each other, as a first step towards matching the numerals with sets of objects: his parents spent a few minutes each day having him match magnetic plastic numerals on the door of the fridge, and recorded progress on the learning chart supplied. He soon reached the success criterion of correctly matching all ten numbers three days in a row, and was able to go on to a new learning chart where he had to recognize and point to the numerals 2 and 3 when asked to pick them out from several alternatives.

Even simpler as a way of managing teaching-to-targets is using a home-school notebook, like the example in Box 6.4.

Box 6.3 Learning chart with parental involvement

Learning Chart

Child's Name: David.

1 **Target for the week:** David will match the numbers 1–10.

2 **Instruction:** Find a number just the same as this.

4 **When to stop:** Not until David gets all ten right on three days in a row.

5 **Rewards:** Sticker from teacher.

6 **Backup resources for independent practice:** Play dominoes with the domino cards with just numbers on them.

Materials: Plastic numbers.

3 **How many times each day:** Ten.

Next pupil target: We'll try David on recognizing numbers.

Mon	Tues	Wed	Thurs	Fri	Mon	Tues	Wed	Thurs	Fri
●	✔	●	✔	✔	✔	✔	✔		
✔	✔	✔	✔	✔	✔	✔	✔		
✔	●	✔	✔	✔	✔	✔	✔		
●	●	✔	✔	✔	✔	✔	✔		
✔	✔	✔	●	✔	✔	✔	✔		
●	✔	✔	✔	✔	✔	✔	✔		
●	●	●	●	●	✔	✔	✔		
●	✔	✔	●	●	✔	✔	✔		
●	●	✔	✔	✔	✔	✔	✔		
●	●	●	✔	✔	✔	✔	✔		

Key: ✔ if correct ● if help needed

Parents' comment: He muddled 2 and 5 but seems to have got them now.

Box 6.4   Home-school notebook

Week beginning:

Target for the week (e.g. counting backwards from 10):

Ideas (e.g. try to spend a few minutes each day counting backwards
10-9-8 etc., when going downstairs, eating ten crisps, or say it together before you start something: 10-9-8 . . . blast-off!):

Parents' comments:

Conclusion

In this chapter we have looked at ways of offering support to children on
those frequent occasions where there is no extra teacher or teaching assistant time available to work with a particular child. These are not just stopgap
resources: as we have seen, involving parents and peers can have benefits
that extend well beyond the surface value of the academic teaching and
learning that take place. Nevertheless, they cannot be the whole story; children should also be entitled to help from trained professionals; it is at this
that we look in the next chapter.

7

Making provision – using additional adult support

Introduction

In most schools today, the provision for children with special needs is not wholly reliant on help from peers or parents; there is usually at least some extra staffing that is used for SEN work – sometimes support teacher time, but more likely dedicated time from teaching assistants.

Using such support effectively, so as to make the best use of the limited amounts available, has in recent years become a major task for class teachers, SENCOs and managers. An increasing amount of research is being directed towards investigating good practice, and providing guidance to schools on how best to deploy additional adult support. It is to this research, particularly in relation to teaching assistants, that we turn first.

Teaching assistants

Teaching assistants are now found working with children with special needs in the great majority of primary classrooms, not only with those who have Statements but also with individuals and groups at the school support level of the *Code of Practice*. There is, however, unfortunately a good deal of evidence to show that they are not always deployed effectively, with positive outcomes for children's attainment and inclusion. All too often they are used as low paid 'minders', coaxing children to comply with an otherwise undifferentiated and often inappropriate curriculum.

Consider, for example, a research report from MENCAP (1999), aptly entitled *On a Wing and a Prayer*. The researchers studied schools reputed to have good practice in SEN and inclusion, and found that all too often the assistant was the child's main teacher, doing all the planning, with few opportunities to liaise with the class teacher. They also noted many cases where the teacher more or less ignored the child, or where the presence of the assistant effectively prevented the child from interacting with their peers.

Consider also the work of Lorenz (1999), who undertook a survey of the experiences of children with Down's syndrome who were included in mainstream schools. Of these children, 60 per cent had somewhere between 20 hours and full-time teaching assistant support. Only 39 per cent of the assistants had received any training in supporting children with Down's syndrome. Only 40 per cent were given time to plan with the class teacher on a regular basis. Of the children, 41 per cent were taught by their class or subject teacher at least once a day, 22 per cent once a week, but 37 per cent were taught by their class or subject teacher 'occasionally or never'.

Put bluntly, what this research means is that teaching assistants can become a convenient device by which the teacher who is responsible for the child's learning can avoid having to adapt their curriculum delivery to take account of the child with SEN – or in some cases avoid having contact with the child at all. Teaching assistants may be deployed on the 'velcro' model, attached like glue to a particular child for long periods, or the 'helicopter' model, hovering over a group of children to make sure they complete their work; either way it is not likely that the support will be as helpful as it might, to anyone other than the class teacher.

What, then *is* good practice in deploying teaching assistants? Much work has been done on this by writers such as Balshaw (1999), Fox (1999) and Shaw (2001); there is also some national guidance (DfEE 2000), which though not specific to SEN roles, provides very useful thinking points.

A good way of opening the debate in school about the roles of assistants is to ask the staff to do an activity where they think of something they as individuals are not good at (for example, swimming), and imagine that they are in a class where everyone is good at swimming except them. Ask them to imagine that they are so bad at swimming that someone tells them they are going to have a special helper. Discussion should follow on how this would feel, and how they would want the helper to provide support.

Staff can also take roles, as teacher, child or assistant, and be asked to complete sentences starting 'Extra adult support works best for me when . . .'. In the role of child, answers may include '. . . when it doesn't make me look stupid in front of my mates' or '. . . when she helps other people too, and isn't with me all the time'. For the teacher, answers could be about setting aside time for joint planning with the assistant, so that they know exactly what is expected. For the assistant, key issues are also likely to be about knowing beforehand what the lesson content will be, what the objectives are for particular pupils and about access to appropriate training, so that they understand, for example, the teaching vocabulary and methodology of the NLS and NNS.

Another way of helping people think about what makes support effective is to make sure that all teachers have an opportunity to act, for a short time, as support teachers in a colleague's class. After experiencing for themselves how frustrating it can be to have poor liaison, or inadequate/absent ground rules (on who is allowed to discipline pupils, for example, or who can give them permission to leave the classroom), they will have a better sense of how to manage support in their own situation.

From activities like these some general principles will arise, which the school can record as a policy document on the use of additional support. In addition, specific roles will need to be negotiated for each support situation.

All too often these roles are restricted to either helping the child or children in a general way to complete tasks set by the class teacher, or withdrawing them to work on basics. Both can be valid ways of working, but they still represent only a fraction of all the possible ways of using support time. They can also mean that the assistant is poorly used in whole-class teaching, sitting passively until the time comes to support a group of less able pupils later on in the lesson. Box 7.1 provides a fuller menu of roles which could be used as a basis for discussions between the class teacher and assistant.

Box 7.1   Teaching assistant roles

- Pre-tutoring: going through work (for example, shared texts) with a pupil or pupils ahead of whole-class teaching, or taking a group for a guided talk session to prepare them for writing
- Helping to manage behaviour: using a behaviour tick list to record children's success in reaching behavioural targets, noticing when a child or group are behaving well and praising them, working with a group to 'coach' behaviours like turn-taking and listening
- Observing particular children in order to gather assessment information
- Ensuring access by using 'bypass' strategies (for example, simplifying or repeating the teacher's language, helping a child formulate answers to questions or using specific resources such as personal number cards or number lines to find an answer, brailling, signing or scribing for the child)
- Taking a group to work on a specific programme such as Early or Additional Literacy Support, an oral language or a thinking skills programme
- Preparing differentiated resources under the teacher's direction (for example, task cards with picture clues, tapes of information texts, simplified worksheets)
- Working with a pupil or group on ICT programmes
- Working one-to-one with a child for ten minutes a day on a teaching-to-targets programme using a learning chart (see Chapter 6)
- Supporting pupils individually or in groups during National Curriculum assessments
- Helping children use self-assessment or to produce evidence of attainment for profiles and progress files
- Alternating roles with the teacher on the 'room management' model (Thomas 1992; Lorenz 1999) where one person takes the role of 'activity manager' (concentrating on the class as a whole, and moving around between groups), a second the role of 'individual worker' (concentrating on working uninterrupted with an individual or a small group), and the third the role of 'mover' (fetching and organizing equipment for the individual worker and activity manager, supervising the preparation or cleaning up of activities, dealing with interruptions, toileting etc.). Where there are only two adults, the role of activity manager and mover can be combined. During any activity period the adults explain their roles to the children, and may wear coloured badges to make it clear who is in which role for that session.

Working with a support teacher

Although less common than access to teaching assistants, some schools are able to identify some extra teaching time for SEN work. This may be through the employment of an additional teacher, or be part of the SENCO's role; where it happens, there is considerable evidence (e.g. Hurry 2000) that children are able to make greater gains than if only teaching assistants are involved.

Some of the key principles in working with a support teacher (such as joint planning and liaison with the class teacher) are the same as those for working with teaching assistants. SEN support teachers, however, should be expected to 'add value' by bringing specific expertise, sometimes quite specialist and based on advanced training, to bear on classroom issues and the needs of particular children.

At the whole-class level, roles for support teachers might include:

- Focused classroom observation and advice to the class teacher on strategies for differentiation or behaviour management.
- Identifying appropriate learning objectives for particular children or groups.
- Joining year group or Key Stage curriculum planning groups to help colleagues incorporate these learning objectives into their lessons, or to consider the bypass strategies that will be needed to enable particular children to access the schemes of work.
- Managing a central resource base and advising on suitable resources – for example, non-fiction books with a controlled vocabulary and simple sentence structure for work on a particular subject.
- Developing or modifying resources – for example, producing writing frames or on-screen word lists for word-processing programmes.
- Advising on appropriate modifications to National Curriculum assessment.
- Modelling particular approaches, such as circle time, which the class teacher can then take on board.

At the level of the individual child or group, roles might cover:

- Assessment to pinpoint areas of difficulty, preferred learning styles and next steps in learning.
- Taking a child or group, either in class or on a withdrawal basis, to work on targeted academic skills – for example, one of the structured multisensory literacy programmes described in Chapter 11.
- Taking a child or group to work on social or emotional skills – for example, individual counselling or group work on anger management.
- Teaching the class so as to free the teacher to observe, assess or work directly with particular children with SEN.
- Teaching in parallel to the class teacher – for example, taking a group for the word level part of the Literacy Hour.
- Pre-teaching: preparing a group of pupils ahead of time so that they can make a contribution to whole-class interactive lessons.
- Drawing up teaching to target programmes (like those described in Chapter 6) for others to implement on a daily basis with the child.

In-class support or withdrawal?

Whether teaching assistants or support teachers are used, schools need to decide on the circumstances under which children will be withdrawn from the classroom in order to access extra help, and the circumstances under which the help will be provided within the classroom. In view of the variable response of Ofsted inspectors to the issue of withdrawal, schools would be wise to document these decisions and the rationale behind them in a written policy.

Both withdrawal and in-class support have their advantages and disadvantages. Withdrawal support enables focused work on individualized targets to take place in an atmosphere of calm and concentration. It can help to economize on scant support time, when children from different classes but with similar needs are drawn together as a withdrawal group. It can provide a welcome break for both class teacher and pupil where behaviour or the relationship is problematic, and provide the child with experience of a range of teaching styles. On the other hand, it may mean that the child experiences a fragmented curriculum, missing just enough of what is going on in the classroom to make it difficult to catch hold of important new learning. If the withdrawal always happens at the same time, the child may miss out on a whole curriculum area. There may be little or no link between the work done in withdrawal sessions and the work in class, so that there are few opportunities to generalize from one situation to another, or to practise skills taught in withdrawal sessions with sufficient frequency to ensure fluency. The child may be stigmatized for going out of class for extra help, to the extent where already fragile self-esteem is shattered. Class teachers may feel that it is now no longer their job to cater for the pupil's special needs; thankfully handing over all responsibility, they may reduce efforts to support the child in class or to adapt teaching styles. There may be few opportunities for the class teacher and support person to share information and skills, and the person doing the withdrawal work may feel personally and professionally isolated.

Advantages of in-class support are that the class teacher maintains a sense of ownership of the problems that are arising for the child, and is encouraged to look at ways of overcoming them through a differentiated curriculum. Pupils other than targeted individuals can benefit from the presence of extra support staff in the classroom, and from the strategies for differentiation introduced as a result of teamwork. The support teacher or assistant sees the child in context, and is thus better placed to understand their needs; the child does not miss work, and – if not obviously the sole client of the support – is less likely to be teased or labelled by peers. On the negative side, the small amounts of in-class support that tend to be available may result in help so diluted as to be ineffective in raising pupil attainment; lack of time for liaison may lead to the kind of situation where support staff are used as just another pair of hands in class, with scant regard to their particular skills and potential contribution. In-class support may come to be seen as solely aimed at helping the child keep up with their work in class, an interpretation which is dear to many class teachers who have plans for what the class will achieve and like to see all children fitting in with these expectations.

There is a real risk in the over-use of in-class support of this kind that it will satisfy teachers' short-term expectations, but seriously disadvantage children for the future, if they end up thoroughly *au fait* with Roman history or the way in which soil is formed, but without the 'tool' skills of literacy and numeracy which they will need in all of their later education. Prioritizing support towards the core subjects, rather than the whole curriculum, is one way of making sure that all available extra adult help is not poured into propping up children so that they can be seen to keep pace with an inadequate curriculum ill-matched to their needs. This does not necessarily, however, mean that children need to be withdrawn (often at times when the things they like best are happening in class) year in, year out to work individually or in small groups on a tedious diet of basic skills worksheets. Instead, it should be possible to use special programmes of work in basic skills on a time-limited basis (for, say, half a term or a term), with clear targets, either in the classroom or out of it depending on whether the programme (or the child) actually requires a non-distracting environment or whether the special work would distract others if pursued in the room. The NLS catch-up programmes provide a model for this type of time-limited support.

It should also be possible to embed any withdrawal programme firmly within the work pursued by the class as a whole: to use a poem the class have studied, for example, as a starting point for work on a spelling pattern, or base work on telling the time on a class science investigation of shadow lengths throughout the day, or build an individual child's self-esteem by doing some preparatory work with them so that they can take an expert role in a class discussion.

However, the important point is that in doing this work the aim of the support teacher or assistant is to teach the children to spell particular words rather than appreciate a poem, to tell the time rather than measure shadows, to grow in confidence rather than gain knowledge of the topic under discussion. The work the whole class is doing forms the background for the additional support, but the support is nevertheless focused on basic skills objectives uniquely relevant to the individual or group being supported.

Some children *will* need some form of more general in-class support: these are the children whose need for bypass strategies, enabling them to circumvent areas of difficulty in order to access the curriculum, is greater than their need for help in acquiring core skills. An example might be a child with a coordination difficulty: in-class support would be necessary if they are to cope with technology lessons involving the accurate manipulation of tools and materials. Equally, a child with a hearing impairment might need in-class support in the form of someone to repeat and clarify instructions.

Other children – those with specific literacy difficulties, for example – may well need bypass strategies and in-class support based on scribing or taping, but may have a greater immediate need for catch-up programmes in English or maths. Only a clear distinction between bypass strategies and remediation strategies, and a process of determining priorities, like the one described in Chapter 5, can help schools decide where to target limited extra adult help. For each child, this will be an individual decision, regularly reviewed in the light of the evidence.

Working with outside agencies

This chapter has so far been about the use of support staff from within the school. It is also important, however, to look at the school's role when working in partnership with outside agencies, particularly LEA or special school SEN support teams.

Well-organized LEA or special school services should be able to offer a range of interventions, which might include:

- Direct work at the individual level – for example, assessment or teaching of a particular child or group with reading difficulties, individual counselling of a child with behaviour problems, or sessions with a group of children on friendship skills and self-esteem.
- Indirect work, still focused on the needs of individual children, but involving consultation with parents or teachers – for example, discussing with parents how to handle their child's anxiety about coming to school, or jointly drawing up an action plan involving daily work in class and a programme at home for a child with a learning difficulty, or discussing with the teacher the implications of a child's special needs for curriculum or SATs access.
- Work that involves demonstrating the use of particular approaches and resources – for example, circles of friends or ICT programmes.
- Work at the consultative level that is focused on the curriculum as a whole rather than the individual child – for example, looking at schemes of work with the teacher and advising on suitable resources for differentiation.
- Work at the organizational level that is aimed, through INSET and policy development, at increasing the school's ability to respond effectively to individual needs.

It is the task of the school to choose, from a menu of this kind, the services that they feel will have the greatest impact in the time available. There will be some overlap between the roles of school-based SEN support teachers/SENCOs and those of LEA support services: the skill in using external agencies is in deciding where the school itself may not have sufficient specialist expertise, and using the external agency to fill that gap – while at the same time ensuring that the agency works wherever possible alongside school staff so as to build, in the longer term, the school's own internal capacity.

One school, working to a model like this, might find that it had adequate internal expertise in behaviour management or literacy, but a gap in advisory expertise – say in the area of mathematical difficulties – that would enable class teachers to draw up differentiated programmes of work. For that year, the school might therefore choose to focus limited amounts of input from external support services on INSET and collaborative action planning for individuals in this area. Another school might feel it was coping well with differentiation and action planning, but was still not succeeding in meeting the needs of a handful of children with severe and intractable reading difficulties. That year, it might choose to use the central support service to get this group going with literacy.

Both schools might well be aware of a real need for specialist expertise in working with the increasing number of children with complex needs –

autism, cerebral palsy or Down's syndrome, for example – who were being included in mainstream classrooms. 'Low incidence' needs like these are ones where teachers are highly likely to need to draw on specialist advice from outside the school.

Effective work with outside agencies, then, depends in part on matching the customer's audit of needs with the provider's menu of services. This negotiation will result, each year, in a written contract specifying the services that have been agreed, along with the criteria that will be used to judge their quality and effectiveness. This is only fair: support teachers, educational psychologists, education welfare officers and other providers expect, these days, to have their work with the customer evaluated – but evaluated in ways that are specific, agreed beforehand, and which enable them to improve the services they offer in the future. If schools will be judging their support teacher on how easy it is to contact them by telephone, on punctuality and the extent to which they succeed in building staff self-esteem, as well as on measured outcomes for INSET or work with individual children, they should say so. In turn, the support teacher should be able to negotiate, for each annual contract, their minimum needs for effective work with the school: for example, time to talk to class teachers, a workspace that is not subject to constant interruptions, or prior information about the content of a lesson in which they will be working in a support capacity.

Sometimes these negotiated agreements will not be between one school and a support agency, but between the agency and a cluster of schools. Increasingly, schools are finding that whereas the small amount of support time available to each of them can do little that is useful on its own, aggregating funding across a group or cluster means that shared support can be bought in, or a shared cluster special needs support teacher appointed.

Finally, in relation to support agencies, schools need to plan how to map the range of support services each class teacher can call on, from outside the LEA as well as in, and the roles they are able to play in schools. The actual roles and services will vary from area to area; a directory of services would, however, normally need to include the roles and contact details of a school nurse and doctor, a child and adolescent mental health service, health service therapists (speech and language therapist, occupational therapist, physiotherapist), social services, education welfare service, educational psychology service, SEN teaching service, and special school and unit outreach.

Setting up a resource base in school

Another way of providing support to children with SEN is setting up and managing some kind of resource base, where teachers (and children) can access books, games, workbooks, software and special equipment to meet individual needs.

The challenge of such resource base arrangements is to make sure they are actually used by class teachers. Storing resources on movable trolleys, which spend a block of time in each classroom in the school in order to introduce all the staff to what is available, is one way around the problem. Another is to index resources explicitly against the school's schemes of work.

It is important that children, as well as teachers, are able to understand and use the indexing system. Storage could be in labelled trays, box files and ring binders; masters for photocopiable materials should be in clear pockets, and clear plastic bags with zip or clip tops should be used for games, sets of materials that need to stay together, and work to take home.

Some of the most useful materials will be those which individual teachers have made to support particular schemes of work: the breakdown one teacher might have done, for example, on how to help children understand the life cycle of flowering plants, or a set of taped materials to support work on the Victorians. These will be supplemented, as finances allow, by commercial materials – software, games, taped exercises, workbooks and worksheets. Many schools have been surprised, when staff looked in cupboards of shared resources, to find out how much was already available (and underused). At the very least, establishing an indexed resource base allows staff to see exactly where the resource gaps lie, and coordinate their own efforts and those of parents and volunteers to make new materials, or to make better use of materials available for loan from local support services and special schools.

Components of a special needs resource base

What should go into a central special needs resource base? It is impossible to be prescriptive, but the following framework may be helpful.

Information for teachers and parents

Many schools choose to subscribe to journals like *Special Children* (Questions Publishing) or *Special!* (NASEN). As well as books and journals, a collection of leaflets and information packs from voluntary organizations dealing with learning disabilities and medical conditions is helpful to parents and teachers alike. ACE (the Advisory Centre for Education) produces information sheets listing names and addresses of organizations to write to for information like this.

Hardware

If the resource base is mobile, and sure to be in constant use, it will be worth considering including a portable computer among the hardware. Other useful equipment would be a cassette player and headphones, simple electronic spellcheckers and the special pens which 'read' words aloud when passed over them. Line-tracker/magnifiers and coloured overlays may also be worth including for children with visually-based literacy difficulties.

Assessment materials

The resource base should include one or more of the small-step breakdowns of National Curriculum attainment targets described in Chapter 4, plus a few user-friendly diagnostic assessment packs in key areas such as behaviour (see Chapter 8), literacy (see Chapter 11) and maths (see Chapter 13).

Materials for developing language skills

For children in the foundation stage there should be a language development programme such as *Living Language* (NFER-Nelson). *Wordplay* (NASEN), *Chatterbox* (LDA) and *Teaching Talking* (NFER-Nelson) are useful for older children with language difficulties. Listening skills can be practised in Key Stage 2 using taped programmes such as LDA's *Listen, Think and Do*, the *Listening Skills Pack* from Questions Publishing and Dee Reid's indispensable short booklet *Some Well Known Tales* from Philip and Tacey. For older pupils, materials include Schofield and Sims' *Oracy* taped materials from their language programme, Learning Materials Limited's *Oral Comprehension* materials and NASEN's *A Rainbow of Words*.

Materials for reading, writing, spelling and handwriting

Texts covering the whole range of reading ability (and coded for reading and interest levels using readability measures and resources such as Hinson and Gains' *A–Z List of Reading Books* from NASEN, or NASEN's CD-ROM *Guide to Reading Schemes*) should be in classrooms and the library rather than in a special needs area. The resource base, however, will need to supply materials that provide an added element of structure and reinforcement. There should be games to reinforce the learning of high frequency words – commercial (such as LDA's *Keyword Fun Activities*) or home-grown. *Games to Improve Reading Levels* from NASEN is a good source of ideas for home-made versions, while an attractive set of photocopy masters from Longman's *Reading World* enables the teacher to make up 50 different games of the lotto, jigsaw and board game type. LDA's *Happy Learning Games* covers the literacy curriculum from reception through to Year 6, while its dice games are another tried and tested resource. For reinforcement of phonic skills, there is an enormous amount of material available: LDA's range is popular with teachers and includes *Sound Beginnings* (to develop phonological awareness), the self-correcting *Stile* phonics and spelling, Sue Palmer's *Word Building Games*, the popular *Switch* and *Track Packs* and, for older children, swipe card games. More specialist are Beve Hornsby's *Alpha to Omega*, Michael Thompson's adventure books and the *Beat Dyslexia* worksheets.

Reading for meaning can be encouraged through materials that use cloze, sequencing, summarizing and similar activities, such as Learning Materials Limited's *Reading for Meaning*, LDA's *False Teeth and Vampires*, Oliver and Boyd's *I See What You Mean* and Oxford University Press' ever-popular *Headwork* series.

To help children sequence ideas and structure stories, there should be sequential picture cards like those from LDA, materials which provide a ready-made structure like Learning Materials Limited's *Picture Writing* and aids to planning like Longman's *Reading World's Super Writers* copymasters and Scholastic's *Essential English* series. Materials for sentence-level work include LDA's *Stile Punctuation* and *Grammar*, and their *Sentence Building Games*.

A range of illustrated word banks, picture dictionaries and supportive dictionaries for the poor speller (such as the *ACE* spelling dictionary from LDA and Christine Maxwell's *Pergamon Perfect Spelling Dictionary* from Nelson) should find a place on the resources trolley.

For teachers rather than children, the literacy section of the resource base should also furnish ideas for parental involvement with reading projects, such as the *Paired Reading Pack* from Kirklees LEA which includes video material and detailed instructions on setting up a project, or the simple but useful *Better Reading Bookmarks* from Questions Publishing, which helps parents listen to their child read effectively.

Finally, for handwriting, easy-to-hold pencils and pencil grips (both from LDA) should be available, along with non-slip materials and perhaps an angled writing board. For practice in pre-writing patterns LDA's *Write from the Start* and the first stage of *A Hand For Spelling* are useful; Collins' *Pencil Fun* is also popular and LDA's *Rol 'n Write* helps children master correct letter formation. For older children, there are Scholastic's *Essential English Handwriting Patterns* and LDA's resources linking practice in cursive script with work on letter strings for spelling.

Materials for maths

It is in maths that there is most scope for collating and indexing resources from a variety of schemes and materials against small steps within the national framework for teaching mathematics.

A useful all-in-one resource which allows teachers to assess children's difficulties and create individual teaching programmes is *Mathsteps* from LDA: this covers all aspects of the early stages of the primary maths curriculum and is especially designed for those who find the gradient of other maths materials too steep. *Quest*, from NFER-Nelson, has a more limited focus but is very useful for assessment and teaching ideas in basic number concepts. LDA's *Stile* materials include sets on money and time and are popular with many age groups.

Most important in the maths resources are games and puzzles for use in the classroom and for home loan. NASEN produce a collection of good ideas for over 70 games and activities for the reinforcement of basic number facts and skills. For ready-made games, materials to look at include the Cambridge Primary Maths scheme *Games Pack*, Learning Materials Limited's games on topics like money and time, Schofield and Sims' *Maths Quest* games, Ginn's *GEM* games and New Peak and Nelson's maths games and resource packs.

Materials for developing thinking, memory and study skills

Well worth including among the more subject-based materials are those which help children learn abstract thinking skills – how to question, how to discuss issues, how to solve problems. The *Primary Thinking Skills Project* (from Questions Publishing) is based on the work of the American philosopher Matthew Lipman and provides a six-week programme of discussion activities around a story-book theme and around work on a houses and homes topic. *Top Ten Thinking Tactics* and *Improving Memory Skills* are other useful packs from the same publisher.

Materials for humanities and science

Differentiated materials in these areas are disappointingly thin on the ground. Hodder Wayland Publishers, however, have broken new ground in producing books with the same content at two different language levels; the Longman Book Project also has non-fiction texts incorporating three levels of reading difficulty. Watts Publishing produce information books with simple sentence structure and controlled vocabulary and there is an increasing range of publications that use pictorial resource material (such as the popular Collins *Primary History* series). LDA are also good for history resources; Learning Materials Limited have their excellent *Support for History Key Stage 2* resources and a good range of easy to read worksheets covering science, geography and common primary topics.

Most useful of all, however, are likely to be the home-grown materials (on-screen word lists, worksheets adapted to different reading levels, cassettes and materials based on the DARTs activities described in Chapter 11) that teachers have made to support their own lessons. Possibly the best invest-ment a school can make is to set up a workshop for the preparation of such materials, followed by time for people to get together to make their own resources.

Materials for personal and social education

SENCOs are increasingly being asked by colleagues for advice and support in helping pupils with emotional and behavioural difficulties, and have a clear role in drawing up IEPs for these children. It is well worth while setting up a resource file of awards, certificates, contracts, behaviour monitoring and self-monitoring sheets. Ready-made award certificates are available (for example in Lucky Duck's *Celebrations*, and from LDA), but personalized versions are easy to create on a word processor. Supplies of reward stickers and stamps for colleagues are also useful. Primary children love the self-inking *Xpressions* stamps from NES-Arnold and the range of stickers from LDA. There should definitely be a range of resources to help develop self-esteem – a good book for teachers is Jenny Mosley's *Turn Your School Around* from LDA – plus structured classroom or small group activities for children, such as Shay McConnon's *My Choice* from Nelson (secondary focused but useful for older juniors too). To help children develop social and emotional skills a wide range of excellent resources are available from Incentive Plus. Together with books on circle time activities (from Lucky Duck and NASEN), the ideas in these resources will cover the whole range of work that may be necessary to help children with special needs in behaviour, emotional and social devel-opment to understand and manage their feelings. It will also be useful to have books for children (such as those in the *Let's Talk About It* and *How Do I Feel About?* series from Watts, those from Child's Play and Cherry Tree Books or the Althea books from A&C Black) which help them to deal with difficult events and issues: divorce, bullying, stepfamilies, bereavement and loss.

Using information and communication technology

When human resources are scarce, the role of ICT in supporting special needs work takes on an extra importance. Aside from its enormous potential in enabling curriculum access for pupils with major physical and sensory impairments, ICT can play a range of roles for pupils with less severe difficulties, from providing extra reinforcement in palatable form in programmes of the drill-and-practice type, to supporting the writing task, stimulating language development and thinking skills through shared work around adventure programmes, and providing information for children to explore at varying levels of complexity for science and humanities work. The range of software is vast and ever-changing. A useful source of regularly updated information is the single-source catalogue for ICT and special needs, covering all the major suppliers, produced by REM.

The first step for teachers who want to meet the whole range of learning needs is to familiarize themselves with the many ways in which word processing can be used to support children's writing. Further discussed in Chapter 12, developments such as predictive word processors, talking word processors, on-screen pictures and word lists to suit the learner's ability and interests enable children to create complex and technically perfect pieces of work quickly and easily.

Second, teachers with an interest in special needs will want to explore software that supports the curriculum in topic work, science and humanities. For children who find it hard to use books for research, animated 'talking' text programmes are proving invaluable – series covering topics from transport to dinosaurs and ancient Greece are available from Sherston (*Look! Hear!* talking reference books) and from SEMERC (*Full Phase* and *Optima*). SEMERC's *My World* series, a framework programme that allows children to discover information and create text through picture screens, is also very popular, as is Crick's *Find Out and Write About*.

Talking books (such as Oxford Reading Tree's *Talking Stories*, Sherston's *Talking Stories*, Bronderbund's *Living Books* and Topologika's *Talking Maths Books*) are increasingly available, and have enormous promise for developing literacy skills.

Finally, it will be useful for teachers with an interest in special needs to explore some of the many materials available to support structured programmes of work in basic skills. Useful maths materials are produced by such companies at Sherston and White Space. In Chapters 11 and 12 we will look at software for practising decoding and spelling words. Often unpopular with ICT purists, these types of material nevertheless have an important role for pupils who require a lot of reinforcement of new concepts, and who find using a computer to practise skills both more exciting and less anxiety-provoking than work with a human helper.

Some particular 'drill and practice' programmes which initially attracted a lot of attention were integrated learning systems (ILS) such as *Successmaker* or *Academy of Learning*, which run on a networked system and aim to deliver a total core curriculum through individual tutoring and practice. Extensive evaluation (Lewis 1999), however, has failed to demonstrate that such systems are effective for pupils with SEN. Despite teacher enthusiasm and some effects on pupil motivation, attainment outcomes were no better with ILS than with other methods. Effectiveness varied with the extent of teacher involvement: the judicious use of carefully chosen software as part of a teacher-led programme appears to be more likely to succeed than totally machine-led learning.

Conclusion

Children can learn from many sources – from computers, games and books as well as people; from parents and peers as well as teachers. Meeting individual and special needs is about finding out – by observation, and by asking – which way works best for each child, and making sure that the system allows for flexibility and pupil choice in matching resources to learners. In the last two chapters, on the management of human and physical resources, we have tried to outline some of the ways in which these flexible forms of support can be offered.

It is now time to move on from the general issues of organizing the school's response to special needs and focus on teachers' more immediate concerns: to consider the main areas of individual need that they most commonly encounter, and the response they can make. We begin, in the next chapter, with the issue that often generates the most concern of all – behaviour.

Managing behaviour

Introduction

Because the term 'special needs' has become, for many teachers, a contemporary substitute used when describing children they would once have called 'slow learners', behavioural difficulties are not always seen as part of the special needs continuum. The role ascribed to the SENCO, for example, frequently stops short of supporting colleagues in relation to pupils who may be quick to learn, but who have difficulty in handling social relationships or in conforming to classroom rules. Yet it is these children who often cause most concern to their teachers, and for whom the special needs framework of assessment, action planning, record keeping and putting in additional resources can be particularly helpful.

Special needs in learning and special needs in behaviour are, moreover, inextricably linked. Teacher judgements of whether particular children have learning difficulties, for example, are heavily influenced by whether or not they demonstrate a particular behaviour pattern of fidgeting, distraction and inability to work in a group (Moses 1982). It has also repeatedly been demonstrated (Westwood 1982) that successful integration for children with learning difficulties into mainstream classes depends relatively little on the extent of the learning problem, but a great deal on whether the child behaves well – follows school rules and routines, does not disrupt in the classroom, shows initiative and self-management when learning and concentrates on the task in hand.

Such research suggests that behavioural needs should often assume primacy when we are planning support for individual children. There is no shortage of advice for teachers on how to go about this: more has been written about behaviour management than any other area of special need. In this chapter and the next we will aim only to provide an overview of some of this work, and describe a framework that will adapt itself to many different behavioural difficulties and many different situations. Two particular areas – aggressive behaviour and poor concentration – will be considered in more detail, since these are among the most common problems which teachers meet and to which they most often seek solutions.

The rules, rewards and sanctions framework

The starting point in any planning for individual children's behavioural needs has to be an overall school framework that specifies the expectations the school holds about the behaviour of all members of the school community, and the systems that will be used by all staff to encourage positive and discourage negative behaviour. Such whole-school behaviour policies have now been developed by many primary schools. The essential steps involve a review of behaviour in school as seen by staff, parents and pupils, and an examination of any factors in school layout, curriculum and organization that may be contributing to behaviour problems, followed by work on the rules, rewards and sanctions that will consistently be applied in school.

Westgate primary school began the process of developing a whole-school behaviour policy by asking pupils to describe the aspects of behaviour that most bothered them in school, and to discuss in small groups what they thought the rules about behaviour should be. Teachers and lunchtime supervisors completed a checklist over several days that helped to identify what behaviour problems they were encountering most often, and in what circumstances. The school had heard about a training programme called *Assertive Discipline* (Canter and Canter 1976) and asked their educational psychologist to organize an INSET day based on its video and workshop material. On the day, teachers and supervisors worked together, using the information derived from their review of behaviour in school to devise some basic rules for the classroom, and some for the playground. This proved easier than expected; by including catch-all rules such as 'Do as you are asked by teachers and supervisors first time', and 'Do nothing to stop others from working', they were able to keep the list down to a manageable number. There was a good deal of debate about whether and how to use rewards, but in the end everyone agreed on a system of special gold certificates presented to children in assembly, to celebrate good behaviour in school – for children who always behaved well as well as those for whom this was more difficult. A hierarchical system of sanctions for breaking rules in the classroom or playground was then worked out: in the playground this involved supervisors showing children a yellow card as a warning and a red 'straight to headteacher' card for repeated or serious misbehaviour. Parents were invited into school to discuss the proposed new system, which was then formalized in an attractively-produced booklet with illustrations by the children.

Another popular approach to the rules, rewards and sanctions framework (Mosley 1993) is to involve children in developing the rules for their classrooms and playground, and link these both to pre-agreed rewards and to a simple sanction system involving missing 'golden time' – a specially constructed Friday afternoon fun activity.

Any systematic attempt to agree whole-school rules and celebrate children's success in keeping to them is likely to reduce substantially the overall level of behaviour difficulties experienced in a school. Users, like Westgate, of the *Assertive Discipline* framework, for example, typically report reduction in behaviour problems of around 80 per cent (Moss 1992). This will often have immediate benefits for pupils with special needs; Safran and Safran (1985) have shown that teachers' perception of problem behaviour in individuals is much affected by overall patterns of behaviour – in a generally disordered class, they found, an individual child was more likely to be seen as the source of any trouble and blamed for it than were children with similar problems in classes that were generally quiet and orderly.

Nevertheless, a whole-school behaviour management system will not eliminate individual children's behavioural difficulties entirely. For these children, individual action plans, using the same rules, rewards and sanctions framework, but matched more closely to their unique needs, may be required.

Assessment

As with special needs in learning, the first step in developing an individual action plan is assessment. There is a natural wish in many teachers to see assessment of behaviour difficulties in terms of discovering the deep-seated causes of the child's failure to conform to behavioural expectations: usually these causes are seen as rooted in the home. There is corresponding disappointment when support agencies appear to discount such forms of investigation and assessment, and instead ask the teacher to look closely at what may be happening in school to spark off or maintain pupil misbehaviour. The reasoning behind this approach, however, is simple and persuasive: it is not that factors and stresses in the child's life outside school are unimportant in the genesis of behaviour difficulties, only that these factors are very hard for teachers (and often other helping agencies) to influence, whereas factors in school are easier to address – and teachers have proved both powerful and effective in modifying children's behaviour when they exert their influence on the things they can change, rather than those they cannot.

Assessment tools for identifying the things that might need to be changed can be very simple. To start with, all that is needed is a two-step process, where step one is data gathering about how the child behaves in a variety of school situations, and step two is finding out what the child's own perspective on the situation is. The questions to ask are:

- In what situations/lessons/times of day/company does the child behave well, and what can we learn from this?
- What things seem to spark off the behaviour problems, and what might the child be getting out of behaving badly?
- How does the child feel – about themselves, about teachers, lessons and friendships (or lack of them)?

Information on the situations in which the child behaves well can be gathered using a questionnaire like that shown in Box 8.1.

In order to find out what sort of things spark off the behaviour problems, and what the child might be getting out of behaving badly, diary observation of targeted behaviour can be used. Here the teacher records incidents as they happen, along with information about the context and subsequent

---

Box 8.1   When does the child behave well?

In what school situations does the child:

- Follow instructions?
- Listen appropriately to the teacher or others?
- Work well in a group with others?
- Work well on their own?
- Play cooperatively with others?
- Appear cheerful and relaxed?

Table 8.1   Behaviour observation diary using ABC assessment

Date/time	(A)ntecedents	(B)ehaviour: what did X actually do?	(C)onsequences: what happened afterwards?

events – otherwise known as ABCs (see Table 8.1). The behaviour to be observed is one that all those closely involved with the pupil (and preferably also the pupil themselves) recognize as a priority problem, using the approach to determining priorities and describing behaviour in precise, objective terms that was discussed in Chapter 5. Behaviours can assume priority either because of their frequency (like the child who constantly calls out in class), or because of their consequences for the pupil's well-being or learning, or the well-being or learning of others (as with the child who occasionally has violent outbursts that put others at risk).

An ABC diary is usually a fairly manageable way of gathering information over a range of contexts. It will provide useful information on possible 'trigger factors' for the behaviour difficulties: for example, that there are often problems when classroom tasks involve a lot of writing or sitting still, or sustained listening – things that could perhaps be changed. It will also help the teacher to see how their response to the misbehaviour may inadvertently be providing the child with a chance to be the centre of attention, or to be sent out and get out of a lesson they were finding hard or boring – factors that may 'reward' the misbehaviour and increase the chance of it being repeated.

The following example of Katy illustrates the application of ABC assessment to a problem that though mild, was happening often enough to jeopardize one child's learning, and also affect the amount of time the teacher was able to give to other children in her class:

The aspect of Katy's behaviour that most concerned her teacher was her constant tearfulness. Several times a day, Katy would be seen weeping in class, and would be quite unable to get on with her work without a lot of reassurance and individual help. Over the course of a week, the teacher noted occasions when Katy cried, along with details of the type of work she was being asked to do, and of her own immediate reaction and that of other children. She also tried to make a note at least once a day of the context and consequences at times when Katy was showing the kind of behaviour everyone wanted from her – getting on happily with her work. With the help of the SENCO, she used her observations to draw up a chart showing what seemed to be happening (see Table 8.2).

Table 8.2   Katy: ABC behaviour observations

(A)ntecedents	(B)ehaviour	(C)onsequences
Happens in class (rarely in playground) Seems to happen whatever kind of work I give her – even very simple work she is really sure of	Katy cries	I usually go and put my arm round her, and ask her what's wrong; she either says nothing or 'I can't do it'. Then I go over the work again or suggest she just tackle part of it. The other children generally say 'Miss, Katy's crying', if I haven't noticed
(A) Often for the last part of the day	(B) Katy does her work happily without crying	(C) Nobody takes any notice of her, I'm afraid!

This discussion in itself led the teacher to plan ways in which Katy could gain physical contact through appropriate behaviour, and to make sure that she was not inadvertently rewarding Katy's inappropriate behaviour by reducing reasonable work demands whenever she cried.

Along with diary recording using the ABC structure, assessment should include an attempt to gain an understanding of the children's perspective of the situation. Do they know, first of all, exactly what it is that is causing concern or getting them into trouble? Open-ended questions like 'Tell me some of the things you do that make teachers (or lunchtime supervisors) pleased with you', and 'Now tell me what sort of things you do that bother them most' are useful here. Then, instead of the usual questions about why they do this, that and the other (which few children can answer), the teacher can ask them to describe a situation in which their behaviour caused concern: the things that led up to it, what they were thinking and feeling at the time, what happened afterwards. Ask, too, for the child's perspective on lessons or 'good days' when they do not get into trouble: what is happening in these lessons? What are they doing instead of the usual behaviour and how did they manage not to get into behaviour problems at that time?

Often this style of questioning can of itself lead to behaviour change, as the child begins to realize that they have some control over what happens and the power to change things if they want to.

To involve children further, they can be asked to do their own research into the good and bad days or lessons, keeping their own ABC diaries, or – if they are younger or have literacy problems – drawing the events leading up to trouble and what happened next on a 'think sheet' following specific incidents. Blank speech and think bubbles will give them a chance to dictate words and thoughts to the teacher, giving further insight into their perspective on events.

In all of this the teacher is trying to get a window – however small – into the child's world, so that planning for behaviour change can go forward as a joint, participative process. There also needs to be some glimpse of how the child sees and feels about themselves – that is, about self-esteem, using, for example, questions like those in Chapter 4 (see p. 59).

Exploration of the child's point of view will often provide valuable insights. For example, that one child who is often in trouble for hitting and kicking is aggressive without feeling angry, as a way of establishing a 'macho' image and some degree of acceptance in a peer group where he has few friends, while another child who also hits and kicks does so in a blind rage, often as a result of being called names.

> For Katy, an individual interview established that she herself did
> not feel her crying was a problem. In her eyes, the problem was
> that she had to do 'too much hard work' at school. She felt her
> teacher was generally pleased with her, adding 'I'm never naughty
> at school'. At home, though, there were quite a lot of things that
> made her mum and dad cross with her: 'I break cups and hit my
> brother and tease my big brother'. Her biggest wish was 'for my
> mum not to tell me what to do', and for teachers 'not to make you
> do hard work'.
>   Katy's teacher had previously interpreted her behaviour in class as a
> sign of lack of confidence. When she listened to Katy's perspective,
> however, she began to see a quite determined little girl, who did
> not like demands imposed on her from outside, and used a range of
> learned coping strategies to re-establish control over a situation.
> The teacher decided to try out with Katy's group a 'plan, do, review'
> system, where children make their own plans for the work that needs
> doing and the order in which they will do it. Katy was given a good
> deal of praise at the review stage with the teacher for following the
> plan she had set herself. The teacher also made a point of asking Katy
> quite often whether she felt she could handle a particular piece of
> work, then modelling and praising her for statements such as 'I can do
> it', or 'I think it's going to be easy for me'. Katy was sent once a day,
> when she had finished all her work, to help Reception class children
> with their reading, and was thanked for being such a sensible, grown-
> up and capable helper. At the same time, the teacher stood firm on
> any attempts by Katy to manipulate her by crying and conveying
> helplessness, and insisted that she would need to make up unfinished
> work in her own time, either at playtime or at home.

Implementing a behaviour plan

After the assessment phase, the next step is to develop targets for change, using the parent–child–teacher meeting described in Chapter 5. Once a small number of targets have been agreed, it is time to think about strategies. A suggested framework for this is given in Box 8.2.

The framework focuses on five key points. Points 3 and 5 – avoiding triggers and setting up a differentiated rules/rewards/sanctions framework – relate directly to the ABC assessment framework. Avoiding triggers means changing the 'As' in the ABC equation – the contextual factors which lead to a particular behaviour. Setting up a differentiated discipline framework means changing the 'Cs' – the consequences that are applied to both positive and negative behaviour.

The five-point plan also includes ideas which go beyond the 'behaviourist' ABC approach. It includes concepts of relationships with teachers or other key adults in the school (Point 1), concepts of self-esteem (Point 2) and the idea of helping children develop any missing skills they need in order to behave appropriately in school (Point 4).

These are all key areas which have been shown to affect the success of efforts to change children's behaviour. Building the relationship with teachers is key because – as we should all know from times in our lives when we have been under stress and not at our best – nothing makes more difference to children than feeling that there are at least some adults in school who value them, treat them with respect and have some empathy for their situation. Building self-esteem is included because research has shown that low self-worth underlies many behaviour problems: if children do not feel good about themselves they approach many situations – both academic and social – with an expectation of failure and a range of negative behaviours that all too often mean their expectations are confirmed, so that a downward spiral develops. Developing the skills needed for good behaviour is included because there is no point in setting up systems to set targets and reward children for achieving them if they lack the particular social skills which they need in order to achieve the target – for example, how to make friends, engage in cooperative groupwork, handle teasing, negotiate their way out of conflict. Often we assume that if children are not behaving appropriately they can be helped to change their behaviour by adjusting the payoffs (the 'Cs') – rewarding good behaviour and ignoring bad. We assume they have a choice. In many cases this is true. In others, however, children cannot make choices because they do not have the alternative, positive behaviours in their repertoire. In these cases, trying to reward good behaviour will be as ineffective as, say, rewarding 'good reading' for a child who cannot actually read. Instead, we have to ask in the assessment phase whether the child can behave appropriately but is choosing not to (for example, if there is evidence of the desired behaviour in some lessons or situations but not others), or whether they can't, and will need to be taught the missing skills.

In the next chapter we will fill out the five-point plan by looking at strategies which schools can use to build relationships with children, develop their self-esteem and teach them missing interpersonal skills. For the moment, we will remain with the basic ABC framework.

Box 8.2   A framework for behaviour plans

Name of pupil:	Name of teacher responsible for plan:	Date for plan to START:	Date for REVIEW meeting:

This 5-point plan records the strategies which will be used to address the targets in the child's IEP

1 Plans to build the relationship between the pupil and a member of staff

2 Plans to build the pupil's self-esteem

3 Plans to avoid triggers which have previously led to problem incidents

4 Plans to develop any missing social skills or self-management skills

5 A differentiated, individualized behaviour management plan

   (a) The key behaviour rule(s) for this pupil (stating what the pupil will be doing to keep this rule)

   (b) What recognition and rewards will be given, in what circumstances

   (c) What happens when the pupil breaks the rule(s): consequences

Avoiding trigger factors

Teachers are generally comfortable with this approach: they often uncon-
sciously work on avoiding trigger factors when they first try to alter a child's
difficult behaviour. Altering a seating position or changing the group the
child usually works with are typical examples: an ABC approach simply takes
this one step further by gathering information systematically on what the
potential trigger factors are, as opposed to working on hunches.

Triggers can be particular lessons, times of the day, learning tasks, pupil
groupings or the way the child is spoken to by adults. Some examples of
common triggers, along with possible ways of avoiding them, are given in
Table 8.3.

Table 8.3 Avoiding triggers

Trigger	Avoidance tactics
Long unbroken tasks	Shorter tasks; opportunities to take breaks
Teacher busy elsewhere in room and not paying child any attention	Agreed signal (e.g. 'thumbs up') given at intervals across the classroom when the child is working well
Unexpected changes in routine	Explain changes beforehand to whole class
Unstructured time, such as lunchtimes	Structure the time with lunchtime clubs, jobs, organized games
Teasing; getting wound up by other children	Circle-time work on teasing/bullying with whole class. Send on prearranged errand to another teacher if child is beginning to get wound up

For some children, such as those who only feel OK if they can engage in
an attention-getting power struggle with adults, directive language ('do this
now, stop, don't do that') will inevitably set off a behavioural challenge. This
particular trigger can be avoided by offering the child choices: 'These are the
three bits of work we need to get done this afternoon – which order are you
going to choose to do them in?' Behaviour, too, can be seen as a choice: 'Are
you sure that what you are choosing to do right now will work best for you?
It would be good I think if you could put that one back in your choice box
and choose another'. The teacher can also change a potentially inflammat-
ory series of 'don'ts' into messages that use a 'when you . . . the effect is . . . and
then I feel . . .' format: instead of 'stop shouting', they would say, 'When you
shout I can't concentrate on helping your friends with their work, and then
I start to feel frustrated and irritable'.

Sarcasm and teacher language which makes the child feel publicly shamed
or small is another common trigger for challenging behaviour; everybody
(from dinner ladies to the headteacher) needs to take care when dealing with
behaviourally disturbed children to use language which rejects the behaviour
but not the person. Work with these children is about encouraging them to
be their best selves, not reiterating negatives; the most effective language is
that which constantly conveys the message 'I like you but not what you are
doing right now'.

A differentiated rules/rewards/sanctions framework

This element of a behaviour plan will focus mainly on altering the 'Cs' in the ABC model: it means working out a system of rewards and sanctions which will positively encourage appropriate behaviour and discourage the behaviour that is causing problems.

What the teacher should aim for is an individual contract, setting out three to five rules based on the positive targets for behaviour change that the joint teacher–child–parent action planning process has identified, a hierarchy of sanctions and some special rewards that really matter to the child. Parental involvement is crucial here. Enlist the parent/carer's help in rewarding the child at home if they meet the agreed targets for a day (younger children) or a week (older ones): the outcome can be a simple contract between child, parent and teacher, like the one given in the following example:

> Jamie was constantly in trouble for a variety of different behaviours. His mother came into school to meet with Jamie and his teacher. Together they agreed that the biggest problems were Jamie disturbing other children's work, calling out in class and swearing. There were problems at home, too, and Jamie's mother welcomed the idea of going with Jamie to the family counselling centre to see what could be done to help with the management of his behaviour. Meanwhile, in school he would be asked to observe a contract. The contract was that Jamie would:
>
> - use acceptable language in school;
> - put his hand up and wait to be asked to speak in class;
> - keep his hands, feet and objects to himself.
>
> Each day that he succeeded in doing all these things his teacher would send a 'good behaviour' note home. When he had five 'good behaviour' notes, he would:
>
> - be allowed to go and help in Miss Edwards' class;
> - be allowed by his mother to choose a small treat from a list he had drawn up with her (going swimming, doing some baking with her, choosing a video, staying up half an hour later on Saturday, having a friend to stay).
>
> The contract also specified what would happen when Jamie did not keep to the agreed rules:
>
> - he would be warned once;
> - the second time (in one day) he would be last out to play at break times;
> - the third time he would be asked to sit and work on his own in class for the rest of the day;
> - the fourth time he would miss choosing time on Friday;
> - the fifth time he would be sent to Mrs Abbott, who would notify his mother and note his name in the bad behaviour book;
> - if his name was in the book three times, he would have an in-school suspension (working all day on his own away from the class).

Box 8.3 Rewards available to primary teachers

- Choice of play activities, e.g. construction equipment
- First out to play/first out at home time
- Taking messages
- Being a monitor
- Cleaning the classroom pets out
- Putting chairs out in the hall
- Being the leader of a group
- Busy boxes: small tubs of interesting things like buttons, magnets, lenses which the child can get out and play with
- Time on computer
- Tidying up an area of the classroom
- Working with a chosen adult
- Ringing the bell at break time
- Helping with the tuck shop
- Taking work (or a note about good behaviour) to show other teachers
- Special praise or an award in assembly
- Classroom game, quiz or wordsearch
- Going to help in a younger class
- House points
- Merit badges, stickers, having your hand stamped with a special stamp/ink pad
- Choosing where you sit
- Certificates or notes sent home to parents
- Individual merit book for each child in the school, in which staff enter positive comments

---

Some children, particularly younger ones, may not be able to go for a whole day or even a whole morning before their positive behaviour is acknowledged under a contract system. For them it is helpful to use some form of chart where a space or square is coloured in, or a sticker/smiley face/star stuck on, every time they succeed in showing a particular desired behaviour. When all the squares are full, the child takes the chart to show an adult of their choice (and receive praise), or – if this is not of itself a sufficient incentive – exchanges the completed chart for an agreed privilege (see Box 8.3). The form of the chart can be adapted to the child's particular interests. Drawings of dragons, robots, dolls, football pitches and wizards have all been successfully used – though visuals that divide naturally into segments (like the scales of dinosaurs) make an obvious choice. Ready-made and freely photocopiable charts are commercially available; many schools have also built up their own banks of copymasters, kept in a ring-binder in the special needs resource centre.

Involving the pupil

Critics of the behavioural approach so far described, with its emphasis on modifying behaviour by altering the consequences that children experience as a result of their actions, have argued that it is manipulative and dehumanizing: treating children like puppets to be controlled by pulling this string or that, and producing superficial behaviour change while failing to reach the inner states and feelings that in the long term determine how we relate to others. This is a valid argument; to avoid the risks it describes we need to make sure we go beyond pulling the strings from outside and devise ways in which children can gain in autonomy through the experience of setting their own goals, working out their own action plans and monitoring their own behaviour.

Such self-monitoring might involve the child in keeping their own record of the number of times each week they are late for school, or in trouble for fighting. It might mean the teacher providing a signal, at regular intervals throughout the day, at which the child notes whether or not they are 'on task'. It might, for older children, mean using a self-rating scale like the one in Box 8.4: before morning and afternoon break, at lunchtime and home time the pupil rates their own behaviour against criteria that have been agreed beforehand and then shows the sheet to the teacher. Teachers will discuss it and add their own rating; each week the pupils set a target of points they aim to earn, pushing the target higher as they feel more in control of their behaviour.

Teachers who want to help children set their own goals and work out their own action plans need to be able to set aside for the moment any kind of blaming response to their negative behaviour and approach the situation with the neutral message: 'There is something going wrong here; let us look together at what we might do about it'. For example, to a child who constantly shouts out in class they might say: 'There is a problem for both of us here. When you keep on talking to the children on your table, I feel worried, because they need to be able to finish their work. Then I start to feel cross. I think it's a problem for you too because it is stopping some children from wanting to be friends with you. I would like us both to spend some time trying to think of all the things we might do to solve the problem'.

From this point, with the pupil's agreement, both parties can work through a problem-solving process, as shown in Box 8.5. In this approach, the child is asked to generate all the possible solutions to the problem, consider the consequences of each and then choose the one that looks most likely to succeed. This is the process that the teacher encouraged in the following example:

> Robert, aged 10, was often in trouble in the playground. He was overweight and frequently picked on by other children. With the help of his teacher he identified the problem he would like to work on: being teased by Paul about being too fat and no good at football. Generating solutions, he came up with the idea of ignoring Paul, teasing him back or losing weight. Ignoring Paul, he thought, would be a good idea because it would mean he didn't get angry, but a bad idea because it wouldn't stop Paul teasing him in the long run. Teasing back had the advantage of helping him feel he was getting his own back, but might make Paul hit him. Robert finally chose his third idea: losing weight would make him able to run faster and get better at football, and though it would be hard to stick to a diet he might manage it with help. He drew up an agreement with his teacher which

Box 8.4   Self-monitoring behaviour sheet

Name _____

My aim _____

My target for points this week _____

Day _____   Date _____

Period	Self-rating	Teacher rating
1	5	5
	4	4
	3	3
	2	2
	1	1
2	5	5
	4	4
	3	3
	2	2
	1	1
3	5	5
	4	4
	3	3
	2	2
	1	1
4	5	5
	4	4
	3	3
	2	2
	1	1

Total for day

I will rate myself and be rated for _____

_____

_____

_____

5 = wonderful
4 = very good
3 = OK
2 = very poor
1 = terrible

(adapted from Long 1988)

Box 8.5 A joint problem-solving process

Ask the child to identify a recent situation with an adult or other children where things went wrong – for example, they ended up in trouble.

Step 1: What was the problem? (e.g. being teased, no one to play with, teacher told me off unfairly). How did you feel? How did others feel?
Step 2: What did you do in this particular situation and what were the consequences?
Step 3: Let's think of all the possible things you might have done in this situation.
Step 4: Now let's look at these one by one. If you did that how would you feel? How would others feel? What might be the consequences?
Step 5: So what do you think looks like the best bet out of all the ideas we have come up with?

---

specified weekly weigh-ins, and a half hour of individual football coaching for every pound lost. In one term he managed to lose half a stone, and began to get on better not only with Paul but also with other boys in his class.

(Thacker 1983)

The teacher's role when pupils set their own goals is to help with recording and review. The child can be encouraged to draw up a self-contract, with headings like 'I want to . . .', 'My plan is . . .', 'My support person will be . . .' and 'I will celebrate success by . . .'. Signed and dated by child and 'witness' (teacher, friend or parent), the plan can be used as a basis for review: the teacher will ask whether the pupil has been able to stick to their plan, praise any successes and help the child adjust the plan if it is not working.

The teacher's role, in helping children acquire autonomy and the belief that they can change their own behaviour, is also to get them thinking about what they may already have achieved in this direction. Questions like these will be useful:

- I noticed then that you could have hit Ben but you didn't. How did you manage that?
- You know you can get this work done; it's about getting yourself organized. How did you set about it last time?
- So you only got sent in from play once this week – last week it was three times. How did you get that to happen?
- Kirsty, can you have a quick word with Melanie about how you got over the problem she's having now?

Aggressive behaviour

Not surprisingly, aggression is the behaviour that worries teachers most and is the most common reason for exclusion from school and referral to special educational provision for pupils with emotional and behavioural difficulties. Theories about causes range from styles of discipline at home to exposure to television violence, but whatever outside influences there may be it is still possible for schools to help children learn non-aggressive ways of relating to others: the ABC model, the charts and contracts and pupil plans are just as valid for aggression as for any other behaviour difficulty.

In addition, however, it may be necessary to use another part of the five-point behaviour plan and actively teach children skills they have never had an opportunity to learn. This will involve work with individuals or groups of children on learning how to control angry feelings and resolve conflicts in non-violent ways. Sometimes it helps to start by making the child more aware of potential trigger situations: by asking them to make a 'boiling point list' of ten things that make them angry, and rank them in order of intensity, or using the traffic-light analogy to help them identify the thoughts, feelings and bodily changes that tell them they are moving from a green light, to a warning yellow, to red for danger in situations where they often lose control. Sometimes it may help to model and teach specific strategies to use when the signal changes from green to yellow: muscle relaxation and slow, deep breathing, counting backwards from ten or imagining themselves as a turtle retreating inside its shell, or taking themselves to a cooling-off spot on the fringe of the activity. Children for whom peer wind-ups are a major trigger for aggressive behaviour can be encouraged to develop 'avoiding the hook' imagery, where they picture themselves as a fish swimming in a river, while all around them on the banks are fishermen casting their hooks and hoping to catch them. They have to choose; either take the bait and be hooked, or outsmart the fishermen and swim calmly by. Finally, work can be done to involve pupils in considering which responses to conflict situations are likely to escalate the conflict, and which to defuse it, and in practising the negotiation skills of saying what you want and why, listening carefully to the other's point of view, then trying to find a compromise that meets both parties' needs. Good sources for teachers planning such work include Shay McConnon's *Your Choice* materials from Nelson, Stacey and Robinson's *Let's Mediate* (1997) and *Anger Management* by Faupel *et al.* (1998). Any strategies that are taught to pupils also need to be carefully explained to parents, who often see aggression as a necessary tool for children's self-protection; they will need to be convinced that alternative approaches are about giving children power rather than taking it away: power to control their reactions rather than be controlled by them, and power to exercise choice about how they will respond. Parents will also need to be convinced, quite rightly, that the school is able through its policy on bullying to make sure that their children will not end up victims of others' aggression if they succeed in controlling their own.

An example will show how self-control strategies can be combined with more straightforward behavioural approaches to reduce aggressive outbursts:

Darren, aged 10, was a tall, well-built and active boy who was often involved in fights and arguments. He could be quite overbearing in class and constantly interrupted other children or adults. His teacher's observations showed that other children on his table tended to irritate or tease him, and when this happened he would become increasingly wound-up and explosive. The teacher had tried sending him out for five minutes on his own whenever there were problems, but this only seemed to make matters worse. A system where Darren earned points for good behaviour in school towards rewards at home had not worked either. Darren's teacher believed in negotiated learning and teacher–pupil conferences, and Darren was accustomed to setting his own work targets. The teacher asked him if they could try a similar system for his behaviour and discussed with him the strategies that might help. Darren showed a strong preference for sanctions rather than any kind of rewards for good behaviour. He was aware that it was other children's wind-ups that often got him into trouble, but felt that bit by bit they made him so angry that he got to the point where he just could not control himself or get himself out of the situation. Between them, he and his teacher agreed on a signal (the teacher taking his glasses off) that could be given as soon as Darren could be seen getting 'steamed up'. At this signal, he would take himself and his work to another room and come back when he had calmed down. If he called out in class and interrupted others, he would – at his own request – have to miss five minutes of the next break. He kept a diary of the times he had to stay in and the times he managed to control his temper by taking himself out of trigger situations; once a week he met with the teacher to review the diary and agree the content of a note home which would let his parents know how he was getting on. His parents were asked to give him a lot of praise and encouragement for even small successes. Darren responded well to this approach and though still not the calmest of children began, over the next few months, to exercise much more control over his angry reactions.

Poor concentration and restlessness

The best predictor of children's academic success is the amount of time they spend on a task without distraction (Keogh 1982). For children with learning difficulties the relationship between concentration and progress is particularly critical; Moses (1982), for example, found that the slow learners she observed were on task for only about half their time, whereas children of average ability concentrated on their work on average for 70 per cent of their time.

On these grounds alone, helping children to concentrate in the classroom is clearly a priority when making plans to meet special needs. It becomes even more important when we consider that things like 'talking out of turn' and 'hindering other children' are the most common behaviour problems in classrooms, and the source of the greatest irritation to teachers (Wheldall and Merrett 1984).

What can be done to help? To start with, it is useful when a child is described as having poor concentration to probe for a more precise behavioural description of what it is exactly that the child is doing, or not doing, that causes concern. Sometimes the teacher is actually describing a child who constantly distracts themselves from the task in hand, or is distracted by others, but sometimes there are other meanings. For example, poor concentration may mean that the child is not able to take in instructions, or forgets what they are supposed to be doing, or is restless only in listening situations like assembly and story time. Sometimes the teacher may be describing not distraction but a learned pattern of overdependence on adults: children who are always back and forth to the teacher with one query or another. An extreme example of this is the little girl who recently came to her teacher to say, 'Shall I have a go at this on my own without asking you?'

It is important to establish what the distracted child is doing when not on task. Are they quietly daydreaming, talking to friends who also want to chat or apparently seeking attention by obviously interfering with others? Are they actually taking in the information and getting the work done, but seeming not to because they are constantly wriggling and fidgeting?

In each of these cases, the strategies adopted will be different: as with all behavioural difficulties, it is important to start with a clear description of the problem.

The extent of children's concentration is heavily dependent on the curriculum – as anyone knows who has watched a child spend 10 minutes finding a pencil and 20 minutes on the first sentence when asked to write, then watched the same child's intense concentration on making a model or working with friends on an adventure program around the computer. Many children's apparent concentration problems could be very quickly resolved if tasks were better adapted to their needs, and particularly if there was less emphasis on writing as the only means of recording in the classroom (see Chapter 12). The teacher should also ask themselves if too much is being asked of the child with regard to sitting still for long periods. How might the teacher react if they were asked to sit in the same chair for most of the day? And what can we learn from watching children at work in their home settings, where they tend to maximize their concentration by moving around – perching on a sofa, kneeling at a coffee table, resting on a cushion? The way the teacher takes these issues into account in managing the classroom can be highly influential in determining how restless the class are.

Nevertheless, the possibility of 'within-child' influences on concentration should not be discounted. The effects of diet are still controversial, but some children do seem to show increased restlessness and inability to settle to tasks in reaction to particular foodstuffs such as additives and colourings, and parents may want to bear this in mind. Some will also want to investigate the medical diagnosis of attention deficit hyperactivity disorder (ADHD) and the effects, also controversial, of stimulant medication on their child's behaviour. Children with coordination problems often have associated difficulties in focusing attention; they may be unable to screen out irrelevant stimuli, so that everything – from a car going past to the work displayed on the classroom wall – is a potential source of distraction. If this seems to be the case, then it may be worth having the child do some of their work in a quiet area of the classroom, facing a plain wall and with a screen placed either side to create a booth (as long as other children also get the chance to take special work they really want to concentrate on to this area too). Children with intermittent hearing loss or language difficulties may find it hard to concentrate when they have to listen closely for long periods, perhaps against a noisy background: they need the kind of help in tuning into important communications that will be discussed in Chapter 10. Problems in short-term memory may mean that the child appears not to concentrate because they have forgotten what to do next: a peer assigned to remind them, or teacher willingness to write down instructions on a Post-it is often all that is needed if this is the source of the difficulty.

Another major 'within-child' influence is the child's developmental stage. Children come into school at very different developmental levels: some have the communication and cognitive abilities of the average 6-year-old, and a concentration span to match, while others are still at a preschool stage. For them it is entirely appropriate for tasks to be short and a certain amount of flitting from one activity to another is to be expected. All Reception teachers know this; many teachers of older children persist in setting tasks of the same length for all, without taking into account the wide range of normal individual differences in concentration span that are part of every junior class.

Planning for children who do not concentrate for long will therefore depend in part on developing an understanding of factors within the child that are contributing to the perceived difficulties and matching strategies to the outcomes of this kind of assessment. However, concentration difficulties are also, as we will see in the next example, amenable to the kind of ABC analysis that we looked at earlier in this chapter, with its emphasis on factors in the environment that may be causing or maintaining problem behaviour:

Duncan, aged 11, was the despair of his teacher: he was, she said, always wandering around the classroom, talking to other children or annoying them by interfering with their things. Her ABC assessment is shown in Table 8.4. She decided that she needed to look at ways of making writing easier for him, by setting shorter tasks and smaller targets and by having him choose words to complete cloze sheets for some of his work instead of writing independently from scratch. She also decided to try and reduce the amount of attention Duncan gained for his wanderings: when she saw him out of his seat she simply put a check on the board, with five checks equalling loss of a playtime. At the same time, Duncan and his friend Andrew agreed to work together on a specific programme which would help Duncan learn to concentrate for longer: twice a day, Andrew would set a kitchen timer to go off after a fixed period (initially ten minutes, but progressively longer as the weeks went on). If Duncan had managed to stay on task for the whole of that period, Andrew put a tick on a chart. When Duncan had earned ten ticks, the whole class was awarded extra playtime – as their reward for helping him concentrate by ignoring rather than joining in with his attempts to cause a distraction.

Table 8.4 Duncan: ABC behaviour observations

(A)	(B)	(C)
Often when task involves writing	Wanders around class: interferes with others	Peer attention. Avoids task. Teacher nags him constantly to sit down
In practical lessons; science, technology	Stays in one place and gets on	No attention unless support teacher is there

The timer method can be used by parents at home, or by children themselves as part of a self-monitoring programme. Self-monitoring need not necessarily be linked to a reward system to be effective; sometimes children becoming more aware of how they are using time is all that is needed, as the following whole-class example shows:

> A class of 11-year-olds were asked by their teacher to write down at the beginning of every hour what they planned to do in that hour; at the end of the period they had to make a private note of whether they had got everything they meant to done. During two separate sessions, the teacher rang a bell every 10 minutes, so that the children could award themselves a tick if they were on task. She did not look at their tick sheets, but asked the children to add up their own as a way they could 'measure their powers of concentration'. The children showed a significant improvement in both quality and quantity of work output as a result of this experimental intervention.
>
> (Merrett and Merrett 1992)

Setting a kitchen timer to go off at random intervals throughout the day is a way of keeping a self-monitoring system such as this going for an individual child or a class over a longer period. If self-monitoring is difficult, children can be paired and use the 'Checking Chums' system (Brown *et al.* 1999) to monitor one another's on-task behaviour. Or the teacher can plan to praise the child and put a tick or a star on a postcard on the child's table every time they pass by and find that the child is working. A set number of ticks can be exchanged for a reward (such as licensed daydreaming time, free choice of activity, the chance to do something active like carry a message or doing a job for another teacher). Slowly the ticks are replaced by praise alone; by this time the teacher will have become accustomed to the idea of praising children when they are concentrating rather than the much less effective nagging of them when they are not.

Another way of monitoring groups for concentration is to put a jar on each table, in which the teacher drops a counter or marble when they see that the children in the group are all on task. The table with the most counters or marbles at the end of the day (or week) will be chosen for a special privilege.

Some young children, whose preschool experience has been a mix of active outdoor play and indoor television and video, may never have had the opportunity to learn to sit still at a sustained task. If this is the case, concentration will have to be taught, in small steps, like any other skill. The child's parents or carers can be asked, for example, to try to engage the child in a settled activity like Lego, or jigsaws, or listening to a story tape for a short (but slowly increasing) period two or three times a week: at first they will need to join in with the activity, but later they should try to stand back and offer praise and encouragement at a distance as long as the child perseveres with the activity. A similar idea can be used for short bursts in class, with the help of a classroom assistant. To start with, the assistant sits near the child and gives continuous attention while the child is on task; later the distance between the assistant and the child can be increased and only occasional praise given.

In all of these interventions, it is the various 'Cs' in the ABC framework which are manipulated in order to encourage concentration. The 'As', however, should not be forgotten. Extensive research (Wheldall 1988; McPake *et al.* 1999) shows that the most common source of distraction in classrooms is seating pupils in a way that invites social interaction when they are for most of the time working on individual tasks. Few, if any, adults would choose to go and sit in a group with their close friends if they had a report to write or some serious planning to do. Yet this is what we ask children to do, day after day, and then tell them off when they inevitably start to chat. For children whose attention is caught by the least extraneous sight or sound, inflexible seating arrangements that group children round tables are a recipe for low work rate. Philip Waterhouse (1990) suggests we turn to the modern office for ideas on alternatives: furniture can be organized as work stations, with four children on a table that has a removable screen down the middle, and resources grouped on wheeled trolleys in the centre of the classroom so that children can access them without walking past (or through) others' work spaces. When children are genuinely engaged in collaborative group work, the screens are taken away; when it is time for individual seat work they go up, and all the children are expected to work without disturbing others. Similarly, arranging the majority of tables in a horseshoe shape, with just two or three grouped together at the side for guided work, will help reduce distractions and allow for whole-class teaching to flow into independent work.

Conclusion

Children differ, like adults, in temperament: some have a shorter concentration span than others, some are less confident, some are more aggressive. To accept such individual differences, however, does not mean accepting that there is nothing teachers can do to modify behaviours that are causing distress, or are stopping the child or others from learning – at least, to modify those aspects of their behaviour that the children themselves have chosen to work on. In this chapter, we have seen how altering the immediate context and consequences can prove helpful, even where nothing more is done to probe causes and stresses in the child's life that may be prompting a behaviour difficulty. This does not mean, however, that schools should see helping children to cope with stress and learn to manage inner feelings as outside their role. There is much excellent work being done in primary schools which falls into this category: it is to this more humanist approach, the necessary complement to the behaviourist strategies we have looked at so far, that we turn in the next chapter.

Communication and classroom relationships

Introduction

It is a common experience to find primary schools where behaviour problems are few and where children and adults consistently get on well together. Not all of these schools are in leafy suburbs or country villages: some are in inner-city areas with high levels of social deprivation. Home life, for many of the pupils, may be stormy or strained, but the school manages to provide a haven and a refuge. Within the school the children learn to deal with their own often chaotic feelings, to care for one another and – most important, to care for themselves. Their special needs for understanding, tolerance, help in expressing and resolving anger and anxiety and sadness, are met.

What is the secret of schools like these? In this chapter we look at some of the organizational factors that help to explain their success and at the range of specific responses they are able to make when children are experiencing stress.

The caring classroom

Arncliffe Down Primary

Arncliffe Down Primary is a large school on a run-down housing estate with high levels of unemployment and a pattern of poor community relationships. Within the school, however, there has been a deliberate attempt to create an ethos of caring and cooperation. Older classes are placed next door to younger groups and each older child takes responsibility for a younger partner on occasions like school trips and assemblies. The older ones have been involved in a project to teach the younger children some of the playground rhymes and games they have collected from parents, grandparents and neighbours. This was part of a wider plan to improve the quality of playtimes by designating quiet areas and providing a range of play equipment from soft balls to dressing-up clothes. In class, all the children are involved in a planned programme of personal and social education lessons: they learn how to recognize and express feelings, how to listen to others, how to resolve conflicts, how to be a good friend, how to keep themselves safe. Older children are trained to act as playground mediators, helping children resolve disputes in non-aggressive ways. There are many informal opportunities for children to express feelings and worries to people who will listen. They are all encouraged to keep a journal, which they can use if they wish for private messages to the teacher. Most classes use circle time, when everyone comes together to talk about the feeling side of their experiences – good and bad things that have happened to them recently, how they are getting on together as a group, how they could sort out arguments and tensions that are cropping up, what is stopping them being their 'best selves', what they have appreciated in one another. Each class has devised its own classroom charter, listing the rights (such as being listened to or allowed to work without disturbance) to which everyone in the room should be entitled. When there are behaviour problems, children as well as teachers will draw attention to the charter. There is a lot of emphasis on mutual support: children are encouraged to nominate one another for special awards if they have managed to overcome a behaviour problem, or been especially helpful to others.

This particular school also has well-developed schemes of work for the National Curriculum, and high academic expectations for all of its pupils. Like many other schools with a caring ethos, it is not in the business of devaluing the *content* of children's learning, only of recognizing the affective context in which all learning takes place, and using that context as a vital tool for educating the whole child.

The common features of schools which, like Arncliffe, succeed in creating an emotionally supportive framework for children could be described as follows:

- Classrooms are organized in a way that allows pupil autonomy and builds self-esteem: children can access the resources they need, set themselves goals for both work and behaviour and assess their own progress with the help of other children and adults.
- Adults try to give children the confidence to handle their own difficulties, either in work or relationships: they help children think out their own solutions rather than sorting everything out for them and reinforce successful problem-solving with generous praise.
- Discipline – through classroom charters, school councils and circle time – is seen as something which is shared with the pupils rather than handed down by the teacher.
- Adults provide models of respect and empathy. Teachers consciously build their relationships with children, find something to value in every child and emphasize effort and progress rather than absolute achievement. They make efforts to listen to children's perspective on school, how they like to be taught and what they think of the work they are asked to do.
- Children's attempts to help and care for one another are explicitly valued and there is much emphasis on mutual appreciation – children and adults noticing each other's positive qualities, behaviours and achievements.

- Time is allocated to personal and social education, and in particular to developing children's 'emotional intelligence' or 'emotional literacy' – that is, their ability to recognize their own and others' feelings and handle them appropriately. There is coherent planning to make sure that key themes are visited and revisited in cross-curricular work or special personal, social and health education time: making and keeping friends, listening and communicating, awareness of feelings, resolving conflict, coping with loss, self-esteem, assertiveness and self-protection.
- Children are given many opportunities to express feelings – through play, art, drama, puppetry, writing and talk.
- There are resources – information and story books, poems, plays and videos – which cover a range of affective issues from bullying to bereavement to family break-up, and which can be used with individuals or groups when a need arises.
- Staff are alert to the signs of emotional stress in children – both the more obvious signs like fighting, stealing or excessive clinging, and the less intrusive ones like aches and pains, lethargy, social withdrawal and poor concentration.
- Staff know how to listen to children – not just to the content of what they are saying, but to the feelings that lie behind the words.

Listening to feelings

When Gary learned that he was going to have to move house, he told his mum that he did not want to go. His mum said: 'Cheer up; you'll have a lovely bedroom all to yourself, and a nice new school, and you'll soon make some new friends'. Gary felt angry and walked off in a sulk. Later on, he got into trouble for fighting with his brother. Gary told his teacher that he did not want to move house. She said: 'I see. So you're wishing you could stay here. Could you tell me some more about how you feel about the move?' Gary said he did like the new house, but he wanted to stay with his friends. His teacher said: 'Yes, I understand that you will miss your friends here. It's sad to lose people'. Gary sat quiet for a while, thinking, and then said: 'I'll come and see them, though.'

In responding to Gary, his teacher used some basic counselling skills that helped him both to express and come to terms with some difficult feelings. What she did was try to listen very hard to what he was saying – his non-verbal signals as well as his actual words – and acknowledge the feelings he was struggling to convey. She took care not to deny or argue with what he was saying, but to reflect back to him her acceptance and understanding of what he was going through, and provide an open-ended invitation to him to say more. In doing so, she gave him the support of being listened to, and space to sort out some of the things that were on his mind.

These skills are not difficult to learn, and are invaluable in helping children with all kinds of special needs to find their way through the difficulties and stresses that beset them. One essential technique is using open questions when talking over problems, rather than closed questions that can be answered in a few words: not 'Did you lose your temper?' but 'How did you feel when that happened?'; not 'Have you had a bad day?' but 'Can you tell me how things have been for you at school today?' Another is mastering the art of paraphrasing or reflecting back communications, in order to show understanding and provide scope for the child to build on what they said. To be effective, this relies on a degree of empathy and informed guesswork about what the child might be feeling: 'So your brother has been talking to you about secondary school and now you're feeling a bit worried about it, perhaps?'; 'It sounds to me as if you feel whatever you do, it's always wrong'; and 'You're feeling very angry about that, I think?'

Most of all, this kind of listening involves teachers in placing a hold on expressing their own opinions for long enough to really hear what the child is saying. Very often, when children talk to us, we block their communication by jumping in with value judgements, instant solutions to their problems, or attempts to smooth over their very real difficulties. Consider this conversation:

Child: My dad's mad at me. I hate him.
Teacher: That's not very nice. What did you do to annoy him?
Child: I dunno – he's just mad.
Teacher: Well I expect he's got a very good reason. Why don't you ask him?
Child: He wouldn't say. He just shouts. He never shouts at Emma.
Teacher: I expect he'll feel better soon. Come on, you go and play with your friends now and forget about it.

Now consider this very different response:

Child: My dad's mad at me. I hate him.
Teacher: So he's cross and you're feeling very angry with him too at the moment?
Child: Sometimes. But . . . he's . . . I don't know . . . it seems like everything I do . . . he really picks on me. Emma's never in trouble. She starts things but he always says it's me.
Teacher: Mmmmmm.
Child: He lost his job. I suppose . . . but why doesn't he take it out on Emma? Why does it have to be me?
Teacher: You're feeling there may be some good reasons why he's often cross, but that it still isn't fair for you to be the one that gets blamed?
Child: Well . . . he's OK sometimes. He's OK. Maybe I . . . I'll have to see.

The second conversation may feel less satisfactory to the teacher: no neat endings, no advice given, no tidying up of messy feelings. In reality, it is much more likely to be helpful to the child than the first teacher's response. By suspending the normal tendency to offer advice, blame or diversion, the teacher is able to convey that they are really listening and trying to understand the child's experience and point of view, even if it may be very different from their own.

Listening respectfully to children like this is one important way of building relationships with them. For children with emotional and behavioural difficulties, their five-point behaviour plans may include setting aside a few minutes each day when the teacher will explicitly use this kind of listening. The plan may also involve creating situations where the teacher can do something enjoyable with the child – for example, using half an hour of supply time once a week so that the class teacher and child can have some special time together.

Creating opportunities for feelings to be discussed

There should not be a need for schools to justify time spent by children in discussing their emotional reactions to their experiences. Helping them to find words for their feelings is a worthwhile educational goal in its own right, that will stand them in good stead throughout their adult lives. It is also the best way of preventing the behavioural difficulties that arise when children's hurt, anxiety or anger go unrecognized and unlistened to. Nevertheless, we can if we wish pin attainment targets and cross-curricular themes to this kind of work: such structured situations as circle time, for example, provide an ideal opportunity to address the English programmes of study by working on children's abilities to 'talk and listen confidently in different contexts, exploring and communicating ideas' (DfEE 1999). We can also reflect on the research (Goleman 1996) which shows that emotional literacy, or emotional intelligence, is a better predictor of lifelong achievement than is conventional intelligence or academic ability.

Opportunities for individual children to open up to the teacher are created in many schools through bubble time, where each child is guaranteed an uninterrupted few minutes 'inside the magic bubble' with the teacher, and through personal journals (of writing, drawings, cartoons, poems) that children can show the teacher if they wish. They will often make good use of this channel of communication, as the piece of writing in Figure 9.1 shows. The response that this piece evokes – unlocking memories of our own about chaotic mornings, family tensions and big event nerves – reminds us of the power that reading or listening to others' writing can have in helping us all to understand and express our own feelings. Literature is a prompt to self-expression: in the caring classroom teachers make sure that carefully chosen poems and pieces of prose are readily available to help children reflect on recent experiences or reach feelings they may have suppressed. There is a poem, for example, which never fails to help children let go of some of the feelings they may have been holding onto. The poem, a translation of one by an 8-year-old Turkish girl, starts,

There is a knot inside of me
A knot which cannot be untied
Strong
It feels
As if they have put a stone
Inside of me.

(Ward and Houghton 1991)

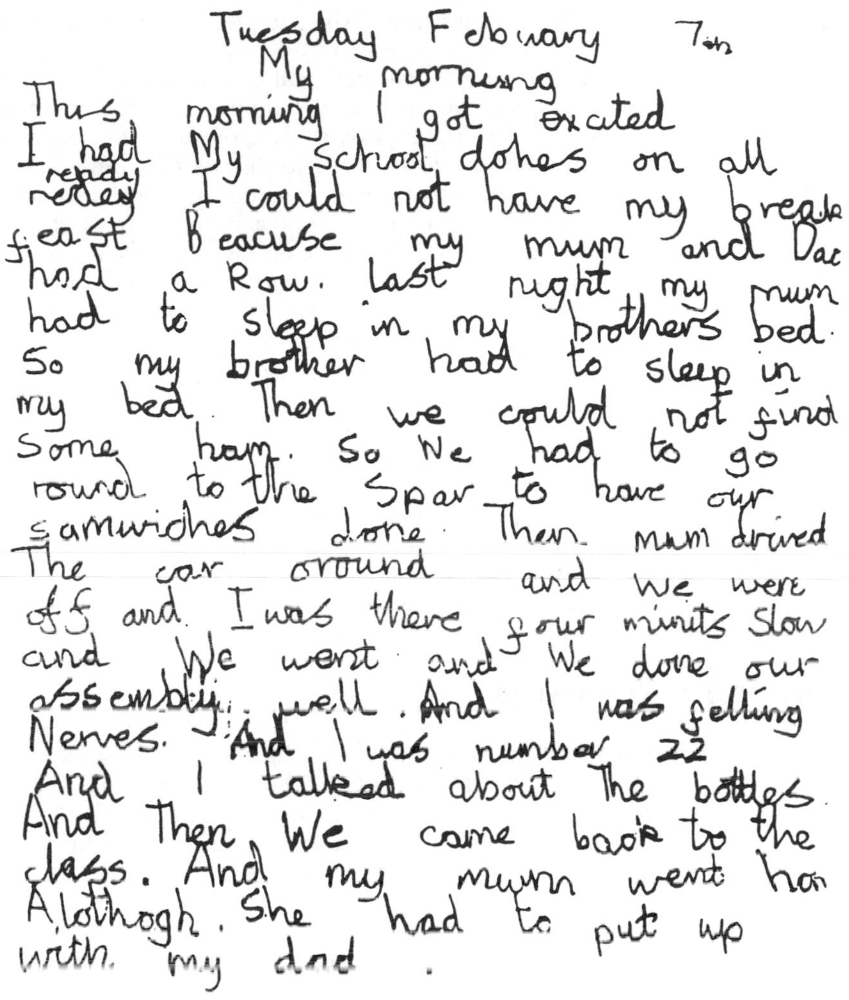

Tuesday February 7th

My morning

This morning I got excated
I had My school clothes on all
ready I could not have my break
feast Because my mum and Dad
had a Row. Last night my mum
had to sleep in my brothers bed.
So my brother had to sleep in
my bed. Then we could not find
Some ham. So We had to go
round to the Spar to have our
samwiches done. Then mum drived
The car oround and We were
off and I was there four minits slow
and We went and We done our
assembly. well. And I was felling
Nerves. And I was number 22
And I talked about The bottles.
And Then We came back to the
class. And my mum went hon
Although. She had to put up
with my dad.

Figure 9.1 Journal writing.

When they identify their own inner knot or stone, children can share their feelings with the teacher, privately, or – more risky but ultimately often more healing – with a supportive group. To help children gain access to this kind of group support, more and more schools are using the idea of circle time. Circle time provides a structure of cooperative activities (games, listening and speaking exercises, drama, puppet and mask work) which get children (and adults) into the habit of talking about feelings and behaviour, and of listening to one another with respect. Children sit in a circle, on an equal footing with the teacher, and initially spend time negotiating some ground rules – maybe that people can only speak if holding a particular object that is passed round, that no one is to interrupt, that no one's ideas will be criticized or put down, and that everyone has a right to pass on any activity that feels uncomfortable to them. A session might start with a round, when each child who wants to will complete the same sentence, such as 'I feel happy when . . .', or 'I get fed up when . . .', or 'If I were an animal I'd like to be . . . because . . .'. Then there will be games, on the surface like party games but always with an agenda of helping the children to listen, to trust one another, to develop sensitivity or grow in self-esteem. These may lead to opportunities for the children to discuss the immediate problems that are troubling them: for example, a game in which a blindfolded child has to negotiate obstacles in order to reach some 'treasure' (Mosley 1992) may allow the children to look at the obstacles (in their own behaviour, or that of others) that prevent them from reaching personal goals in their own lives. Or it may be possible to discuss and tackle a problem (like teasing or 'breaking friends') that has recently arisen in class.

Sources of ideas for circle time are readily available in publications from Lucky Duck, LDA and NASEN. A particularly useful variant (Evans 1992) is the idea of 'end-of-day' activities where children spend a few minutes at the end of each school day on rounds such as 'If you could change places with someone, who would you be?', 'You're being bullied; who would you tell?', 'I am good at . . .', 'I've had a good/bad day because . . .'. Any child can pass on any round, but there is an open invitation for children to stay and talk to the teacher afterwards about any item that provoked a strong reaction or made them feel uncomfortable.

Handling tricky issues

When children are actively encouraged to communicate in school about the things that trouble them, issues will come up that leave staff also uncomfortable, and often unsure about how to respond. For some issues, such as disclosures by children of emotional or physical abuse, there are well-established systems and guidelines in place in most local authorities to help teachers know what to say, what to do, and how to seek support for both the child and for themselves in handling such emotionally charged events. Coping with disclosures about bullying is another area where schools are developing internal guidance on similar lines (Robinson and Maines 1997). But other difficult and commonly occurring issues, such as how to help children cope with family break-up, are less well charted.

The principles for these tricky issues are the same as for any other open discussion of feelings with children: listen; do not make judgements or take sides (or if you do, keep them to yourself), provide support, if the child is willing, in the form of sharing the feelings with other children (who may well have had similar experiences themselves), and in the form of reading or listening to what others have written.

Children going through a family break-up need to know that this happens to many people, and that they should not feel ashamed or different. They should be told that many children feel it is somehow their fault when parents split up, and that it is natural and normal if they feel like this – though almost certainly completely unjustified. It is also natural, but unjustified, to see themselves as unworthy or no good because a parent who has left appears to have rejected them as well as the adult partner. They should know that it may take some time before they can get used to the division of their family, and that meanwhile they are likely to feel intense longing for things to be the way they were, mixed perhaps with anger at one or both parents, and perhaps feelings of needing to take sides or look after a parent who once looked after them. They need to be told that the teacher will understand if they find things hard in school for a while, but would want the child to come and talk over how they are feeling rather than bottle it up so that it comes out in other ways.

If a step-parent appears on the scene, the feelings that may need acknowledging by the sympathetic teacher could include sadness because this means an end to any hopes that the parents who split up will get back together again, bitter jealousy if a mother's or father's attention seems to be devoted to a new partner, anger on behalf of the parent who has been replaced, or guilt and split loyalties if the child finds they feel positive about the step-parent. Irritation and exhaustion at having to form a whole new set of relationships – often with step-brothers and sisters as well as the step-parent – may also be part of the reaction, as well as relief for the child that they are part of a 'normal' family again.

Supporting children after bereavement can prove particularly hard for teachers. There is often a tendency to shy away from mentioning the loss, for fear of upsetting the child or causing embarrassment. Like adults, however, children need to be encouraged to express grief in order to be able to work through it: to say what it was about the person who has died that they most valued, to relive memories, to look at photographs, to cry if they need to. Teachers can help by not avoiding talking about the loss and by providing a quiet, private place where the child can go when they need to be alone. Teachers need to let the child know that it is normal to experience many bewildering feelings after a loss – not only sadness but also anger (at being abandoned), guilt (about the things they feel should have been done or left undone, said or left unsaid), worry (about what might happen to other people they depend on), or even periods of numbness and no feeling at all.

Helping children cope with anxiety

As well as the major stresses of abuse, family break-up and loss we have looked at so far, children can need their teachers' support in coping with anxieties about many lesser events – often school-related, such as worries about moving on to secondary school, speaking in front of a group, going swimming and so on.

Teachers can help anxious children by mapping out with them a series of small steps that will lead them bit by bit to master particular fears. A child who is worried about giving a talk to the class, for example, might need practice in speaking to a partner, then in threes, then a slightly larger group. Children who are anxious about water might need to spend the first swimming lesson sitting on the edge of the pool splashing with their legs, the next jumping briefly into the arms of a helper in the water, the next spending five minutes in the water. For each step completed, the teacher will praise the child enthusiastically, using words that build up the child's picture of themselves as a competent person in control of events: 'You did really well to stick to your plan' or 'You should feel proud of the way you coped with that situation'.

Anxious children also benefit from being taught how they can control their own emotional reactions. Some work in science on the evolutionary significance of the body's physiological response to threat will help children to recognize physical signs, like increased heart rate, sweating, experiencing a dry mouth or knots and butterflies in the stomach, as indications that their bodies are getting ready for swift action (the 'fight-or-flight' response) by shutting down unnecessary systems (such as the digestive system) and pumping energy to muscles. From there, they can be taught how to slow down these physiological responses through slow, deep breathing and progressive muscle relaxation. They can practise, in PE lessons, tensing and tightening each group of muscles in turn, then letting them go floppy and loose, until they are able to let go of muscle tension quickly and easily. Relaxation tapes, to give extra practice at home for children who are particularly vulnerable to anxiety or anger, can be made by the teacher or parent. An example is shown on p. 143 (Box 9.1).

Children who become so apparently anxious about school that they sometimes refuse to come at all can benefit from both relaxation strategies and a small-steps approach, under the guidance of a psychologist, welfare officer or behaviour support teacher. Often, however, the school and the classroom teacher can prevent such school anxieties from escalating to the point where outside intervention is needed by the messages they give to the child and to parents. It is necessary to promise that any worries the child may have will be thoroughly listened to in school, and acted upon, but at the same time the message should be that the child must come to school rather than stay at home and have the worries mount up. If the child is reporting morning aches and pains or stomach upset, the parents can be reassured that the teacher will monitor them closely and send them home if obviously unwell. If the parents seem unable to get children to go to school, it can work wonders if someone from school comes firmly once to collect them. The principle is quick intervention before the child gets locked into a pattern of anxious non-attendance, or a belief that whether or not they go to school is under their own control.

Helping children with friendships

Children who are anxious and withdrawn are also very often children who are lonely and isolated from their peers. So too, very often, are children who are aggressive or disruptive in an attention-seeking way in the classroom: it is surprising how often problems in making and keeping friends lead to behavioural difficulties of all kinds.

Teachers seeking to help children with friendship problems can:

● Work with the whole class on creating an ethos where all children support each other, through circle time and playground systems like the 'friendship stop' – a place where children can wait if they have no one to play with, with the whole class in the habit of including anyone who is waiting there.

Box 9.1

This tape will help you to practise relaxing. It will show you how to breathe slowly and deeply, and how to relax different parts of your body. You should listen to the tape many times, and practise slow breathing and relaxation over and over again. When you are lying in bed at night is often a good time to listen to the tape and do your practice. If you practise often, you will soon find that wherever you are, and however worried and tense you feel, you will be able to use the breathing and relaxation to make yourself feel calm. This will mean you never have to panic; you will always know what to do to calm yourself down. You will feel in control.

Now let's begin to practise relaxing. Make yourself as comfortable as you can: close your eyes; just let yourself relax. Enjoy the feeling of letting go; breathe in and out, in and out slowly and deeply. Put your hand just above your stomach. Keep breathing in . . . and out. Feel your hand being pushed away from you as you breathe in . . . and out. Slowly and deeply. Now imagine there are lots of little tiny holes in the bottom of your feet. As you breathe in . . . and then out you push all of your worries down through your body and out through the soles of your feet. Breathe in . . . and out, letting all those worries down through your body and out through those holes. Keep breathing in . . . and out, letting all the tensions ease away. Let all the muscles in your face relax completely; let go of all the tightness in your head . . . forehead . . . mouth . . . neck. Let it all go loose and floppy. Keep breathing slowly in . . . and out. Concentrate on your shoulders. Let them go floppy. Now your arms and hands. Tighten all the muscles in your hands; clench your fists . . . now let go, and feel your arms and hands go heavy and floppy. Every time you breathe out feel more and more relaxed. Now your legs . . . tense the muscles in your legs . . . in your feet . . . curl up your toes very tight . . . now let go. Breathe slowly and feel your legs and your feet all heavy and floppy. Let yourself feel more and more floppy and comfortable. Let all your muscles go. Lie still for a while.

Now I'm going to count backwards from seven to one. When I get to one, you will be alert but still relaxed. Seven . . . six . . . you're waking up now . . . five, four, three . . . ready to go now . . . two . . . one.

- Involve them in collaborative work with a carefully chosen group, giving them specific roles and putting in preparation so that they are able to make a success of their contribution.
- Involve them in a lunchtime or after-school club.
- Try to raise their status in the class by giving them responsibilities or having them play a key role in a project where they have a special interest, knowledge or skill.
- Involve them in peer tutoring.
- Ask an educational psychologist or behaviour support teacher for advice on using the circle of friends technique (Newton and Wilson 1996).
- Help them to identify the things they do (like being aggressive or critical, impatient or fickle) that stop other children from wanting to be friends with them, and making these the subject of a personal plan.

- Identify specific friendship skills they may need to be taught, or praised for demonstrating, using for example the questionnaire suggested by Long (2000).

A friendship skills course for a group of children is a time consuming but very worthwhile form of intervention, as this example shows:

At St Anne's Primary, a member of staff with a special interest in children's behaviour difficulties decided to run some lunchtime sessions for six children who were a source of concern to their class teachers, because they seemed withdrawn or, in some cases, unpopular and involved in bullying. She started each session with an ice-breaker: for example, a name game where each child had to call out another's name before throwing a soft toy to them, or a game (called 'untangling the knot') where everyone stood close together and, with closed eyes and crossed arms, took hold of someone else's hands, then opened their eyes and tried to unscramble themselves into a circle without letting go. The group worked out some ground rules and reviewed them each week to see if any of them needed to be changed. The theme of Session 1 was 'What makes a good friend?' The children collected their ideas on a spider diagram. The teacher then put a pile of cards onto the floor, saying things such as, 'I can keep a secret', and the children had to decide whether each card should go into a 'good friend' pile or a 'not good friend' pile. Homework for the week was noting and bringing back to the group examples the children saw of people being 'good friends' to one another in school.

Session 2 began with a round: 'This week I was a good friend because . . .', and 'This week I wasn't a good friend because . . .'. The teacher introduced a game about helping, where all the children had to move around balancing a beanbag on their heads while following instructions to hop, skip, move forwards, backwards, slower, faster. If the beanbag fell off somebody's head, he or she was 'frozen' until another child picked up the beanbag and put it on their head. The object of the game was to keep as many people as possible unfrozen. At the end, the children were asked how it felt to help and be helped, and how we should respond when people help us. They went on to watch two children act out a scene where they have been playing a game and one has lost three times in a row, discussing what the winner might say to help the loser feel better, and how the loser should try to behave.

Session 3 was about listening, with the children working in pairs and taking turns to pretend to be a 'good' listener and a 'bad' listener while the other talked about their interests and hobbies. The teacher collected their ideas about what makes for good and bad listening on a flip chart, and set the children to practise some of their 'good listener' ideas for homework.

In Session 4, the topic was giving and accepting compliments. The children drew round and cut out the shape of their hands. Each 'hand' was passed round for the children in turn to write something they liked or admired about its owner on one of the fingers. The children spent some time looking at what others had said about them, and could if they wished take their 'hand' away to keep (all but one of them chose to do this).

Sessions 5 and 6 were spent thinking about in-group/out-group processes, put-downs, name-calling and teasing. The teacher asked the children to talk together in threes in gobbledegook, taking it in turns to be left out by the other two. As a whole group they discussed how it felt to be left out and what could have been done to make the outsider feel better. The teacher then said she was going to read them a story about a day in the life of a boy called Paul, who wakes up feeling happy and good about himself. She gave them each a piece of paper, and said this stood for Paul's feelings inside: 'I'm happy, I'm good, I'm OK'. As she told the story of his day, they had to tear off a little piece of paper every time something happened that took away the 'I'm happy, I'm good, I'm OK' feeling. In the story the boy was shouted at by his father, teased by his sister, ignored by a friend, called names at school and so on. At the end, most of the paper was in bits on the floor. The children were very quiet. The teacher went on to ask them to suggest ways in which people in the story could have helped Paul to feel better about himself, picking up a piece of paper from the floor for each suggestion. The group made a list together of 'put-downs' that children in school use towards one another, and another list of 'build-ups' that could be used instead. They cut up the build-ups and pasted them down one by one over the put-downs. At the last group meeting they shared with the group the put-downs they most often received, and the one taunt or criticism that each felt was guaranteed to hurt or wind them up most. They thought of ways of reacting to put-downs and decided together which were most likely to make other children go on teasing, and which might make them stop.

The children finished with a round: 'Something I've liked about being in this group' and a final game of 'untangling the knot'. All of them said they would miss the group and that it had been good fun. Their class teachers felt that it had in small but significant ways helped all of them to get on with others, and asked for the group to be repeated with different children in the next term.

Building self-esteem

A factor that is common to most children with friendship problems, behavioural difficulties and learning difficulties is low self-esteem – defined as the difference between the way the child would like to be and the way they actually perceive themselves. If the difference is very great, children cannot feel good about themselves. And if they do not feel good about themselves, they approach many situations – both social and academic – with an expectation of failure and a range of negative behaviours that all too often mean that their expectations are confirmed.

What can be done to help children escape this downward spiral? Increasingly, research is showing that it is possible for schools – using relatively simple interventions – to begin to alter pupils' perceptions of themselves, and that the resulting gains in self-esteem are directly linked to improved behaviour and academic achievement. One example is the work on peer tutoring, described in Chapter 6, where very significant improvements in children's rate of progress in learning and classroom behaviour were achieved through no other means than asking them to help teach younger pupils – with all that meant to them in terms of feeling valued and important. Another example is the pioneering work of Dennis Lawrence on the effects on children's reading achievement of providing them with a counselling relationship with a volunteer adult helper, whose job was simply to affirm the child's worth by showing a positive interest in their activities, encouraging them to express feelings and opinions and showing that those opinions were valued in a non-critical way (Lawrence 1988). These findings were later replicated in a study where the volunteer helpers were older pupils: again, there were very significant improvements in the children's reading and spelling, compared to a control group who also had extra help with literacy skills, but whose self-esteem was not nurtured in the same way (James *et al.* 1991).

This research involves volunteers; teachers, of course, are an even more potent and ever-present influence on children's self-esteem. Clark and Warlberg (1968), for example, showed that when teachers made a point of praising children with reading difficulties very frequently for their reading, and having the pupils record each positive comment, their rate of progress shot up as they began to incorporate into their self-image a picture of themselves as 'good readers'.

Sometimes it is apparently casual comments from the teacher which alter self-image. The teacher who says 'I hear from your mother how grown-up you've been since the new baby came' may find the child starting to affirm a 'grown-up' image in all sorts of ways in the classroom; the teacher who says of a piece of writing, 'You've got a real feeling for words' may find the child producing better and better poetry as a result. Many teachers can think of a particular child they have taught whose self-image they were able to alter, with spectacular effects; even more so, most parents can think of the special teacher who succeeded in turning a particular key for their child which unlocked whole areas of potential that had previously lain hidden – by nothing more complex than simply making the child feel good about themselves.

Sometimes the key is not with one teacher, but is turned by a whole school staff working together, as this example shows:

> Brendan was 6, and failing in school. He had a complicated early history, with many operations for a series of heart and digestive complaints. He showed early developmental delay, particularly in language. At 4, he joined a small assessment class in a special school, but later on at his parents' request he moved to a local primary school with a good reputation for 'caring'. When he was in Year 3 he was referred to the educational psychologist: he was not progressing with reading, had great problems with handwriting and was very easily distracted and unmotivated in the classroom. He said of himself at this time: 'I'm no good at my work and no one wants to play with me'. It was decided to make raising his self-esteem a priority in the school's

action plan: a greater priority even than specific help with reading and written work.

Two terms later, the psychologist returned to review Brendan's progress. In the interim, he had been chosen for the part of Joseph in the school Nativity play. He had also been selected to serve at Mass when it was celebrated in school. He was now sitting between two very able boys in the classroom, and often given responsibilities as the 'oldest boy in the class' (which he was). He had done quite a lot of writing on the computer; this had helped him to produce work that looked good, of which he could feel proud. All the staff made a point of singling him out for special notice; even the headteacher, whenever he went into the classroom, would say, 'Where's that boy who's so good at setting my watch?' and give him the job of doing so.

When she reassessed his basic attainments, the psychologist found that Brendan had improved at twice his previous rate. Even more important, he was concentrating for much longer periods in the classroom, and mixing indistinguishably with other children in the playground.

As with behaviour management, self-esteem interventions for individual children need to be set in the context of a school-wide framework for enhancing the self-esteem of *all* pupils. This will involve looking at issues of curriculum, discipline and classroom management. Does the curriculum allow opportunities for all to experience success? Does teacher language, marking and display place a value on absolute achievement, or does it instead emphasize the importance of effort and individuality? In addition to individual praise, are group praise and class praise used to foster a sense of belonging? Are mistakes reframed as good opportunities for learning, and are teachers open about their own mistakes? Is there a structure for children to make positive comments on each other's work and behaviour?

Then there is the balance of rewards and sanctions, and the ways in which these are applied. In the average primary school, pupils receive about four and a half times as many negative comments about their behaviour as positive (Merrett and Wheldall 1987), leaving them with little chance of developing an image of themselves as well behaved, kind, helpful or hard-working. It is, however, quite possible for teachers to reverse the ratio by following the adage 'catch them being good', and explicitly praising pro-social behaviour rather than taking it for granted. This needs to be done much more frequently than might be imagined: it has been shown that, just to keep children's self-esteem at a steady level, a ratio of five positive remarks to every one negative is needed. To *raise* self-esteem, in children who do not think well of themselves, requires a ratio of nearer ten to one.

When children do need telling off, this can be done in ways that avoid humiliation, sarcasm and personal criticism. Teachers can use language that shows they reject particular behaviours, without also rejecting the child (Maines and Robinson 1989a). Saying 'You are a bully' will only reduce self-esteem and provide both teacher and child with a convenient label that will direct much of their future behaviour, while 'Hitting other children is not allowed in this school; you have been hitting, and the consequence will be . . .' leaves the child with the chance to learn from the sanction and change their behaviour next time. Children can sometimes be bullies, liars, spoilsports, cheats or fusspots, but there is nothing at all to be gained from calling them any of these things (even in the privacy of the staffroom). Instead, teachers can make use of the more helpful, 'When you . . . then I . . .' or 'I . . . message' framework (Gordon 1974): 'When you tell me a lie, I feel let down and also angry that I have to spend a lot of time now sorting this out'; 'When you keep coming to ask me questions about work I know you can do, I get irritated because I can't get on with the work I've planned for this group'; and 'When you spoil the game the others get angry with you and won't want you to play next time'.

The final aspect of a whole-school framework for building self-esteem concerns classroom management. Systems that deprive children of the right to exercise choice and independence in the classroom can be very damaging to self-esteem: when the goals and the means to achieve them are always set by others, children never develop the sense of self-direction that is the main characteristic distinguishing those who have high, from those that have low, self-esteem. Then there is pupil grouping: fixed pupil groupings that make it very clear to the pupils who the teacher views as achievers, and who the no-hopers, are a major source of low self-esteem for many pupils. So are special needs interventions that single children out as obviously different from their peers – having to fetch their reading book from another part of the school, having a classroom assistant who works with them and never anyone else, having special equipment that others are not allowed to try out and share as a special privilege. Yet differentiation can be achieved without such blows to self-esteem: witness the classrooms where resources at different levels are available, but the children themselves choose which they think are most appropriate for them, or the teacher who arranged matters so that her teaching assistant worked regularly with groups of gifted and talented pupils as well as with children with learning difficulties.

Schools that have looked at their overall curriculum, their discipline and their classroom management systems in terms of the effects on children's self-image are generally very successful in reducing the frequency of behavioural and learning difficulties. Even the best of them still find, however, that there are children who need a more individual and intensive attempt to boost self-confidence.

These are the children with very low self-esteem, who can be recognized by certain characteristic behaviour patterns: they typically find it hard to concentrate or are apathetic in learning situations, they avoid taking part, remain on the fringe of groups, set themselves low goals, continuously ask for help and reassurance or compensate for poor self-image by trying to appear powerful to other children, exaggerating achievements and possessions or refusing to conform to classroom norms (Gurney 1988).

Teachers can explore individual children's self-perceptions using published self-esteem scales (Lawrence 1988; Maines and Robinson 1989b), or the discussion format described in Chapter 4: these will identify children whose global self-worth is low, and highlight the particular areas (such as academic achievement, appearance, friendship skills) where they most need help in formulating a more positive self-image.

The strategies that can be used for children low in self-esteem are many – for example:

- Adopting a policy of positive 'noticing' of the child by every adult in the school.
- Finding out what the child is good at or knows a lot about, and having them share this with the rest of the class or school.
- Helping the child to become an expert, or develop skills in a particular area – which may be extracurricular: becoming a judo orange belt has worked wonders for some children, as has being given the responsibility of organizing a lunchtime or after-school group, such as a stampbug or nature-watch club.
- Compiling with the child a book of 'Things I Can Do Now', or 'Things I Am Good At'.
- Choosing the child for special responsibilities.
- Asking the child to tutor another with their work.
- Choosing the child to be part of a group that supports or counsels other children – for example, those who are having problems in the playground, are being bullied or are new to the school.
- Making much use of praise, stickers, certificates and notes home to highlight achievements in behaviour or learning.
- Giving the whole class a favourite activity or five minutes' extra playtime when the target child has done well in either work or behaviour.
- Having the child set themselves small, attainable targets within a special 'success area' they choose to work on; keeping a 'Success Record Book' such as the one suggested by Long (2000).
- Helping the child to keep records of reaching these targets, and dated samples of work (for example, a 'first of the month' book kept throughout the year), so that they can clearly see progress and show the evidence to others.
- Asking the child to record one success, however small, in a special praise book at the end of each day.
- Having the child keep a book of positive staff comments about their work or behaviour, and discuss it with a helper at the end of each week.
- Photocopying good pieces of work to take home.
- Having the child 'overhear' you tell another adult how they have grown up/surprised you/excelled.

It is also possible to construct a series of planned activities for a small group of children who share problems of low self-esteem. One teacher, for example, set up what she called the 'I can club', which had a special membership badge; the children took part in a series of affirming activities such as taking photographs of one another, displaying them on posters surrounded by positive comments they had made about each other, completing lists of things they were able to do well and telling a friend about one special achievement they were proud of. Other children have enjoyed making an 'I can tree', either at home or at school, where they stick paper leaves on a cutout tree trunk, each leaf recording a skill they have mastered – or some of the everyday things they manage to do well.

Children with low self-esteem will find it hard to think about what they are good at, but can be helped by prompts (in rounds, or on worksheets) such as 'I am liked because . . .', 'The best things about the way I look are . . .', 'Things I've made are . . .' or 'I'm a good friend because . . .'. Or they can finish sentences like these in pairs, then form a group where each child describes some of the positive things they have learned about their partner. Again, using one of Jenny Mosley's ideas, they can be helped to get into the habit of acknowledging positives by choosing a piece of work each week to stick a coloured label on and present to a small group or to the class at circle time with an explanation of why they are proud of it (Mosley 1993).

Teacher praise for children with low self-esteem needs to be given with care. If it is to succeed in restructuring the child's self-image in any long-term way, praise for a particular piece of work or behaviour needs to be linked with more general attributes and strengths: not just 'That's a lovely painting' but 'That's a lovely painting; it shows you have good powers of observation'; not just 'Good girl for getting that finished' but 'Good girl for getting that finished; I can see you are a real hard worker'. It is also import-ant to make it clear that the child has succeeded entirely because of their own efforts or qualities. Research has shown that children with special needs come to believe that while the failure they encounter is the result of their own inadequacies, any success they may experience is due to chance or the actions of others (Dudley-Marling *et al.* 1982). If I can do a task, the child feels, it must be because the task was easy, or I had help; if I fail, it is because I am stupid or bad.

To challenge successfully this kind of conviction, teachers need to emphas-ize permanent inner factors in the child when praising success. Conversely, when they have to correct the work or behaviour of a child who is low in self-esteem, they need to stress external and temporary factors. They can convey to the child that if there are mistakes in work it is because the task was too hard, or the teacher had not explained it properly, or even because the child chose, on that particular day, not to try very hard. They can convey that problems in behaviour have arisen because the child chose to react in certain ways to external circumstances – but another time would be able to adopt a different strategy. It is important *not* to let the child feel that you think them permanently slow, or lazy or aggressive, but instead to emphasize factors that are changeable and specific to the situation.

This may call for considerable revision of our own attitudes to children with SEN. Despite much evidence to the contrary, there is still a belief in many teachers that some pupils just will not succeed, ever. And if they hold such low expectations of certain pupils, they appear according to research to adopt certain behaviours towards them that actively contribute to these expectations being confirmed – restricting the breadth of curricular experi-ences, for example (Blatchford *et al.* 1989). If pupils' self-esteem is to be raised, we need to monitor effects like these very carefully, and reverse them where necessary – as did the teachers in one study (Good and Brophy 1977) who, when they were told that they were offering less praise and more criticism to children they designated as low achievers, immediately altered their responses and found that the behaviour and performance of the low achieving group improved rapidly as a result.

Finally, it is important to remember that teacher praise alone will not be enough to raise a child's self-esteem. As McNamara and Moreton (1997) point out, 'the three shapers of children's self-esteem are parents, peers and teachers in equal parts'; we need to make sure that good news is constantly shared with the home, and build into our plans ways of helping peers, as well as the teacher, give positive feedback. This will be easiest in a climate where all children are trained to notice one another's strengths and successes, and pay each other compliments via structured circle time activities.

Conclusion

In this chapter we have looked at ways in which schools can support children's affective development. At a time when teachers are overwhelmed with pressures from the academic curriculum, this may seem inappropriate: time for listening to children's feelings and helping them to relate to one another is hard to come by with so much curriculum content to be covered. The argument has to be, nevertheless, that if we do not pay enough attention to these issues, the time children can spend learning and teachers can spend teaching will be eroded by the resulting behavioural challenges to the teacher's classroom management, and children will continue to underachieve because of feelings of low self-worth. Let children see themselves as valuable, capable of handling stress and sorting out problems, however, and they can get on with their school work – and a good deal more besides.

10 Special needs in speaking and listening

Introduction

The importance of oral language skills as a vehicle for learning and a means of communicating what has been learned is central both to the Early Learning Goals for young children and to much of the National Curriculum documentation. As well as having an attainment target to itself in English, talk is also prominent in programmes of study in other subjects – with children working in groups, discussing ideas, reporting back to an audience and learning by listening to one another.

For some children with SEN, particularly those with difficulties in writing, an emphasis on oracy is immensely helpful. For others, the speaking and listening programmes of study are themselves a stumbling block: these are children who, for whatever reason (whether because of inbuilt factors or classroom demands ill-attuned to their natural language patterns), find it hard to listen and remember, to express their ideas, to ask and answer questions and to recall experiences and describe events.

In this chapter we consider ways in which teachers can differentiate the National Curriculum programmes of work in speaking and listening to meet such children's needs, and ensure that they can access work in other subjects wherever it relies on well-developed oracy skills.

Two children

David, aged 6, has been with the same teacher throughout his first two years of school. When he started in the Reception class, his speech was barely intelligible and he talked very little: only in a whisper to the teacher, and never in small-group or class discussion times. Over the next two years he became more confident in speaking to one familiar adult in school, and his articulation problems all but disappeared, leaving only slight immaturities such as 'tissors' for 'scissors'. He was making almost no progress with reading and writing, however. He found it hard to follow instructions in class and would often be found sitting daydreaming instead of getting going on a task. He still was not consistently participating as a speaker in group activities: he would speak when asked a direct question but not spontaneously relate 'news', or describe something he had done or planned to do in school. The teacher decided to work on this, with the help of David's parents, by keeping a home–school diary: she used the diary to ask David questions when the class were together on the carpet (initially closed questions, but becoming more open as he developed confidence). He was also asked to draw pictures in the diary and use these as a support when talking about his news. Other children in the group were encouraged to ask David questions about his pictures, to promote a less teacher-directed exchange.

This plan had some success, but it was slow. David's teacher felt there was enough evidence of language difficulties to ask for a speech and language therapist's assessment: David had had some speech therapy in his preschool years, but had been discharged because his parents failed to keep appointments.

The speech therapist confirmed that David was still a long way behind his peers in many aspects of language. She observed that he had particular difficulties in word-finding: he might know perfectly well what something was called, but be unable at times to recall the name for it. When he looked at a picture of a cup and saucer, for example, he struggled for a long time to name it, saying: 'It's a plate . . . no, it's a teapot . . . a dish'. She felt this might partly explain why he was so reticent in classroom situations where he felt 'on the spot' to produce the right words. He also showed a lot of difficulties in following and processing complex language: he would often pick up only part of a sentence, responding for example to an instruction like 'Before you give me the car, give me the red van' by handing over only the van. Simple mathematical language such as 'Find two the same' or 'How many can we have each?' was quite beyond him, but if the instruction was demonstrated by gesture and example he could cope easily with the task.

This assessment helped David's teacher to understand why David often seemed so slow to catch on in the classroom; the speech therapist's advice helped her to plan ways of adapting her classroom language to meet David's needs.

Emily was 10, and a source of concern to her teacher mainly because of her poor written work. She had been late in talking in her preschool years, as had her elder sister and brother. She had had consistent, high-quality extra help with reading throughout her primary years and was now a reasonably skilled reader. She had mastered a core spelling vocabulary by learning the words by heart alphabetically, naming each letter to herself over and over until she remembered them. Words outside this vocabulary were often spelled in a bizarre manner – 'pisall' for 'pencil', for example, and 'rasey' for 'rice'. Her stories and written work were often disjointed and her teacher could not make sense of them.

She had always tended to jumble her words and substitute one word for another: 'hockeysocks' for 'hollyhocks', 'eiderup' for 'eiderdown'. If one listened closely to her speech, it was missing little joining words and word endings; when asked to describe what a wheel was in a word game, for example, she said: 'On a car. It black, it round, like a little tube'. She seemed quite unable to understand everyday idioms and metaphors; when her teacher said things like 'Are you with me?' she would always answer 'yes', because she *was* with the teacher, literally at least. She seemed puzzled by indirect instructions, saying 'No thank you', for example, in response to the teacher's 'Would you like to join the story group now, please Emily'.

A multidisciplinary assessment of Emily's needs concluded that she had marked and specific language difficulties. Her problems with written work were important, but secondary to the wider language problem; commenting on her spelling, for example, the educational psychologist observed: 'Emily finds it hard to discriminate, reproduce and sequence speech sounds in words, and has not as a result been able to reliably map the written symbols onto these patterns of spoken sounds'.

What do these two children need in terms of help from their teachers? Both require ongoing literacy support, it is clear, but also more fundamental support with spoken language.

First, they need specific programmes of work within the speaking and listening programmes of study, perhaps planned with the help of a speech and language therapist and SENCO. For Emily, this might focus on non-literal uses of language, and expressing her ideas grammatically and in sequence; for David, work on processing the complex language he hears in the classroom and on expressing himself fluently in group situations is needed.

Second, both children need 'bypass' strategies that make sure they have full access to, and a fair chance to succeed in, the *whole* curriculum despite their communication difficulties. Many of these bypass strategies will relate to teacher language. David's teacher has to make her instructions short and back them up with demonstration and gesture; Emily's teacher to explain and clarify metaphor, jokes, irony and idiom. For David, too, there will be a need to find ways in which he can demonstrate his learning other than by contributing to group discussion.

Identification and assessment

How can teachers become more aware of children, such as Emily and David, with special needs in language? We are not speaking here of bilingual children, for whom English is not the language of the home: these children have traditionally not been considered to come under the special needs umbrella, and this is the convention followed here. The focus here is, rather, on children who have difficulties in acquiring – or using appropriately in the classroom – a single language, and who show one or more of the following behaviours:

- unclear speech;
- difficulty in listening to and understanding what they hear in school;
- inhibited or restricted expressive language.

Such difficulties are common. Some years ago, for example, it was estimated that 1 in 20 children started school unable to make themselves understood (Hersov and Berger 1980); now that more and more 4-year-olds are in Reception classes, the figure is likely to be very much higher. The difficulties can also have long-term consequences for the child's development: the overt signs of language problems may not be so evident when the child is 7, or 17, but there is often a legacy of emotional, behavioural or learning difficulties that persists over many years. In one study (Sheridan and Peckham 1975), over half the children identified as having language problems at 7 still demonstrated residual language problems, learning, social or emotional difficulties at 16; difficulties in reading are particularly likely (Aram and Nation 1980).

Straightforward articulation problems and unclear speech are the easiest form of language difficulty for the teacher to pick up – but at the same time, it seems, the least likely to lead to long-term learning difficulties (Snowling *et al.* 2000). It is important for the teacher to be able to screen for more subtle forms of language impairment, using a knowledge of the normal course of development of language in young children (see Table 10.1).

They should also be aware of some of the behavioural patterns that might be pointers to language difficulties. This will mean watching out for children who may be always one step behind when following instructions (for example, in PE, where they may be watching the other children to see what they have to do), for children who have difficulty with rhyming and word games, for children who are restless and inattentive in listening situations like assembly, for children who respond at a tangent in conversation or pick up only the last part of things you say to them. If young children are showing possible signs of language difficulty, it is always wise to have their hearing checked and to refer the child (with the permission of parents or carers) to a speech and language therapist for assessment and advice.

For older children, it can be more difficult to pick up evidence of special needs in language. Children of 7 or over who have had an earlier history of communication difficulties may still have difficulty in articulating the finer sounds (such as consonant clusters), in sequencing events when retelling a story, dealing with complex tenses and structures (especially passives, as in 'More roads had to be built'), and making adequate 'how', 'why', 'what if' and 'what next' inferences. They may talk or write in a roundabout way, not completing sentences, or repeating themselves. Their writing may contain odd grammatical structures, with little grammatical joining words or word endings missed out – as in 'He go somewhere to get a ladder and try to open the window. He go to his friend house and phone his mum and dad'.

Again, children with very specific language impairments such as these are likely to benefit from referral to a speech and language therapist so that a special programme of work can be drawn up and implemented – perhaps at school – in order to meet their needs. There are also commercially available resources (such as *Teaching Talking* from NFER-Nelson) which enable schools

Table 10.1 Screening for language difficulties in the early years*

A 4-year-old should be able to (at a minimum)	A 5-year-old should in addition be able to (at a minimum)
Follow simple directions directed specifically at him or her	Follow general instructions given to class; manage to listen and play/work at the same time
Listen and attend to a short, simple repetitive story with pictures	Listen with interest to a more complex, unfamiliar story with pictures
Repeat correctly a sentence, such as 'We're having a visitor tomorrow' (10 syllables)	Repeat correctly a sentence like 'We're going to visit the market tomorrow' (12 syllables)
Give three objects in order – for example 'Give me the pencil, the book and the scissors'	Give four objects in order – for example 'Give me the book, the crayon, the pencil and the scissors'
Respond correctly to simple sentences with four information carrying words – for example 'Put the big balls in the box'	Respond correctly to simple sentences containing five information carrying words – for example 'Open the book and colour a ball red'
Understand concepts of size (big/little), and prepositions (in, on, under, behind)	Understand comparisons (bigger/heavier) and harder prepositions (in front of, above, between)
Understand and use what, where and who questions	Understand and use when and why questions
Use an average sentence length of 4–7 words	Use an average sentence length of 5+ words, but is often able to use even longer sentences with connectors such as 'and', 'but', 'so that' and 'because'
There may be omissions – for example 'The boy (is) running fast'	There should no longer be omissions
Can relate events concerning self	Can relate stories; beginning to know the difference between fact and fantasy
Can use speech sounds m, n, p, b, t, d, w and sometimes f, v, k and g	Can use k, g, f, v and sometimes s, z, sh, l, ch, j and y but may not, until the age of about 7, use r, th and clusters of consonants (sp, fr, pl, etc.) correctly

* Adapted with kind permission from *Speech and Language Norms*, a guide for teachers produced by The Bath and District Health Authority Speech and Language Service.

to assess children's language difficulties themselves, in all but the most serious cases, and use their assessment to set priorities and plan language work to be done in a small group.

For the purposes of differentiating speaking and listening tasks within the National Curriculum, the most useful forms of assessment will chart the child's progress on small steps within the three key strands of the Key Stages 1 and 2 programmes of study. These are:

- speaking for different audiences;
- listening and responding;
- discussion and group interaction.

Within the discussion and group interaction strand we find, at Key Stage 1, the objective 'asks and answers questions'. Breaking this down into small steps, we might have:

- Understands and uses what, where and who questions.
- Can answer a simple direct question which requires the child to tell about their own experiences.
- Can answer a simple open question which requires the child to talk about a TV programme or story.
- Understands and uses when, why, how and which questions.
- Uses grammatical inversion – for example, 'I can go' – 'Can I go?'
- Uses restructuring of sentences – for example, 'I need my coat' – 'Do I need my coat?'
- Can answer (in turn) a question put to everyone in the group.
- Puts simple questions to peers in order to make contact, or obtain information about immediate events.
- Can ask each person in the group a specific question in order to collect data – for example, about favourite foods.
- Can role-play the teacher, asking questions of others in the group.
- Can ask others for ideas in a group project.
- Uses questions to obtain information about abstract concepts and remote events – for example, plays 20 questions.
- Can devise questions in order to follow a line of enquiry – for example, plan an interview.
- Can respond to others' questions in order to guide them in completing an activity, designing or making something.
- Can in response to a question advocate and justify a point of view.

Another strand, listening and responding, might in relation to stories and poems start with listening to simple repetitive picture stories on a one-to-one basis, go on to listening to a picture story in a small group, then in a class, then longer stories without pictures. The responding aspect would begin with joining in familiar rhymes, then go on to answering simple questions about stories and drawing pictures to illustrate them or acting them out. The next step would be contributing to group retelling or 'finishing off'. At the next level, the child would discuss the characters and events in a story or poem, and say whether they liked it and why.

The objective 'follows instructions from the teacher' within the listening and responding strand is particularly important in that if children have problems in this area they are likely to fail right across the curriculum – and sometimes to get into trouble for apparently naughty behaviour as well. Teachers would do well to assess the stage reached in responding to instructions as a matter of course when any child presents learning or behaviour problems, so that they can adapt their classroom language appropriately, and also if necessary plan ways of gradually extending the amount of information the child can take in, remember and act on. A possible sequence of small steps might include:

- Can respond to directions if the adult goes up to the child and turns them to face the adult before speaking.
- Can respond to instructions when the teacher gives a preliminary alerting signal, names/looks at the child, and the child is not occupied.
- Responds to instructions containing three key information-carrying words – for example, 'Put the *book* on *my table*', and to a single instruction – for example, 'Choose the colours you want'.
- Can give a friend simple one-step instructions in pretend or constructional play.
- Responds to instructions containing four information carrying words – for example, 'Put the *big balls under* the *table*'.
- Responds to general instructions given to the class when all are asked to stop what they are doing and listen.
- Responds to general instructions given to the class while doing something else at the time.
- Can take a written message to another teacher.
- Responds to complex sentences with five information carrying words – for example, '*Find* your *book* and *colour* a *teddy red*', and to a two-step instruction – for example, 'Put your book away and then line up'.
- Can pass on the meaning of a simple instruction to another person, child or teacher – for example, 'Ask her for the register please'.
- Can follow a simple three-step instruction – for example, 'Get out your maths book; find the page with the picture of buttons, and write in the numbers next to each set'.
- Can give two-step instructions to another child in pretend or constructional play.
- Can give two-step instructions to another child or group, which they follow in order to make something or complete a set task.
- Can respond to complex multi-step instructions such as 'Find a flower you'd like to use for your art work; decide what materials to use and then get to work in the area just outside the classroom'.
- Accurately conveys verbatim messages and telephone messages.
- Gives and follows precise instructions for playing a game, making a model or conducting an experiment when pursuing a task individually or as part of a group.
- Guides other pupils in designing something.

In making a small-steps assessment of the stage that children have reached in speaking and listening skills, the teacher may choose to observe their response to standard tasks such as those suggested for teacher assessment within the National Curriculum. It is also very important, however, to try to discover from parents more about the range of language the child uses at home, since many children have language capabilities which they do not display in the school setting. It is also useful to gather information about the child as a speaker and listener over time, in a variety of contexts, using methods such as notepad jottings of verbatim quotations, audio- or video-taped samples of talk, or having an older child scribe a whole piece of talk about a picture or an artefact the child has made.

Developing expressive language

The National Curriculum programmes of study for speaking and listening involve talking confidently in language which increasingly approximates standard English when appropriate and is adapted to the needs of the listener. The current consensus among specialists in the education of children with speech and language disorders is that all these skills are best learned in a meaningful context where the child has a powerful reason to communicate, rather than through any form of drill.

This conclusion is based on research into the factors that seem to promote language development in young children (Wells 1981; Wood 1986). This has shown that both at home and in nursery classes, children make most progress when available adults foster real conversational interaction over a shared activity: when they take time to listen to the child's contribution, add something of their own, hand the conversation back to the child and give them space to respond, and then expand and paraphrase what the child has said in sentences just a little more linguistically complex than they are yet able to use. By contrast, language development is slowest when adults are unresponsive, or control the conversation with a string of closed questions, or with requests to the child to repeat something in correct form.

For children with expressive language difficulties this means that the first element in an action plan should be finding for them a regular, sympathetic adult listener or 'talking partner' (whether volunteer helper, parent, grandparent or classroom assistant). The adult helper will foster conversation over all those classroom activities that are the traditional vehicles for talk: making things, finding out, cooking, drawing, role play in the home corner or home corner 'conversion' to hospital, café or bank. The helper can also be asked to read to the child, as often as possible, since we know this to be another major contributor to language development, and to share books with lots of detailed pictures to talk about, books without text where they can make up a story together, and interesting non-fiction.

There should be good access to story tapes at the listening centre, so that the child can recreate at will the experience of listening to a special story that has been read to them, and have extra repetition of its vocabulary and language structures.

Sentence-level work within the Literacy Hour will be helpful for these children. While the majority of children in the class are working on the written forms of verb tenses, plurals, possessives etc., the child with expressive language difficulties can simultaneously be practising these structures at an oral level. Oral 'transforming' tasks (for example, transforming a sentence from positive to negative, past to present, statement to question, expanding simple sentences into complex ones) are particularly useful.

However, such work may not be enough on its own. Specific language structures the child needs help with may need to be practised on a one-to-one or small group basis, usually under the guidance of a speech and language therapist or language support teacher, in the context of turn-taking and games. For example, if the child is learning to use questions with inverted word order, the helper might unveil a complex picture bit by bit while the child has to guess, as each new piece is revealed, 'Is it a . . . ?' Or, for regular and irregular past tenses, the child and helper might take turns to mime an action and ask each other, 'What did I do?'

Another technique that can be used to help the child learn new structures is that of forced alternatives. Here the helper or teacher asks questions which offer the child a choice of responses and an appropriate adult model. A child learning to describe future actions using 'going to' might, for instance, be asked 'Are you going to draw now or are you going to play with the sand?'; if they produce only 'play sand' the adult can still expand this into the correct the form – 'Oh, I see; you are going to play with the sand', so that the child will have heard the correct model not just once, but twice. Similarly, a child learning vocabulary of 'bigger' and 'smaller', say, can be offered two pieces of paper and asked not 'Which one do you want?', but 'Do you want the bigger piece or the smaller piece?': the possibilities of the technique for expanding children's language skills in naturally occurring classroom situations are obvious.

Children with difficulties in word finding (retrieving words they know) – like David, whom we met earlier in the chapter – need to be encouraged to express themselves in whatever way they can: the emphasis should be on getting meaning across, even if in a roundabout manner. If, for example, the child says 'You know . . . the place where . . . where you do the cooking and all that', the sympathetic listener will say 'Oh yes, in the kitchen, go on . . .', rather than build up tension and anxiety by waiting for the child to find the right word. These children can also practise, on other occasions, the skill of explaining word meanings – perhaps by giving a partner clues in a guessing game: 'It's an animal. You see it in the zoo. It has a hump and lives in the desert'. If they have to be asked for the name of something in class, they should be cued in with an associated word or phrase ('needle and . . .', 'we cut wood with a . . .') if they are struggling to respond.

For most children, however, difficulties in expressing themselves fluently in school are more likely to be due to the lack of an appropriate vocabulary rather than to word-finding problems. The teacher's role is then one of helping to expand that vocabulary, most importantly by making sure the child has a chance to *listen* to a wide range of taped stories and non-fiction that uses mature vocabulary, and where the meaning of new words can become clear from the context.

For children who read reasonably well, reading itself will be the main means of vocabulary enrichment, but encouragement to make use of a thesaurus and dictionary when redrafting writing will also help. Setting a daily puzzle ('What would you find in a belfry?') or asking children to research and find alphabetical adjectives (as in the old game 'the parson's cat is an avaricious/boisterous/corpulent cat') or alphabetical things to tell other children to do (amble, brag, canter) will expand vocabulary while providing practice in dictionary use at the same time. Children will also enjoy making glossaries for information texts that do not have them, or 'Call My Bluff' books where each page has a word and three or four possible definitions, only one of which is correct.

Visual concept maps (spider diagrams), in which children take a target word and write or draw pictures or words which relate in some way to the target word, are also helpful in consolidating understanding of new vocabulary.

Some children with expressive language difficulties need not so much help in acquiring new vocabulary and structures, as encouragement to use the language they already possess in order to convey meaning more precisely. Activities where one child has to give instructions to another in order to complete a task are helpful here, for example:

- Using computer software where one child creates and prints a picture, and then has to give instructions to a partner at the keyboard ('Put a witch on the hill . . . put a dragon under the bridge') so that the partner can recreate the scenario without showing the other child their picture.
- Using a box of materials varying in colour, texture, pattern, shape and size: one child silently chooses a piece and tries to describe it so that the other can pick the right one.
- Having one child make a tape of instructions on how to make a model or how to use a particular piece of equipment, and seeing how successful the instructions are when a partner or group of children try to follow them.

Riddles and word games are another way of helping children to use precise language for particular purposes, and need not descend into drill if the children have the opportunity to invent their own puzzles for one another as well as respond to the teacher. Older children enjoy 20 questions, or games where they pick a pair of objects on the grounds of conceptual similarity and challenge the group to find out why they have put them together. Younger children like making up silly sentences ('Water is dry . . . cars have four wings . . .') for others to repeat in correct form, or hiding objects and giving each other clues to help find them ('It's under something that tells the time . . . it's behind something square').

So far we have looked mainly at work that will help children to convey information and ask questions. What about another National Curriculum objective, that of telling real and imagined stories? Often this is the area requiring the most careful differentiation of teaching approaches, with some children able early on to construct and tell an elaborate make-believe story to a group, and others hardly progressing beyond an 'and then . . . and then . . . and then . . .' account of real experience.

At the earliest stages, children should be able to recount recent events at home or school to a small group, perhaps with the prompt of a set of pictures or photographs, or of direct questions about experiences recorded in a home–school diary.

When it comes to talking about *imaginary* events, a small steps way in for some children may be asking them to describe, with support, 'pretend' events that happen to their favourite teddy bear or soft toy. For others, it may be retelling simple, familiar stories in a round, taking turns with the teacher, then dramatizing the story and finally retelling it to a partner or parent with the help of pictures or drawings.

After preparation of this kind, children will be ready to work on storytelling in mixed ability groups – the child with language difficulties is placed in a small group where the other children are good communicators but also good at making space for others and listening to them supportively. Children can be assigned roles within the group: those who find speaking and listening difficult are asked to retell a story the teacher has introduced, others are assigned to predict things that might happen after the story ends and others lead the group in trying to make up their own new twist or version.

Alternatively, the children can work in pairs or threes of similar language ability; differentiation here will take the form of supplying less or more structure and props, according to need. One group might work around ICT software which provides a high degree of structure in the form of choices between sets of pictures: 'Once upon a time there was . . . a princess/soldier/ mermaid who had a magic . . . finger/ring/box that could . . . ?' Another group might be given a title and a set of stimulus pictures to sequence, while another would have the title alone.

Reluctant talkers

The emphasis on talk within the National Curriculum has made teachers increasingly concerned about children who are quiet in class and hardly talk at all. Some of these children may have specific language difficulties; others may have different reasons for reticence – their language capabilities are as good as other children's but their personality or experiences make them reluctant to communicate. In extreme cases this may amount to total refusal to speak to the teacher, or to other children, at all.

Assessing the needs of such children requires careful observation. Do they talk freely in group activities but not to adults? In the playground? At home? To whom do they talk? Is there evidence of real language difficulty in taped or scribed samples of their talk? Are they anxious and inhibited in a variety of situations, with many fears? Or are they strong-willed by temperament, withholding speech stubbornly because they hate to give in?

Children who talk to peers but seldom to the teacher will need a slow process of relationship-building, and graded opportunities to communicate in non-threatening situations: talking on behalf of a puppet or from behind a mask, making a regular tape recording for the teacher to listen to in the car on the way to school, talking in a whisper or answering forced-alternative questions as a step towards more spontaneous communication.

Sometimes children fall into a pattern of not talking to adults at school because they never need to – like this little girl:

> Charmaine was 6 and, according to her mother, 'a real chatterbox' at home. She spoke freely to a small group of friends at school but never to the teacher. If she needed anything, she would send one of her friends to ask: 'Charmaine wants to go to the toilet', 'Charmaine's not feeling very well'. Her teacher felt Charmaine was anxious and shy, and let this go on, hoping that eventually she would be able to win Charmaine's confidence. But Charmaine never did speak to the teacher, and a year later in a different class was still sending her friends to talk for her.

Teachers of children just starting school can often help to avoid later problems by pre-empting, at an early stage, the pattern of silence – like one Reception teacher who decided (successfully) to hold onto one mute little boy at breaktimes and ask him at first to whisper 'Yes' when she asked if he wanted to go out to play, later to speak in a normal voice and later still to make the request himself.

If the pattern of withholding speech is entrenched, however, it is generally wise to seek advice, usually from an educational psychologist; one of the possibilities that will always need to be investigated is that a child's reluctance to speak is linked to the silence and secrecy that surrounds physical or sexual abuse.

Children who *do* talk freely to the teacher, but are self-conscious and quiet in group situations, require a different set of strategies. They need to have a regular 'talking partner' with whom they regularly share ideas and talk things out. Any group discussion can follow the twos/fours/eights pattern: a friendship pair start off by talking to one another, then join another pair to share their thoughts and conclusions, then another foursome. Becoming an expert on a particular topic and passing on knowledge to younger classes or other visitors will often help the reluctant talker to gain in confidence. The jigsaw group work pattern described in Chapter 3 is another way of casting quiet children in an expert role. And again, opportunities to take part *in role* in a group – behind a puppet or a mask as part of a group-composed story, or in drama – can free a child from the constraints of self-consciousness and allow them to use language with a new freedom.

Speech difficulties

Speech and language therapists draw a distinction between what they call *language* difficulties (where children have difficulty in understanding spoken language or expressing themselves in appropriate grammatical structures and vocabulary), and difficulties that are confined to *speech* or *phonology* (articulating sound and words). Speech difficulties are in a sense easier for teachers to deal with than language difficulties, in that the problem is immediately evident, and very often short-term: relatively few children who start school with unclear speech are still unintelligible by the time they are 6 or 7. In another sense, however, speech difficulties are harder for teachers to manage: they feel immediately very concerned if they are unable to grasp what the child is saying, unsure of whether or how to correct the child's speech, and aware that the child may react to not being understood by withdrawing or exhibiting frustrated, angry behaviour.

Many of these difficulties can be avoided by using particular strategies:

- Encouraging the child to use gesture, drawings or showing a picture from a display or a book to help with communication.
- Trying to make time to offer several versions of what the child might be saying.
- Trying not to get into the habit of asking the child questions that can be answered with yes or no. Instead use forced alternatives – for example, 'Did you go by bus or in the car?'
- Correcting speech by repeating back what the child has said – for example, if they say 'It lellow', say 'Oh, it's yellow, I see'.
- Keeping a home–school diary so that the teacher knows what the child is trying to say about events at home, and the parents know what the child is saying about events at school.

- Making plenty of opportunities for the child to talk to the teacher over a shared experience; when both are doing the same thing the child's meaning will be clearer and they will be able to feel that they are being 'understood'. Examples are the teacher joining in a pretend game, or joint story composition in shared and guided writing.
- Speaking slowly and clearly to the child, so that they will be able to see and hear the sounds being made.

It will be sensible to have the child's hearing checked regularly, particularly if they are prone to colds and catarrh. In addition, advice on how to help the child achieve clearer speech should be sought from the speech and language therapist. The therapist is likely to emphasize developing listening and discrimination skills before moving on to work on specific sound production.

Some children with unclear speech may be later in learning to read and write than other children, but not all. As long as they are never put into a situation of failure by being expected to read aloud *to* an anxious or impatient adult before they are ready there is no need to postpone ordinary early literacy activities. Shared or paired reading at home and at school, particularly of familiar and frequently repeated stories, and making books that build on the child's own language in conjunction with photographs and drawings, are likely to be helpful to children with all kinds of expressive language problems. Nor is there necessarily any need to avoid the teaching of sound–symbol relationships: indeed, since many children with speech difficulties have the kind of poor phonological awareness of sound patterns in spoken words that is implicated in many cases of severe and persistent reading difficulty (Bryant and Bradley 1985), there may be even more need than usual to include in their early teaching a wide range of activities to promote phonological awareness and mastery of sound-symbol links. Such activities will be described later in this chapter.

Within the literacy hour itself, work on rhyme, segmenting words into sounds and blending sounds into words will all help the child with a speech difficulty. Tasks may need to be modified slightly, however. If, for example, other children are being asked to generate rhyming words, the child with a speech difficulty might start with very simple words with no initial, or else no final consonants (words like 'see', 'it', 'go'). Or the child might be asked to answer yes/no questions ('Does tea rhyme with see?') rather than generate rhymes. When it comes to segmenting and blending, it may be better to start with the 'long' sounds (sss, fff, mmm) which are easier to hear and blend than sounds like d, g, or b, and again use words with two phonemes (sea, am, if) rather than three. Instead of asking for a spoken response, the teacher can use pictures – for example, asking the child to point to one of a selection of pictures for a word they are blending, rather than saying the word itself.

Developing receptive language

Children who do not seem able to listen to, understand or remember what is said to them are harder to spot than those with expressive language difficulties, but are often even more disadvantaged in making progress within the whole curriculum.

Receptive language difficulties can arise because the children are following a normal course of language development but at a slightly slower rate than their peers – perhaps because of the quality of the language they have experienced in the past, or perhaps because of a family pattern of language delay. Or they may have fallen behind in their language because they have had a period of hearing loss: even minor, fluctuating losses caused by repeated ear infections or intermittent catarrh can have long-lasting effects on a child's developing vocabulary and listening skills. A very small group may have a very specific language disorder, which means they are more than just a bit late in understanding complex language: they are actually developing differently and can have major problems in making sense of what they hear.

The teacher's main task for any child with comprehension difficulties, however caused, is to make sure that messages are getting across in the classroom so that the children are not at a loss in learning from the start because they do not understand what they are supposed to do, or how they are supposed to go about it. It may help to:

- Get the child's attention. Before you speak, call the child's name, make sure they are standing still and looking, or give a signal like 'Listen carefully'. Give directions before, not during, an activity.
- Avoid speaking out of the blue and out of context: try to establish a background to the conversation so that the child will be cued in from the start.
- Go up close to the child to speak, rather than talk across a busy classroom.
- Place the child in a position where they can pick up what is happening by watching the other children, but also where the teacher can easily keep a look out to see if they have understood.
- Say it again – give the child time to respond and then, if necessary, repeat what you said *in the same words*, as rephrasing may only confuse.
- Use pictures, demonstration and gesture to help get a point across.
- Use visual summaries of discussions, like spider diagrams.
- Break long and complicated questions or instructions into shorter units – for example, convert 'When you've coloured the stars cut them out and stick them on the black paper' into 'Colour the stars. Cut them out. Then stick them onto the black paper' or 'Show me the long red pencils' into 'Show me the pencils. Show me the long pencils. Now show me the long, red pencils'.
- Put the main message last. Make sure that the important parts of a message are at the end: not 'Fetch your PE bags; you'll need to take them with you to the hall straight after our television programme' but 'After the television programme, you're going straight to the hall, so fetch your PE bags now'.
- Check for understanding by asking the child to explain to you what they've been asked to do, and watch them start any new task. Give praise whenever the child asks for an instruction to be repeated or explained.
- Watch your words. Always ask yourself if the child is actually understanding words you use – for example, in maths work do they know what 'each side of', 'altogether', 'larger number', 'the number before . . . after . . .' mean? Be consistent with the vocabulary you use, and make sure there are visible reminders, such as wall charts of key vocabulary.

- Let the child's friends help. When you are busy, appoint a friend to repeat instructions and if necessary demonstrate the task.
- Be prepared for bad behaviour if the child has to spend a long time listening to language they cannot understand. When you can, give them another task during long assemblies and stories. When you cannot, warn the child of the need to sit still and be ready with a small reward – like a gold star – if they succeed. Try if possible to have a helper or parent go over a shared text or tell a story to the child by themselves, or in a small group, before they are expected to listen in the whole-class situation.

To help develop children's ability to respond to stories and poems, to listen in a group and follow instructions, teachers might want to consider setting up a small language group, made up of children with receptive language difficulties, who work with a volunteer helper or teaching assistant for a short period each day, as did St Agnes Primary School:

> The Reception teacher described her main difficulty with the class as 'getting them to sit still and listen'. There were several children whose attention span was short, who seemed oblivious to classroom instructions (despite normal hearing), and unable to participate in group discussion of any kind. With the help of a visiting support teacher, she worked out a programme of listening games and activities which her very good teaching assistant was able to do for 10–15 minutes most days over an eight-week period. Work started with very simple activities: listening to a tape of sounds the children might hear in the house and identifying them, listening with eyes shut to various musical instruments and picking out the one that was played, playing the game called 'Keys to the Kingdom' where keys are passed round a circle with one child blindfolded in the centre trying to point to where they think the keys might be. Each session ended with a short story told or read to the group.
>
> Over the next few weeks, games with words were introduced. The children played a shopping game with grocery packets, responding to and giving one another instructions to 'buy' two, three or four items. They played 'Simon Says'; they passed whispered messages around the group and enjoyed the ever-popular Smarties game: the helper would drop three or four coloured Smarties into a tube, saying each colour as it went in, and the child would have to remember and replicate the order with their own tube in order to get to eat the contents. They played 'Eligibility': 'Stand up everyone who is wearing grey socks', 'Stand up everyone who is wearing grey socks and has long hair'. In their special story time, they now had to listen for deliberate mistakes, or spot target names or words whenever they cropped up in the story.
>
> Finally, the group went on to games like 'Kim's game' (with words rather than objects), to following sequences of instructions in order to build a model or complete a drawing, and to listening to each other recount news. At this stage they were able to listen to some stories without many pictures, and begin to be able to predict outcomes and discuss events and characters.

For schools that have listening centres, there is a good range of listening skills/language comprehension materials on cassette, from publishers such as LDA and Learning Materials Ltd. Teachers can also make their own short tape recordings relating to duplicated pictures ('On your picture you will see a row of houses. Colour the first door red. Now find the largest window and give it some frilly pink curtains'), things to draw ('Draw a round pond. Then put some water lilies on the pond, and some reeds all around the outside'), or constructional materials ('Make a wall two bricks high out of green Lego bricks. At one end add a square tower of red bricks'). There should always be a model ('Here's one I made earlier . . .') so that children can check their success in following the tape.

Remembering instructions and information: problems in short-term memory

In older children, the most restricting legacy of earlier language difficulties is often poor short-term memory for things they hear. Each of us has only a limited capacity for taking in and remembering information while we process it – either by acting on it immediately or transferring it to our more permanent long-term memory. For many children with SEN, instructions all too often exceed the limits of what can be remembered; their capacity may be smaller than that of their peers, or their strategies for rehearsing information within the short-term memory store to keep it available may be less well developed. Research (Gathercole and Pickering 2001) has shown that impairments in short-term or 'working' memory are extremely common in children identified by their teachers as having SEN, whatever the nature of their particular special needs.

The easiest way to assess short-term memory is to ask the child to repeat either strings of digits (at a rate of about one per second), or short sentences. The average 4-year-old can recall three digits in correct sequence, or a sentence containing 10 syllables. The average 5-year-old can recall four numbers and a sentence of 12 syllables or longer; the average 6- to 7-year-old recalls five numbers and the average 8- to 9-year-old six or more numbers.

Children with poor short-term memories can also be spotted by their difficulties in following instructions and organizing themselves for learning. Given an instruction about several tasks they have to complete during the day, they may forget all or part of it; they may also find it hard to hold a sequence of events in mind, so that they constantly forget to bring their swimming kit on the right day, or always appear at the wrong place at the wrong time with the wrong equipment. Their written work, relying as it does on the child holding an overall plan and the parts they have already written in short-term memory, may appear disjointed and disorganized. They may seem, often wrongly, like all-round slow learners, because what the teacher says does not stick in their minds for long enough to make the necessary transfer to long-term memory.

With the right bypass strategies, however, many of these difficulties can be overcome. The first essential is for the teacher to adjust the complexity of their language when giving instructions. It is surprising how complex, in terms of memory load, is much of the language we use in school. A recent five-minute sample in a Reception/Year 1 class in an infant school yielded the following examples:

> 'When you come in from washing your hands you should sit at the back not the front because if you sit right at the front all the others have to climb over you to find somewhere to sit.'

> 'Now, tomorrow or maybe the day after that depending on whether the weather's good and we have sports day we'll ask the juniors to write some prayers for us to say at our assembly.'

Shorter, simpler instructions are one way round the problem of memory overload; the teacher should be prepared to highlight key points, sequence the items clearly and avoid excess verbiage that will only serve to confuse the issue. When children are able to read reasonably well, key points can be written down on a postcard or Post-it and attached to their desk; for younger children a series of drawings might be substituted. Another approach is to give children with poor organizational skills a special diary, with each page divided into sections; to begin with the teacher writes just one task in one section, having them bring the diary and their work back when this is complete, so that the teacher can write the next instruction. The teacher then slowly builds up the number of sections filled in at the start of the day, until within a few weeks the child is using the diary to help them organize and sequence an entire morning's work.

For writing, using a story planner sheet at the planning stage helps get over the problem of the child not being able to hold the whole story in mind as they write; some children have also had success by tape-recording their whole story, then playing it back bit by bit in order to write it down.

Short-term memory can be improved, for example by regular practice in taking messages and playing memory games like 'I went to market and bought . . .' or 'I'm going on a trip; in my suitcase I put . . .', where each child repeats the preceding items and adds one of their own. Some children may benefit from an intensive memory training 'course', such as *Mastering Memory* or *Acceleread, AcceleWrite*, both of which are effective but require one-to-one support.

Despite all this, to some extent, limited memory capacity is something children and teachers have to learn to live with; the challenge is to help children find their own independent ways around the problem – like always carrying a notebook and pen to jot down instructions and make lists of things to do, or learning to repeat instructions to themselves over and over again as they go to carry them out, or being very organized about checking calendars and timetables carefully when sorting out equipment that is needed for school.

Curriculum access for children with communication difficulties

So far we have looked at ways in which teachers can use bypass strategies to help children with difficulties in understanding and remembering complex language to access the curriculum – mainly by adjusting the way they them-selves talk to individuals or groups in the class.

The important principle in all this is that children should not be held back by language barriers from getting to grips with the curriculum. For example, in maths they should not be prevented from exploring division operations because they do not understand the meaning of the word 'each' in problems of the kind, 'How many can they have each?'; in science they should not be prevented from exploring the properties of objects because they have not yet mastered negatives and do not understand the question, 'Which ones will *not* float/keep out water/get hot in the sun?'; in history they should not be kept from appreciating a sequence of events because they have not grasped the language of 'before' and 'after'. There are always other ways of getting these concepts across, using language that all of the children will be able to understand.

Similarly, when it comes to expressing their own ideas – particularly in plenary sessions and assessment situations – it is important that children are not disadvantaged by linguistic constraints. Often we ask children to use language to 'group', 'compare', 'describe' and 'discuss': all activities which will penalize some children, unless their teachers remember that there are multiple ways in which children can convey what they know: not only talk or writing, but also pictures, models, posters, drama, holding up sentence cards and so on. Children with language difficulties should be encouraged, whenever possible, to develop an oral response when one is required by using pictures and props to aid their talk, and by practising first with a 'talking partner'.

Playing with language: awareness of sounds in words

A final aspect of work on special needs in language concerns the auditory skill of awareness of sound patterns in words that underpins successful devel-opment in reading and spelling. Many young children with language diffi-culties have problems in this area. They are uncertain when words sound the same: when they begin (alliteration) or end (rhyme) with the same sound. They may not realize, for example, that a word like 'cat' is made up not of one sound but of several, or that it has something at the beginning that sounds like the start of 'cup' and something at the end in common with 'bat' and 'rat'. Without this kind of awareness they are unable later on to segment words into their component sounds, and accurately map written symbols against their spoken equivalents. They go on, as much research has now demonstrated (Goswami and Bryant 1990; Share 1995), to do less well in literacy development than their peers.

Again, this is a pattern that is preventable, given appropriate intervention in the early years of school. Research (Bryant and Bradley 1985) has shown that even small amounts of special practice with rhyme and alliteration in relation to letter patterns, for children initially assessed as having poor phonological skills, appears to produce substantial and long-lasting gains in later measured literacy skills. In these studies, 5- and 6-year-old children who were initially poor at picking the 'odd one out' of groups of spoken words by rhyme or initial sound were given six to ten hours of training in these skills,

---

Box 10.1 Checklist for identifying children with little awareness of alliteration and rhyme

1 Can think of a word to complete an unfamiliar rhyme
2 Can identify a part of their body that rhymes with
    peg   sand   rose
    or pick an object from a group supplied that rhymes with an object picked from a feely bag
3 Responds with understanding to wordplay such as deliberate errors in familiar rhymes, e.g.
    Little Miss Muffet   *Old King Cole*
    Sat on a chair   *Was a merry old* man
4 Can succeed in a group lotto game where each child covers pictures that start the same as the one the teacher holds up
5 Can join in, correctly, a game of initial sound 'I Spy' using objects placed in front of the group
6 Can line up on the basis of alliteration – 'all those whose name starts like *Rhinoceros*'

---

spread out over two years. At the end of this training they were on average in reading 10 months ahead of children who had had extra individual attention but not specifically rhyme and alliteration work. In spelling they were 17 months ahead. What is more, these initial gains seem to be maintained over long periods: four years after the training ended, the children who had the special teaching were approximately two years ahead of the control group in reading, and at least 14 months ahead in spelling.

To reproduce these effects, teachers can use a simple checklist (like the one in Box 10.1, or those provided in NLS materials) to pick out those children in infant classes who have poor awareness of sound patterns in words. These children will need a rich diet of rhymes and wordplay – everything from alliterative alphabet books to nursery rhymes, counting rhymes and finger rhymes – for sharing at home. Parent workshops might also include sorting or spotting games with objects and pictures, where children are helped to find the ones that start with the same sound, and traditional games like 'I Spy', or 'I'm thinking of something in the room that rhymes with . . .'.

In school, there should be time spent on class projects on rhyme and wordplay. Children will enjoy creating their own class rhyming slang to baffle visitors, or composing tongue-twisters and limericks. Much exciting work can be built around tape-recorded and written compilations of playground rhymes, from other generations as well as current favourites.

Class books can be made based on alliteration of the children's names ('Laura likes lollipops, Surinda likes sweets'). Children can play circle games – for example, all thinking of a word beginning with 's' in a particular category like food, or all the children's names they can think of beginning with a particular phoneme. Feely bags with collections of objects that start the same, or rhyme, are good to feel and guess at. Many other traditional games, such as snap, or grandmother's footsteps ('Take two steps forward if you can say a word that rhymes with bed') can be adapted to rhyme and alliteration. Children can alter well-known songs and rhymes in the manner of 'Happy birthday to you, Squashed tomatoes and stew'. They can swap initial sounds around in jokes and riddles ('What do you get if you cross a labrador and a poodle – a pabrador and a loodle'), and illustrate the results. They can experiment with taking away initial sounds on a day when every-one has to address each other by name with the first sound deleted – 'om' for Tom, 'iss' for miss. They can work in groups with a set of pictures in the middle: one child says the name of a picture sound by sound and the others have to guess which one they mean.

Good sources of ideas for developing phonological awareness are to be found in NLS materials: the original training 'lunchbox', *Progression in Phonics* and the early literacy support activities. Also useful are the work of Layton *et al.* (1997), and commercial materials such as *Sound Beginnings* from LDA, the Oxford Reading Tree *Rhyme and Analogy* material and *Launch Into Reading Success* from the Psychological Corporation.

As a result of activities like these, children should be able to analyse the spoken sounds that make up words they hear, tell when words start the same, or when they rhyme, and categorize picture cards accordingly. It only remains to help them make the links with written symbols, in the manner of Bryant and Bradley's original (1985) research: the teacher or helper puts out plastic letters to make one of the words in a rhyming or alliterative set and asks the child to choose another picture and make the word themselves. Initially the child will sweep away all of the letters of the first word and start afresh; over time they learn, for example, that the plastic letter 'p' can stay in place for a set of words like 'pen', 'pig' or 'pot', or the 'all' letter string stay in place with only the first letter changing in rhyming words such as 'ball', 'fall', 'call'. In this way, the child discovers some of the principles that underlie the way written language works: their difficulties in oral language become less likely to spill over into the kind of long-lasting literacy difficult-ies that are the subject of the next two chapters.

11 Special needs in reading

Introduction

Paul and Daniel are both 9 years old. Both struggle with reading and written recording, though they are both as bright as most children their age, and in some areas (technology, science) are more able. They go to different schools. Paul is lucky. In his school, there is a part-time special needs support teacher, funded from the school's own budget, who works with him for half an hour each day, four days a week (sometimes within the Literacy Hour, sometimes outside it), on a carefully planned programme which mixes reading lots of exciting books with learning letter–sound relationships in a highly structured and cumulative way. The support teacher also works closely with Paul's class teacher to make sure that he has help with texts and written recording in his class work.

Daniel is not so lucky. His teacher feels that he is 'just a slow learner', and that he perhaps hasn't learned to read because of lack of support from home. She tries very hard to give him extra help by giving him some time with the teaching assistant who is sometimes available to support the class in the Literacy Hour. However, she is unsure how to match work to his level when he is so far behind the others. He seems to be switching off more and more from any effort to improve his skills. Increasingly, he is unable to participate in ordinary classroom work because he cannot read information books or instructions.

These two children are typical of many with literacy difficulties. The outcome for each of them, in terms of future educational success and post-school opportunities, is likely to be very different: the inequities are stark, but not at all unusual. That they persist is a scandalous indictment of our educational system, which fails to fund the kind of provision that we know could prevent the misery of long-term reading failure.

Literacy difficulties are very common. Nationally, 1 in 20 children fail to achieve even a Level 2 in English SATs at the end of Key Stage 2: enough to mean that most primary teachers will have at least one or two children in their class who are unable to read and write well enough to cope with the most basic curricular demands. What is more, the great majority of these children are of perfectly ordinary general ability, and not particularly 'backward' or slow learning: they have difficulties that are *specific to literacy*. In other subjects they can do well – although all too often their difficulty with texts prevents them achieving their potential. What do ordinary classroom teachers need to know about teaching these children? First, it is important that they be aware of the high frequency of specific literacy difficulties, and that they take care to avoid any assumption that poor readers necessarily need a slower pace to all their learning than children who pick up reading and writing quickly. Instead, the children may only need access to the kinds of bypass strategies that will be detailed later in this chapter: strategies that will make sure they can still get on with their work and have a chance to succeed despite their problems in coping with texts.

Second, every class teacher needs to be able to work out an action plan for teaching the child to read and write, using the NLS objectives as the framework, and using strategies which have a track record of evaluation behind them. These effective, proven strategies fall into four broad groups, which we will consider in more detail later in the chapter:

- those aimed at increasing the child's contact with print;
- those aimed at extending the number of channels through which the child can learn to read;
- those aimed at ensuring over-learning of core sight vocabulary and letter–sound relationships;
- those aimed at increasing the learner's self-esteem and overcoming the anxiety and loss of confidence that often accompanies reading failure.

Finally, the class teacher needs to be able to make a careful assessment of children's literacy skills, and monitor closely the outcomes of any intervention. Such assessment and monitoring has become easier as a result of the NLS framework, with its carefully sequenced objectives, which are as useful for placing individual children on appropriate programmes as they are for class planning.

Assessing reading difficulties

The basic tool for assessing children's word, sentence and text level skills is miscue analysis. Here the teacher analyses the child's errors or 'miscues' when reading aloud, in order to discover which of the cueing strategies or 'searchlights' used by a fluent reader (visual, phonic, meaning and grammatical) the child is able to apply when they meet an unknown word. The analysis will show whether the child is an 'overpredictive' or an 'underpredictive' reader. Overpredictive readers are good at inventing what they think the words should say (using meaning and grammatical cues), but not at checking their predictions against the graphic cues on the page. They appear fluent, but are often wildly inaccurate. They need to have their attention directed, when reading aloud, to initial and final letters, letter strings and word length – anything that will encourage them to focus on visual detail. Underpredictive readers (a larger group) need the opposite kind of support. They tend to read word by word, with little expression, sounding out words a letter at a time when they come to them and paying little attention to the overall meaning. They need to do a lot of talking about what they are reading, to listen to books on cassette and to tapes of themselves reading, to engage in oral cloze work using context and first letter to predict words the teacher leaves out, to read back passages and always ask 'Did that make sense?'

Miscue analysis needs to be supplemented, for the purpose of establishing appropriate readability levels for texts the child is asked to cope with in class, and for the purpose of monitoring progress, with a norm-referenced assessment that will yield a measure of reading age. Several of the more up-to-date assessment tools (such as NFER's *Individual Reading Analysis*) incorporate both miscue analysis and an assessment of the child's overall reading level. They take only about 5 to 15 minutes to administer and fall comfortably into the province of the classroom teacher rather than the SENCO or reading 'specialist'. They have the additional advantage of providing separate scores for the child's decoding and comprehension skills, enabling the teacher to pick out those children who may be expert at decoding but have no idea what they are reading about, or those, conversely, who have good enough language skills to get the general gist of texts even though they have a very limited sight vocabulary and stumble over almost every word.

Other straightforward assessment tools available to the classroom teacher include the NLS lists of high-frequency sight words, and lists of regular words exhibiting the main phonic conventions – from three-letter consonant–vowel–consonant words to consonant clusters, vowel digraphs, silent e, silent initial letters and prefixes/suffixes. A recent publication from LDA (Gross *et al.* 2000) provides a complete toolkit of materials which teachers can use to assess exactly where children are on the NLS framework objectives – across all three strands of word-, sentence- and text-level work.

Using tools like these, the teacher will be able to establish which of the small steps on the road to fluent decoding the child has mastered, and what the next steps in the teaching programme might be – whether improved use of a particular cueing system, or a new set of high-frequency words to be practised, or a new phonic convention introduced.

Beyond the assessment of reading age, use of cueing systems and sight vocabulary/phonic skills, we enter the realms of 'diagnostic' assessment, to which a great deal of (largely unnecessary) mystique has attached itself. The mystique has been based on an earlier assumption in the world of reading remediation that in order to construct an adequate teaching programme for children with reading difficulties it was necessary to establish their profile of strengths and weaknesses in underlying perceptual and memory skills – to diagnose the root cause of the reading failure in order to discover the appropriate remedy. This meant the use of elaborate packages of tests, based on complicated theories of the reading process, which many teachers found daunting.

As we saw in Chapter 4, however, research has failed as yet to support the effectiveness of this model. In its place, we can for the moment put a much simpler notion of 'diagnosis', based on the small steps idea. If a child seems unable to learn something, we can ask what are the necessary prior skills or sub-steps which make that piece of learning possible, and try to find out where in the chain the point of breakdown for a particular child might be.

As an example, it is no good expecting a child to acquire a sight vocabulary if they cannot yet reliably discriminate a word from others that may look quite similar. So if children are having difficulty in remembering words out of context, it would be useful to assess this level of visual discrimination by having them match individual words on cards with those in their reading books (particularly words with visually confusable letters like i/l, h/n, f/t, b/p/d, r/n and c/o/a), and introduce extra practice if necessary. It would also be useful to look for signs of visual sequencing difficulties: children who constantly lose their place on the page, skip lines or misread the order of letters in words may benefit from using a linetracker or visual tracking magnifier, and a brightly coloured card placed down the left-hand side of any page they are working on to act as a reference point for the left to right sequence. A referral for a full assessment of the child's vision (to include investigation of convergence, accommodation, tracking, binocular control and reference eye as well as the conventional tests of visual acuity) should also be considered.

If visual discrimination and sequencing are not the problem, the point of breakdown in acquiring a sight vocabulary may be further down the chain, at the level where the child has to remember what the words look like. Showing single words and asking the child to pick them out on a page from memory is one way of assessing this skill of visual recall, which if weak can sometimes be improved by giving practice in the look–cover–write–check strategy for learning spellings, or by asking the child to try to 'carry a picture' of a word in their head from a word bank, picture dictionary or piece of paper, while they go back to their seat rather than copy-write it directly.

So far we have looked at visual skills; for many children, however, the point of breakdown may lie elsewhere – in auditory skills. Since learning to decode printed words involves learning to match a pattern of written letters with a pattern of spoken sounds, children need to be able to discriminate and recall what they hear as well as what they see. They need to be able to detect similarities and differences between spoken sounds, to segment spoken words into their constituent parts (so as to be able to work out independently how these parts are represented in print), and to handle the opposite process of blending separate sounds and syllables into whole words.

Tests are available for assessing auditory discrimination (for example, in NFER's well-known *Neale Reading Analysis*), but more informally the teacher will be able to spot children with difficulties by the errors they make in reading and spelling – confusing similar-sounding pairs like d/t, m/n, k/g, p/b, a/u and e/i. If a child has very pronounced auditory discrimination problems, a hearing check should be requested, though more often than not the difficulty is one of central processing rather than peripheral 'hearing'. Children with poor auditory discrimination need to be helped to find ways around the problem, by learning for example to articulate the words very clearly to themselves as they write, by using visual mnemonics (the letter 'a' made to look like an apple, or the letter 'u' like an umbrella) to help them master the confusable short vowel phonemes, or moving on to learning the easier to discriminate long vowel phonemes even though they may not have fully mastered the short vowels.

Ways of assessing children's ability to segment words into their constituent phonemes, and to recognize when and how some words sound the same, were described in Chapter 10, along with strategies the teacher can use to help children improve their phonological awareness. For sound blending, the child can be asked to guess a word the teacher says slowly, sound by sound (at a rate of about one sound per second): i-n, u-p, l-i-p, b-a-g, etc. The aim is to find out whether the child can cope with blending two sounds, or three, or four: if less than three, there is little chance that they will be able to benefit from phonic teaching (beyond predicting words from their initial letter) without some extra practice. This can be achieved by having the child work with a helper to blend – at a purely oral level – short and then longer words they are about to meet in their reading books. Children can also be taught how to circumvent the difficulty by blending not separate sounds when reading but an initial and final letter string (f-ill, s-eat), or blending no more than two sounds at a time ('frog' as f-fr-fro-frog, for example).

The model of diagnostic assessment that is suggested here (summarized in Figure 11.1) does not pretend to be comprehensive. It is practically oriented, aiming to supply information on only those aspects of prior or underlying skill that are critical to the child's progress, and which we can actually do something about. If the model is applied to every child with a reading

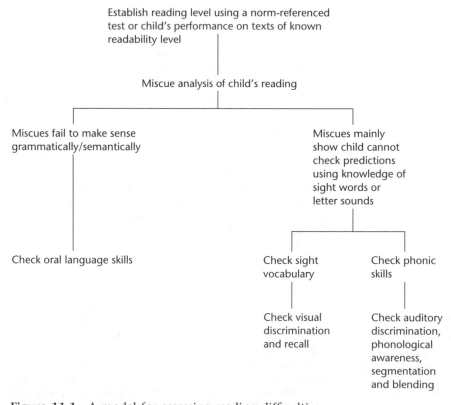

Establish reading level using a norm-referenced test or child's performance on texts of known readability level

Miscue analysis of child's reading

Miscues fail to make sense grammatically/semantically

Miscues mainly show child cannot check predictions using knowledge of sight words or letter sounds

Check oral language skills

Check sight vocabulary

Check phonic skills

Check visual discrimination and recall

Check auditory discrimination, phonological awareness, segmentation and blending

Figure 11.1   A model for assessing reading difficulties

difficulty it should, however, enable the class teacher – perhaps with a little help from the SENCO – to develop individualized teaching strategies that are more finely tuned than those required by the child who is making normal progress in reading.

Increasing the child's contact with print

The first of these individualized strategies will almost always need to include a plan to increase the amount of practice the child has in reading –that is, to increase their contact with print. This is because most children with literacy difficulties need to see a word far more often than other children do in order to remember it. Despite this, without deliberate intervention by the teacher they actually end up with *less* exposure to print than their peers. It has been shown, for example, that children making slow reading progress in their first year at school read only an estimated 5,000 words, compared to the 20,000 read by children who are making good progress (Clay 1979). In another study, Feiler and Webster (1998) found that struggling readers had significantly fewer entries in their home and school reading diaries than their classmates; as children get older, and the better readers begin to read for pleasure at home, the gap widens further (Juel 1988). The effects of reading failure thus rapidly become cumulative.

The Literacy Hour alone is not sufficient to redress the balance. Nor are other classroom or school-wide systems which aim to increase the amount of time spent on reading-related activities likely, of themselves, to do much to improve the skills of poor readers, even though they remain vital for fostering interest in and enjoyment of books. Poor readers lack sufficient decoding ability to be able to get to grips with texts alone. What they need is some form of regular, frequent *supported* reading practice.

It is unlikely that the class teacher, or even a support teacher, will be able to partner the child in supported reading with sufficient regularity and frequency to be worthwhile. Once a week guided reading will need to be supplemented with alternative ways of providing supported reading practice – peer tutoring, parental involvement, volunteer helper schemes and schemes that require no helper present at all, such as taped libraries and computer-aided reading.

Paired reading

One approach that offers children maximum exposure to print, with the chance to learn from a correct model, and read with as much or as little support as they feel they require, is paired reading (Topping and Wolfendale 1985). Not to be confused with the many other kinds of reading practice called shared, or shared-and-paired reading, paired reading 'proper' follows a particular, tightly structured format:

- Peer, parent or volunteer helper commit themselves to 10 or 15 minutes of reading with the child, preferably daily, for a fixed period (usually of about six to eight weeks).

- The child chooses the reading material, which can be anything at all that they want to read, however difficult.
- The helper and child begin by reading simultaneously, with the helper pointing to the words as they go along.
- When the child feels able to read a little on their own, they give an agreed signal, like a knock or a nudge, and the helper stops reading.
- The child reads alone until they make a mistake or get stuck. The helper then gives the correct word (not leaving the child to struggle with it for more than about five seconds); the child repeats it and the helper joins in again until the child next signals a wish to read independently.
- The helper praises the child frequently for reading words correctly and for signalling to read alone.

Paired reading has been extensively evaluated (Topping and Lindsay 1992); typically, children make progress in reading over the tutoring period at three or four times the normal classroom rate.

When done by older children for younger children, paired reading can also free the teacher for a short time each day to give additional group support to children with the greatest difficulties. A model for this is provided by Thompson (1992). In his school the bulk of children in the younger age groups (Years 2 and 3 children with reading ages over 7) read with an older (Year 6) partner for a quarter of an hour three times a week, while the children still at the very beginnings of literacy remained with their teacher for small-group work. All the children in the scheme made better than average reading progress; those who had the extra time in a small group with their own teacher made progress at twice the usual rate.

Apprenticeship approaches

Some researchers have questioned whether the formal structure of paired reading is a necessary ingredient in successful supported reading, and produced evidence to show that other more 'relaxed' approaches to reading together can be equally effective. Felicity Craig (1990) recommends immersing poor readers in good quality children's books, with the adult reading *to* the child (preferably daily) for about 15 minutes, encouraging the child to follow the print by running a pencil or finger under the words, then stopping for the child to read back a particularly exciting couple of paragraphs aloud: if the child gets stuck on a word it should be supplied after five seconds or so, with no attempt to make them 'work it out'. Again, there is an emphasis on frequent, enthusiastic praise.

In other approaches the child and helper can alternate pages, or paragraphs, or the child can engage in 'repeated reads' (Reason and Boote 1995): first the peer or helper reads a page or short piece to the child, then child and helper read it simultaneously, then the child reads it with prompts where necessary, and then (if the child would enjoy sharing the book with others), they read it to parents, or siblings, or a partner in a younger class, or to a friend.

The essential element in all these approaches is the absence of any possibility of failure, or of any element of performance or being on show – that is, until the child feels really ready for it. The aim is to get through as many exciting books as possible, quickly and enjoyably, rather than struggle painfully through a reading book. Other elements may well be needed in the total reading programme, to provide perhaps more opportunities for over-learning of a key sight vocabulary, or explicit teaching of sound-symbol relationships, but supported reading in one form or another, *in quantity*, is the very first thing to try, and the one essential that must run alongside any other type of programme, so that the child (and teacher) don't lose sight of what real reading is all about.

Books on tape or CD-ROM

Sitting in the book corner or at the listening centre and following text that has been put onto cassette lacks the interactive element of sharing pleasure in a good book. Nevertheless, when human help is limited, it can be an effective alternative means of providing supported reading practice. In one project (Dring 1989), for example, pupils who had regular story cassette input (while following the print at the same time) made twice as much progress in reading as children who also had extra small-group language support with a special needs teacher, but without the extra practice with tapes.

Providing a cassette library need not be expensive or time consuming for the teacher. Having older, more fluent readers work in groups to prepare the tapes will give them practice in reading for a purpose, and in research and design as they experiment with, for example, appropriate reading speeds and end-of-page pauses. It will also, if some of the tapes they prepare are not story tapes but tapes of reference materials, have the added bonus of increasing curriculum access in science and humanities for children with reading difficulties throughout the school.

CD-ROMs can provide a motivating way of increasing contact with print, which are also more interactive than taped books. More and more publishers are presenting texts with an associated speech synthesizer to 'say' any word that the child points to with the mouse, often with a range of back-up activities to help the child explore the text as well as 'read' it. Ones to look out for include Sherston's Talking Books, Oxford Reading Tree's Talking Stories, SEMERC/Nelson Thorne's Sound Start, Broderbund's Living Books and Carron's Electronic Library.

Extending the number of channels through which the child can learn to read

The debate about the 'best' way to teach reading has often ignored the wealth of evidence that children acquire reading skills in many different ways, using different channels for their learning. Some use their good oral language skills to make maximum use of prediction from context; some apply their good phonological awareness to pick up an early extensive knowledge of letter–sound relationships; some have little need of phonic skills because they have such good visual recall that they only have to be told a word once to remember it.

Children with literacy difficulties may have problems in any or all of these areas. Many struggle with the visual memory element: perhaps, it is increasingly thought, because they perceive the words in a shifting, unstable fashion, with the letters of a word arriving at their processing system all at once instead of in a sequential, stable form. This means that one word – like 'felt', for example – may look like a mixture of 'left', 'flet', 'telf' and so on; many different visual patterns have to be attached to the corresponding spoken word rather than just one. These children may need much more exposure to a word before they remember it than those with neat, sequential, left-hemispheric perceptions.

We know that very many children with reading difficulties have poor phonological awareness. They are unable to deduce for themselves, without help, the relationships between written letter strings and spoken sound patterns, because they do not perceive the commonalities of sound that are the foundation of the written code.

Some unlucky children appear to have poor phonological awareness and an absolute inability to remember what words look like. For them, the outlook can be grim, even with consistent extra help.

One day it may be possible to accurately assess each individual child's cognitive profile and match teaching strategies to the learning channels from which they are most able to profit. Some useful work has already been done in this direction, for example a computerized screening program for dyslexia. At the moment, however, our knowledge is too inexact to make such individual programs really useful to the classroom teacher. What the class teacher *can* do, however, is make sure that the child's reading programme makes use of all the available learning channels, so that they can make use of strengths and circumvent weaknesses, rather than being constrained by one method that does not suit them. This means going beyond the kind of extensive contact with print that we looked at in the last section (since this relies almost exclusively on visual and sequential channels), to working, through the auditory channel, on sound–symbol relationships and even – for the small minority of children with poor auditory *and* poor visual skills – use of the kinaesthetic channel: learning words, via tracing and writing, as patterns of movement.

Using the auditory channel

With the many children whose sight vocabulary grows only very slowly, and who characteristically 'can read a word one minute and forget it the next', it is essential to tap the auditory learning channel and to teach them to make good use of sound–symbol relationships for cueing unfamiliar or forgotten words. If assessment shows that they have a good auditory awareness of the sound patterns in spoken words, all the more reason to focus on phonic skills; if it shows they have difficulties in auditory perception, then there will need to be work (of the kind described in Chapter 10) on phonological awareness alongside the teaching of letter–sound relationships.

Most teachers will by now be familiar with the NLS group-based early literacy support and additional literacy support materials used to help children catch up on phonic skills; also well worth considering is using Phonographix, a complete scheme suitable for children of any age, which teaches letter sounds in carefully thought out groups alongside extensive practice in splitting words into their component sounds and in blending. THRASS (teaching handwriting, reading and spelling skills) is another widely used structured approach to phonics, particularly suitable for use in Key Stage 2.

Using short periods of daily practice and materials like these, there is no reason why any child cannot learn all the main phoneme–grapheme relationships in a relatively short time. As all teachers of reading know, however, mastery of sound–symbol relationships is no guarantee that the child will actually make use of them when reading. There is evidence (Adams 1990) that children's willingness to use phonic cues is a direct function of the success they experience with them early on in their learning: if they are exposed to books with a high proportion of phonetically regular words they are more likely to go on later to apply their phonic knowledge than if they are exposed mainly to phonetically irregular text. For this reason, it is essential to spend time modelling the use of phonic word attack skills in shared reading time, and making sure that the child is exposed in their own reading to plenty of appropriate texts. Such texts tended in the past to be stilted and contrived, but with the advent of pattern, rhyme and analogy strands in all the major schemes, the teacher now has a wide choice of lively, natural text which stresses sound–symbol regularities.

Structured multisensory approaches

Recognizing that children with literacy problems often need to bring all their senses into play when learning to read, teachers in the specific learning difficulties world have traditionally relied heavily on a range of off-the-peg approaches collectively called 'multisensory'. In these approaches, sound–symbol relationships and irregular sight words are taught in a set order, and learning involves seeing a word or letter, saying it, hearing it, speaking it and – importantly – *feeling* it, either by tracing or writing.

The approaches include the Kathleen Hickey method (Hickey 1992), Units of Sound on CD-ROM, Beve Hornsby's *Alpha to Omega*, and Keda Cowling's *Toe by Toe*. All ideally require about two hours of individualized teaching a week (although group programmes, such as the multisensory teaching system devised by a team at Manchester Metropolitan University, are also now available), and a teacher or teaching assistant who is thoroughly familiar with the materials. Given these conditions, good progress is reported. Whereas children with specific learning difficulties who have only regular classroom teaching and no special help with their reading have been found to fall progressively further and further behind their peers, making on average only 5 months' progress in reading age in the space of a year (Thomson 1989), those who do get help in the form of a structured multisensory teaching programme can make better than average progress, of the order of 18 to 24 months per year (Thomson 1989; Hornsby and Farrer 1990).

Teachers can devise their own multisensory programmes to fit into the Literacy Hour. Margaret Hunt and Jennie George (1999) describe a five-step programme of group activities, suitable for the independent and group work phase of the hour, which can be used with any reading scheme aimed at struggling readers.

Ensuring over-learning

As well as increasing contact with print, and making sure that any approach used is multi-channel rather than single channel, there is a need with almost all children with reading difficulties to build in an element of 'over-learning' into the reading programme – that is, constantly repeating variations on the same material over and over again so that the knowledge and skills become automatic and resistant to forgetting.

Parents and teachers often find it infuriating that poor readers seem to know a word one minute, but not when they meet it further down the page or the next day. They may blame forgetfulness or laziness, or put it down to inattention; the myth of 'he could do it if he tried' stems from this character- istic pattern of inconsistent recall. In fact, however, adults can recognize the same pattern of inconsistency in themselves, if they think back to the early stages of learning any new skill – like learning to drive. When skills are new, and not 'over-learned' to the point of automaticity, performance is erratic: competent one minute and chaotic the next. The harder the learner tries, and the more tense they become, the more likely it is that things will be forgotten and mistakes made.

The remedy is practice, continued well past the point where the child seems to have mastered the new piece of learning. The challenge, for teachers of children with learning difficulties, is how to make the practice sufficiently motivating for them to want to persist.

Traditional reading schemes – especially those developed for the slower learner, such as *Fuzzbuzz* or *Wellington Square*, rely heavily on the principle of over-learning. A core vocabulary is visited and revisited throughout such schemes, and practised also through a range of supporting materials. Children do not forget earlier words or sound–symbol relationships because they keep on meeting them. Because they recognize the need for such built-in over- learning, many teachers' first step when confronted with a child with read- ing difficulties is to move them from less structured reading material onto a scheme or combination of schemes – often with good success.

Direct instruction programmes (such as those marketed by SRA – *Reading Mastery* for younger pupils and *Corrective Reading* for top juniors and the early secondary years) carry the principle of overlearning to its most extreme. These schemes use a short daily group reading lesson of a very formal nature: children chant new words and sounds together and read contrived texts around the group under tightly controlled conditions. Each new piece of learning builds on the last, and there is constant built-in repetition of every skill taught. A points system ensures pupil motivation. Preparation and plan- ning are minimized; the teacher works to a prescribed script.

The rigidity of direct instruction programmes, and their old-fashioned air, means that most teachers initially approach them with great suspicion. Those who get as far as trying them out often persist, however, when they find that the children enjoy the novel formality of the lessons, and that even the most switched-off do learn to read by these methods after years of failure. There is considerable hard research evidence to back up these teachers' experiences of success with direct instruction (for example, Somerville and Leach 1988; Byron 1991).

The advantage of direct instruction schemes is that they provide the teacher with a ready-made structure. Over-learning can be achieved without them, but it takes more work. The teacher needs to be prepared to keep an ongoing record of the child's mastery of key sight vocabulary and sound–symbol relationships, and to provide a range of games and worksheet-type activities to reinforce each learning step – such as those suggested in Rea Reason and Rene Boote's excellent *Helping Children with Reading and Writing* (1995). Children can trace or copy word strips from the books they have read and reread, cut them up, jumble and reassemble them, if necessary by matching them with the book. They can choose a part they liked from the story book to illustrate, add a caption or speech balloon with words they find and copy from the text, or read and illustrate captions and speech balloons the teacher supplies. They can cover up a word or phrase on a page with Blu-tack, then swap with a friend who has to work out what is underneath, and help each other order photocopied pages of favourite books. They can play board games, happy families, lotto or dominoes based on the core vocabulary or letter–sound links. They can test each other on sentence strips in pairs, trace words or letters on friends' backs for them to guess at, or go through a pack of single sounds or consonant clusters (with a clue word and picture on the back of each card) together on a daily basis. Or they can create sentences and clue pictures for a small number of hard-to-remember abstract high-frequency words, then test each other daily in pairs, at first with and later without the clue pictures. Research (Moran *et al.* 1996) suggests that this is a particularly effective way of learning key words, as long as it is the children who make up the sentences, not the teacher.

Another way in which children can obtain the necessary repetition and rehearsal is through work on the computer, using a mix of open-ended content-free software and (in small doses) programs of the drill and practice type. Word processing using a prepared concept keyboard overlay of words to be over-learned (taken from a book the child has enjoyed), or an on-screen grid from the very useful Clicker software, will provide repeated practice in reading and using a core vocabulary. The Talking Computer Program (also known as *Acceleread* or *Accelewrite*) allows children to use word processing alongside phonics-based practice to achieve substantial, well documented gains in literacy levels (Brooks 1998).

Most of the drill and practice type of programs are phonically based; they aim to increase the speed and fluency with which the child can apply newly-learned decoding skills by providing large amounts of individual, closely monitored practice. *HI-Spell* from Xavier provides a complete suite covering the whole range of phonic skills from single letter sounds to prefixes and suffixes. Other suitable programs come from Sherston (especially their *Talking Animated Alphabet*), White Space (*Wordshark*), Fisher Marriott (*Starspell 2001*) and Inclusive Technology (*GAMZ2*).

Increasing self-esteem

Wesley, at 7, was a non-reader: the only child of devoted parents, with a mother who ran a successful small business but had herself struggled with reading and writing throughout all her school years. Wesley's teachers found him a nuisance in class; he was restless, unable to work successfully in a group, and always coming to them to ask for one thing or another. His mother was desperately worried about him. He was beginning to show signs of reluctance to come to school, saying that other children called him names and wouldn't play with him. He refused to read with her at home, something he had once loved. One day, she found under the bed a card he had made for his father. It said 'To bad, best wisis from Welsy'. When she asked why he had never given it to his dad, he said it was because it was all wrong and his writing was no good. He was stupid (hadn't his teacher told him not 'to be so stupid' that same day, when he refused to go out to play?) and everyone else in the class could read and write except him.

Then Wesley got a new special teacher, who worked with him twice a week on his reading and written work. She could see straight away that his feelings about himself were very negative, and that there was little chance of him learning anything while he felt this way. Instead of asking him to read to her, or write, she worked with him on oral storytelling. Using her as a scribe, he began to produce stories that were astonishingly vivid and well thought out. He ought, his teacher told him, to write a proper book, a long story, for others to read. Together they began on a long project. In each session Wesley dictated a new chapter, which the teacher would type up on the computer later. Sometimes Wesley asked to type up some of his story himself. The book was produced, illustrated and shared around the school. The other children were impressed. The book was sent to publishers; several wrote back to Wesley to say how well he had done. These letters became reading material he would return to again and again. He began to read more, and read more fluently. After talking with his teacher, he also began to be able to say he 'just had a problem with remembering words', but there were many, many things he could do really well. This message was by now getting across to the other children too. Although he still had a long way to go in mastering the mechanical skills of reading and writing, Wesley was well on the way. He had begun to believe in himself.

Adults who take their own literacy for granted sometimes find it hard to get in touch with the feelings of the child who is struggling with reading, especially the extent to which failure in this one area can come to permeate their whole self-picture. It is because of this pervasive effect, perhaps, that interventions that work *only* at the level of raising the child's self-esteem can contribute significantly to improving reading skills (Lawrence 1973; Wooster and Leech 1982).

Combining skills-based approaches with planned work on raising self-esteem seems to work best of all: using interested, sympathetic adult listeners who showed that they valued the child in a series of regular meetings Lawrence (1988) showed enhanced gains in reading age for a group who had regular remedial help plus extra counselling sessions when compared with a group who had the remedial help only.

Many of the strategies to build self-esteem described in Chapter 9 can be relevant to children with reading difficulties, particularly if used to pave the way for later skills-based interventions. It will be important also to make sure that reading material looks sophisticated and not too childish: ICT and non-fiction can help here. Reward systems can be devised to record and celebrate progress – high-frequency words mastered, phonics learned, books read. But as with Wesley, the most significant possible boost to the self-esteem of the poor reader (or writer) is of course being told you are not, as you may have thought, stupid or slow or lazy: that you are, in fact, a perfectly able and acceptable person who just happens to have a specific difficulty with written words that is not in any way your own fault. This remains one of the main arguments for using emotionally warming labels like dyslexia with children and their parents, when a child is struggling to acquire literacy.

Current definitions of dyslexia are broad-based, for example: 'Dyslexia is evident when accurate and fluent word reading and/or spelling develops very incompletely or with great difficulty. This focuses on literacy learning at the "word level" and implies that the problem is severe and persistent despite appropriate learning opportunities' (British Psychological Society 1999). These definitions do not rely on proving a discrepancy between overall intelligence and reading or writing ability: research (for example, Brown *et al.* 1998) is increasingly showing that children across the ability range who experience literacy difficulties share common features (such as difficulties in phonolo-gical processing) and benefit from similar teaching approaches.

With this in mind, teachers do not need to rely on elaborate psychological assessments to diagnose dyslexia. The magical 'test' that will show whether a child is or is not dyslexic does not exist. Instead, they can themselves make judgements about whether a child has persistent difficulties with word-level work despite adequate instruction. They can also make use of a set of loose indicators, all research-based (see Box 11.1), which can help establish whether the child might lie somewhere on a continuum of dyslexic-type difficult-ies. And if they do appear to show many of these indicators and lie some-where on the dyslexia continuum, it seems sensible to try to explain this to both child and parents, so that the child can make a fresh start unburdened by whatever guilt or blame may have accumulated over years of failure. Using a checklist of indicators of dyslexia may also be helpful to the teacher when they want to evaluate the need to move towards a somewhat more structured teaching programme, with a strong multisensory element, for a child who seems to be making slower progress in literacy than others in the class.

Accessing the curriculum

The extent to which the teacher is able to raise the self-esteem of children with reading difficulties will often depend on their inventiveness in devising bypass strategies, which will make sure the child is able to succeed in the main body of the curriculum even though their performance within Eng-lish may be problematic. Too many children fall behind in areas they could otherwise do well in, simply because they can't read instructions, follow worksheets, use information books, cope with classroom notices or read what the teacher has put on the blackboard. Often they are afraid or embar-rassed to ask what things say – like Richard, aged 10 but with the reading

Box 11.1 Indicators of specific learning difficulties/dyslexia in the primary school

Early warning signs
- Child was a late talker, or speech not fully intelligible on starting school.
- Child had not fully established left- or right-handedness on starting school.
- There is a family history of reading or spelling problems.
- Child has poor ability to analyse or synthesize the sounds in words, e.g. cannot by 6–7 tell when words rhyme, blend three sounds of a word spoken to him/her at one per second, identify first and last sounds in a word s/he wants to write.
- Child has poor short-term memory – for example, for a series of instructions, or for a series of spoken digits (a child of 4 should be able to repeat three digits spoken at one per second; a child of nearly 6 should manage four digits).
- Child has difficulties in remembering the names for objects.
- There is a history of early clumsiness.

Indicators in children over 7–8
- Persisting letter and number reversals, particularly 'b/d' confusion.
- Inability to remember the 'look' of even short, common words; phonetic spelling which persists over 8–9 years – e.g. 'cum' for 'come', 'duw' for 'do', 'hav' for 'have', 'enuf' for 'enough', *or* in children with the most severe difficulties, spelling which bears little relation to either the look or the sound of the word.
- Persisting minor speech (e.g. 'w/r', 'f/th') or auditory discrimination difficulties (e.g. 'e/i' confusion).
- Difficulty in repeating unfamiliar polysyllabic words, e.g. preliminary, statistical, corollary.
- Letter sequence errors in reading of the 'was–saw', 'of–for', 'spot–stop' type.
- Poor auditory short-term memory: the average nine-year-old should be able to repeat four digits in reverse order, rising to five digits at 12 years.
- Problems in basic numeracy, though not so severe as in literacy: confusion of +, −, ×, ÷ signs, poor memory for number bonds and multiplication tables.
- Poor rote memory for sequential information such as the alphabet, days of the week, months of the year.

skills of a 6-year-old, who said: 'I can't always read what it says in my maths work; I do ask my friends but they get fed up if I keep on doing it. I ask Gareth most and he's OK but if he wants to get his own work done he tells me to shut up and leave him alone'.

For some children, it works well to quietly appoint a regular 'working partner' for them, who has explicit instructions to read words and supply spellings: it is necessary, though, to rotate the helper role so that no single child is overburdened. In other classrooms children are making use of new technology (the 'Quicktionary' pen), which will 'read' a word out loud when the pen is run over it.

Some really committed schools have used older children (reading for a purpose) to prepare a bank of tapes of the text of maths worksheets, and information books for the use of any child who wants support with the reading element. Other schools run regular checks on the readability levels of the materials each class is working from: using samples of text and a simple computer formula (Sawyer and Knight 1991), or a chart like the one in Figure 11.2, they can assess how well the materials are matched to individual children's needs. Even simpler as a readability measure is the so-called 'five finger exercise': the child is asked to put a finger on each word on a page

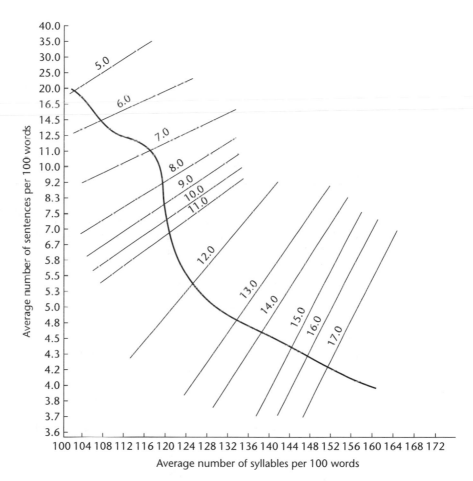

Figure 11.2 Assessing the readability level of text. (1) Choose random samples, each of 100 words. (2) Find average number of syllables, and average number of sentences per 100 words. (3) Plot on graph, and read off the readability level, the minimum reading age needed to understand the text (Fry 1972).

Box 11.2 Texts will be easier to read if the following apply

- Short sentences are substituted for long and complex ones
- Short words are substituted for long
- There is a word bank giving definitions of difficult words in a box at the end, and all the words in this word bank are underlined or written in bold type when they occur in the text
- Pictures, diagrams and flow charts are used to clarify the text
- Instructions are made to stand out clearly from the text – for example, by being put in boxes, or in a different typeface
- The layout looks uncluttered, with a wide border round the edge and not too much text on each page

An example of text modification might be:

Original text
Ammonites, aquatic creatures from the distant past, are frequently found as fossils. The fossils were formed when the shell of the ammonite became buried on the sea floor under the mud, which subsequently hardened around it.

Modified text
Ammonites lived under the sea long ago. When an ammonite died, its shell sank to the bottom of the sea. Mud buried (hid) it. The mud hardened (got hard) into rock around the shell. This made a fossil.

---

that they can't read – if the number exceeds the number of fingers, the text is likely to be too difficult to be read without support. If this is the case, then there are several ways of offering help. The teacher can have the children work in pairs, pairing the child with reading difficulties with a better reader. Alternatively the child can pair-read the text with a fluent partner before they work on it on their own. Or the text can be modified, ahead of time to make it easier to read (see Box 11.2).

Materials with several levels of readability can be prepared for the topics or schemes of work regularly used in a school; published materials that will be helpful here include Ginn's 'Sharp Eye' high interest level/low reading age information books, anthologies and stories (on common themes such as homes, myself, creatures, school and going places), and information books from Watts Publishing, the Longman Book Project and Wayland. A useful idea that is being taken up by more publishers is supplying books with audio-cassette as well as text versions, and the good range of CD-ROMs now available to support multimedia learning.

Accessing the Literacy Hour

The Literacy Hour structure has been helpful to children with reading difficulties, particularly because the shared text work in the first 15 minutes enables them to work at a text level above that which they can manage independently. The regularity of the hour, with its daily short bursts of focused teaching, followed by practice and reinforcement, provides ideal conditions for learning for all children with special needs; the training and guidance on quality teaching of word-level work means that all teachers are now developing the skills needed to teach children who need over-learning and need to learn through a range of channels.

Nevertheless, the Literacy Hour also presents many challenges for these children, where they are substantially 'out of step' with the teaching and learning objectives for the class as a whole. Planning is needed if they are to participate fully in class work, while at the same time pursuing the particular objectives appropriate to their needs.

During the shared text time, for example, the teacher may need to direct these children's attention to aspects of the text appropriate to their particular level, and pre-plan ways in which they can take an active role in the lesson – by asking them, for example, to frame a letter or word with a masking device, circle a capital letter, draw round a word or grapheme with a pen on an acetate overlay or hold and read a prepared question card. At the same time, the teacher should be able to give them opportunities to shine through their oral contribution to question and answer sessions, and through the ideas they can contribute to shared writing.

All children, no matter what their needs, should be able to participate in the shared text work. For the word-level 15 minutes, it may (if there is extra adult support available and where an individual child or small group are working well outside the objectives for the class) be better to run two sessions in parallel.

Where there is a group of children with literacy difficulties, guided reading is easily accessed, as long as care is taken to choose books carefully so that they are at the group's instructional level (no more than 10 words in 100 they can't read) and so that they are appropriate to the children's age and dignity. The NASEN *A to Z: A Graded List of Reading Books* (also available on CD-ROM) will help with this. It is also important that the books chosen for the guided read have back-up activities for independent work, to reinforce the vocabulary. Most of the major publishers now produce a strand for less skilled readers to meet this need.

Where there is not a group with similar needs, but an individual 'out of step' child, they can still take part in guided reading, if additional adult help or parent support is available to pre-tutor the text, if the child listens to the text on tape first, or if books are chosen which have text at different levels. Some information books, such as those from Wayland, have the main text summarized in simple language elsewhere on the page. Several publishers produce plays with parts at different readability levels: for example, Ginn's 'Penguin Plays' and LDA's 'Act One'.

It is important to remember, however, that the child will still need their own instructional reading, at the correct level, at other times of the day or week, and that one guided read a week will never be sufficient practice for children with difficulties. They still need the increased contact with print described earlier in this chapter; just as before the introduction of the Literacy Hour no one would have assumed that all the needs of struggling readers could be met within their regular English lessons, so it follows that additional support needs to be arranged outside of the hour as well as within.

The Literacy Hour does not mean that teachers have to throw out tried and tested support programmes for children with reading difficulties in order to make 'everything' fit within the hour. Some highly effective strategies, such as Reading Recovery, or Family Literacy (involving sessions for parents as well as for their children) are too valuable to lose and can be timetabled outside of the hour. Others can readily be fitted in to the independent and group work 20-minute slot, so that a group of children can work with a teaching assistant or volunteer helper up to four times a week on a structured programme. The NLS' own additional literacy support is the prime example of this, but many of the programmes on phonological awareness we looked at in Chapter 10, and the phonic programmes described earlier in this chapter, are ideally suited to the daily short bursts of practice which the Literacy Hour provides.

For independent work, struggling readers can spend time individually or in pairs working on software like the *Talking Computer* program or *Wordshark*, they can work on the back-up activities from their guided reading books, they can work in pairs to test each other on high-frequency word packs, they can play board games like LDA's excellent Track-packs, or use self-checking materials like LDA's *Stile* or *Paperchains*. Alternatively – and it is very important that this happens for at least some of the time – they can undertake differentiated activities which the teacher has planned to follow on from the shared text and the class teaching focus.

These activities will use alternatives to traditional paper and pencil tasks: making captions and posters, story boards, ordering cut-out words, sentences or paragraphs, matching words to pictures or pictures to words, text marking (highlighting words with a particular spelling pattern, for example, or words/ phrases describing a particular character or setting, or all the verbs in a passage), making words with plastic letters, punctuating text with counters or sticky dots, using word cards to complete cloze exercises where words have been missed out of a piece of text, matching speech bubbles to text or pictures, making notes in the form of a picture or 'mind map'.

Using 'active learning' techniques like these (Berger and Gross 1999), supported by simplified worksheets and extra adult support when available, children who are struggling with literacy can participate fully in the independent and group work part of the hour. In the plenary, they can easily talk about their work or show the visual product. They should also be encouraged to reiterate key points from the lesson for others, ask other children questions and give them feedback using prepared cards.

Children with reading comprehension difficulties

So far this chapter has mainly concerned itself with strategies the teacher can adopt for children with poor decoding skills – the ones who just don't know what the words say, and can't seem to remember them when told. Many of these children have an oral language foundation for reading that is at least adequate, and sometimes superior: they are able to use context and their knowledge of language to predict unknown words and to understand what they have read (if, that is, they are able to decode enough words, rapidly enough, to maintain the overall gist). But there is another group of children

with reading difficulties whose needs are very different: they can decode fluently, and at speed, but they do not understand what they read.

For them, the text level objectives from the NLS framework will be particularly relevant. Their work within the Literacy Hour should include:

- group discussion of the words that should go in text with deletions;
- correcting deliberate mistakes in a passage;
- pairing sentences and pictures;
- pairing sentences of similar meaning;
- following recipes and written instructions;
- sequencing sentence strips or longer chunks to make a story, poem or series of events/instructions;
- discussing and choosing a headline for a newspaper article, or a title for a story;
- writing their own table of contents and 'blurb' for the back of a book;
- making up questions about a text for a friend to answer;
- completing a story map (setting, problem, action, outcome) after reading a story;
- underlining key events, ideas or words on acetate overlays;
- discussing and choosing appropriate subheadings for paragraphs;
- composing a telegram of words relating to the main events in a story;
- discussing and choosing the best of three summaries provided for a piece of text;
- using techniques for activating the child's prior knowledge and extracting information from text using KWL grids, one of the many exciting ideas from the Exeter Literacy Project (Lewis *et al.* 1994), now incorporated into the NLS:

What I know	What I want to know	What I've learned

Another way of increasing children's comprehension is taking part in DARTS (Lunzer and Gardner 1979). DARTS activities are a means of both increasing children's understanding of what they read and of improving reading fluency by engaging them repeatedly, in an interesting way, with the same piece of text. Some DARTS activities require text modification and prior preparation:

- A passage is reproduced with blanks in place of some (teacher chosen) words: the group of children discuss and try to agree what should go in the blank spaces.
- A passage (poem, recipe, historical or scientific account of events or pro-cesses) is cut up into sections or strips: the group of children try to reorder them in a way that will make sense.

Other DARTS activities can be done with the text as it stands (a copy per child), and teacher support:

- Underlining categories of information in the text with different-coloured pens.
- Labelling key ideas in pages or paragraphs.
- Transferring information from the passage to a chart, hierarchical table, family tree diagram timeline, flow diagram, bar chart or series of labelled pictures.

Evaluation of the use of DARTS techniques suggests that they are a highly effective form of intervention for children with reading difficulties:

> A learning support teacher, when asked to 'do something' about a group of eleven year old children two to four years behind in their reading, decided to use DARTS to support the children's science work. They researched the big cat family, taking a book on tigers and underlining, on overlays, facts about tiger size, colouring, food and hunting methods in different coloured pens, then transferring the information to a tabular chart. They labelled a drawing with information about the body of a tiger. They retold, in a series of pictures, a story about a boy and a cheetah, which the class were studying. Over the nine month period of support (for two and a half hours a week in a group of four), the children gained on average seventeen months of reading age.
>
> (Pearsall and Wollen 1991)

Conclusion

Without reading skills – both at the mechanical decoding level and at the higher-order level of comprehension – children become increasingly and enormously disadvantaged throughout their school career. It is possible to prevent this; there are plenty of schools and individual teachers with such a strong commitment to each child's right to read, and such confidence in their ability to teach reading, that persisting reading failure is almost unheard of. In this chapter, we have taken a look at the kinds of strategy and materials that contribute to success of this kind.

Many of these strategies involve children learning words as written patterns: reading and writing are, in both multisensory teaching and in the kinds of activity that promote over-learning, often inextricably linked. So too are the children's actual difficulties in both reading and written recording: it is very rare to find children who cannot read well who do not also have writing and spelling difficulties. An action plan for reading must inevitably involve one for writing too. In the next chapter, we will consider how such plans can be made to work.

12 Special needs in writing

Introduction

Ideas about teaching writing in the primary school have come a long way in recent years. Writing has become a craft to which children are apprenticed, learning from the models provided by shared and guided work until they are able to operate independently.

All this is very helpful for children with special needs, as is the explicit teaching of the 'secretarial' aspects of writing – handwriting, spelling and punctuation. Nevertheless, for many of them, writing remains a chore and a focus for negative self-image, as for this boy, who wrote:

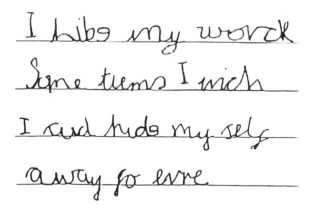

Figure 12.1 Writing by Darrell, aged 10 years (*Dyslexia Institute Annual Review*, 1986).

This chapter is concerned with children like Darrell, and how we can help them overcome the very considerable obstacles which writing presents for them.

Assessment and teaching strategies

Spelling

As with reading, the assessment of spelling difficulties should include a normative measure (such as the *Vernon Spelling Test* from Hodder & Stoughton) for the purpose of establishing the extent of need and monitoring progress. It should also include formative assessment linked to the NLS framework objectives, such as that published by LDA, which includes miscue analysis of the child's own writing and 'tests' in the form of dictation lists of words. The assessment will show which spelling objectives the child has mastered, and what the next steps are in their learning.

Miscue analysis of a child's own written work, repeated over time, is essential in providing the teacher with clues about the point of breakdown, for that individual, in acquiring spelling skills. Is it awkward, ill-formed handwriting that prevents them from using kinaesthetic and motor cues to aid spelling recall? If so, they may benefit from practising a fluent cursive script, or from working on spelling materials with a strong handwriting element such as Charles Cripps' *Hand for Spelling* from LDA. Is it poor phonological awareness, so that the letters the child writes bear little relationship to the sound patterns in words? If this seems to be the problem, the child may need to work at an auditory and oral level on 'hearing' correctly when words rhyme, what their constituent sounds are and how they can be tapped out as chunks or syllables. Or is it a difficulty in visual memory, evident in older children as phonetic misspellings (such as 'duw' for 'do') of short, irregular high-frequency words? If so, there may be a need for systematic and structured phonic teaching coupled with some activities to improve visual skills – finding small words within larger ones (*Wordscore* from Taskmaster is useful for this), making collections of words with the same visual patterns, using look–cover–write–check on a regular basis, learning new words by linking them in groups and target sentences with words that share the same visual pattern/letter string, and using supporting commercial materials such as LDA's *Stile Phonics and Spelling*.

As with reading, teaching strategies for children with spelling difficulties do need to be multisensory. Methods that work for the majority of children may not work for those with specific difficulties. Thomson (1991), for example, has showed that while a visual inspection method of learning spellings worked well for children whose reading and spelling was developing normally, poor spellers did much better with a multisensory technique called simultaneous oral spelling (see below). A range of different approaches to learning spellings need to be on offer: too much emphasis on a wholly visual approach will fail children who cannot form accurate visual images of words; too much emphasis on sounding out phonemes will fail those who cannot, no matter how hard they try, accurately analyse the sounds that make up spoken words.

One way of finding out which approach will work for a particular child is to make use of recent research on individual learning styles (Brooks and Weeks 1999). This research compared a number of different ways of learning spellings:

- Neurolinguistic programming: here the child 'takes a picture' of the word to be learned, using an imaginary camera in their head. The word is written on an A4 sheet and held in the child's top left field of vision – about 3 feet away, 1 foot to the left of and above the child's face. The helper talks about the word: its visual appearance, words within words, tricky bits. The card is then taken away and the child has to keep looking up, picture the word in their mind, say the letters in order from left to right, then backwards from right to left, and finally write the word down from the mental picture, checking it against the original.
- Onset and rime: based on breaking the word up into onset and rime components (b-ig, pl-ay), making the 'chunks' with plastic or wooden letters, pushing the onset and rime together to say the whole word, then writing the word.
- Look–cover–write–check: looking carefully at the word for about 10 seconds, covering it up, writing from memory and then checking and talking about any mistakes.
- Own voice: speaking the whole word into a tape recorder, then the individual letter names, then the whole word; listening to the tape before writing the word again and checking it is right by listening to the tape one more time.
- Tracing: tracing over the word on sandpaper, then writing on paper before checking against the original.
- Simultaneous oral spelling: writing the word, saying each letter name as it is written, then saying the whole word and checking for correctness.
- Words in words: identifying any smaller words within the word to be learned – for example, the 'all' in 'smaller', the 'or' in 'memory'.
- Mnemonics: making up a mnemonic like 'big elephants can't always use small exits' for the word 'because'; reciting the mnemonic then spelling the word.
- Picture links: writing the word and turning some or all of the letters into a picture.
- Phonics: making the word with plastic or wooden letters, saying each separate phoneme and touching each corresponding letter or letter group, then saying the whole word. The child then writes the word, saying each sound as it is written, and writes the whole word once more (again from memory).
- Look-say: looking carefully at the word for about ten seconds, then saying it.

An excellent short booklet, developed from the research on these different methods and available from the Helen Arkell Dyslexia Centre, gives instructions on how to find out which method is most successful for an individual child. The child uses a different method each day to learn a list of ten words; the number of words they get right each day is graphed and compared. Using this straightforward assessment technique, the researchers found that children approximately doubled their normal rates of learning spellings once they were using the method most suited to their particular learning style.

Children will also need to learn that different methods are useful for different types of word. For irregular high-frequency words, for example, highlighting the 'tricky bits' and using mnemonics may work best. These might include repeatedly re-pronouncing the word phonetically – 'people' as 'pee-o-pull', for example, to help with remembering the 'o' in the middle, or 'Wednesday' as 'Wed-nes-day'. Or it may mean making up a mnemonic like '*B*ig *e*lephants *a*re *u*gly' for the beginning of 'beautiful', or '*We* *d*o *n*ot *e*at *s*weets day' for 'Wednesday'. Again, it may involve learning a cue sentence ('A *bus* is always *bus*y', 'W*hat hat?*', '*You* are *you*ng', 'A *pie*ce of *pie*') that links a known spelling with the tricky bit of the new word. Joy Pollock's *Signposts to Spelling* (Heinemann) and the *Mnemonic Spelling System* from Senter are useful sources of ideas for such mnemonics, for teachers and children alike.

If the mnemonics are to be home-grown, it works well to pair a poor speller with a peer or parent helper for a short period of daily work on devising cues for a list of words to be learned, and practising saying the cues while writing the word. A video training pack on this approach is available from the Kirklees Paired Learning Project (Oxley and Topping 1988).

Using mnemonics has been shown to be highly effective (Veit *et al*. 1986) – more so even than direct instruction and overlearning – in ensuring long-term recall of difficult spellings. Once again, if peer tutoring is used the experience seems to benefit teacher as well as taught: children in the Kirklees project made highly significant progress in spelling after using the technique three times a week for half a term, at a rate of twice the normally expected gains for tutees, and three times for tutors.

Turning now to phonetically regular spellings as opposed to irregular key words, the same systematic, multisensory approach needs to be applied. The teacher's choice is whether to devise an individualized learning programme, based on mistakes from the child's own written work and/or words they really want to learn (noted in a spelling journal), coupled with meticulous record keeping of what has been covered, or whether to use an off-the-peg spelling scheme that will take the child through a set sequence of letter patterns and spelling conventions.

An example of the first tailor-made approach was given in Chapter 6, where the teacher targeted a list of words containing a particular spelling pattern or following a particular spelling convention each week, and had a pair of children practise that pattern using a different activity each day, as part of their independent work in the Literacy Hour. The daily activities can include:

- Using the particular method, such as onset/rime, or making the words with plastic letters, that has been shown to be effective for that particular child.
- Filling the words into blanks in sentences made up by a partner.
- Making up and illustrating a silly sentence, rhyme or rap that links as many of the words as possible.
- Using supporting computer software, such as *Wordshark* or *Starspell* from Soapbox, *Sounds and Rhymes* from Xavier or *GAMZ* from Inclusive Technology.
- Using worksheet material.
- Testing each other on the word list.

A tailor-made approach like this is only really possible where the school's special needs resource base has a wide range of worksheet material and software catalogued according to letter strings and spelling conventions. It is, however, relatively light on teacher time once this initial organization has been done.

More demanding on teacher or teaching assistant input, but useful for those wanting a complete all-in-one scheme, are the structured multisensory approaches listed in Chapter 11. These are as relevant to the teaching of spelling as they are to reading, since they all employ a basic methodology of having the child learn each new sound–symbol relationship by writing it, first on its own and later as part of word lists, then reading back what has been written. Other structured multisensory schemes specific for teaching spelling include Violet Brand's *Spelling Made Easy* and the *Wizard's Spelling Toolbox* workbook and cassette scheme from Barnstormer Books.

Teaching spelling patterns and high-frequency words is one thing – having children apply this knowledge to their own writing is another. There is so much for them to think about when they write – generating ideas, structuring sentences, remembering punctuation – that the overload means something has to give: often, if new spelling patterns have not reached the point of being automatic it will be spelling. Fortunately, the process of drafting and editing can help with this. Children can be taught to apply their new learning about how words are spelled at the editing stage – initially by looking for a small, specified number of errors on one or two particular high-frequency words or spelling patterns targeted by the teacher (ones they should know from previous teaching sessions), later still for an unspecified number of errors on a target pattern chosen by the teacher, later still for errors on a self-chosen spelling pattern or patterns. Ultimately, children should be encouraged to pre-empt the editing process by underlining words they are not sure of as they write, and checking back later using a simple dictionary, word bank or personal word book.

Handwriting

When assessing children's handwriting, it can sometimes be difficult to get away from the global impression of untidiness, and pin down exactly where the difficulties lie. Take the piece of work, from an 8-year-old shown in Figure 12.2. What is it that he is doing, or not doing, that makes his writing so hard to read?

A simple checklist, used by the teacher or by children themselves, can help pin down problem areas. It needs to cover the four 'Ss' of handwriting: shape, spacing, sizing, straights. First, are the letters correctly shaped and formed? Do they start and finish at the correct point – for example, are the circles in the a/o/d/g/q group adequately rounded and closed? For spacing, is a space approximately the width of the child's little finger left between words? Letters should be aligned to a baseline, with correctly positioned ascenders and descenders; all the small letters should be the same size as each other, all the tall and capital letters likewise; the writing should be neither too large nor too small. Straight lines in letters should be vertical or have a slight, even slope towards the right.

This kind of checklist, applied to the piece of writing overleaf, would show that this child had problems in spacing, letter sizing, placing letters relative to a line, and with the formation of the circular shape in some letters.

Figure 12.2 8-year-old's handwriting.

Assessment should also include watching the child writing, looking for factors such as how they hold a pen or pencil and position the paper, and whether they steady the paper with their non-writing hand. Right-handers should hold a pencil in a tripod grip, with their fingers about 20–25 mm from the point; left-handers need to hold the pencil slightly further from the point – about 30 mm away. For a right-handed child, the paper should be at a 30° angle, tilted to the right; for left-handed children the paper should be tilted 30° to the left (so that they do not cover the work as they write, and develop a 'hooked' grip).

It is not easy to alter established habits, but special pencil grips, or for older children who want to appear no different from their peers, three-sided

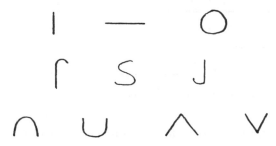

Figure 12.3   Basic shapes of letter formation.

pencils and pens (from LDA and Berol) can help those who hold a pencil wrongly or too tightly, as can placing taped guidelines on the child's table or in the writing corner (clearly marked to show which are for right handers and which for left-handers) to show how the paper should be positioned and angled. Beyond these simple structural measures, improving children's handwriting is a matter of getting the child to do short periods of regular practice that targets any problem areas highlighted by the checklist. Young children may need to practise the basic shapes of letter formation as shown in Figure 12.3. The basic shapes should be practised large and small, with eyes open and eyes shut, on the black- and whiteboards and on big sheets of paper, with paint, chalk and big felt-tips. To make the practice more interesting, the shapes can be turned into pictures to trace, copy and complete – handles to put onto umbrellas, a picture of waves in the sea to finish, railings on a fence, noses on clowns, dotted lines down the middle of roads. There are many commercially available materials to support this kind of approach.

Once the basic shapes are mastered, children with handwriting difficulties need access to varied worksheets on letter formation, perhaps supplemented by using *Rol 'n Write* from LDA to consolidate their knowledge of where to start letters and which direction to go in. Letters should be taught in groups with a similar pattern of movement – a c d g o q, b f h k l t, i m n r u y, j p, v w. They should be practised in small groups of three of a kind, never a whole line of one letter – it is impossible to sustain a rhythm of correct letter formation along an entire line, and the writing inevitably deteriorates towards the end. Many children find it helpful to have pointed out to them, from the beginning, the difference between the 'giraffe' letters (b, d, l, etc.), the 'turtle' letters (a, c, e, etc.) and the 'monkey' letters (g, j, p, etc.), and to practise placing them relative to the line.

It makes sense, when practising letters together for joined writing, to choose meaningful letter strings rather than random groups. Learning to write, for example, 'an' and then practising it in a list of words like 'can', 'pan' or 'ant' will benefit the child's spelling alongside handwriting.

Once children have had some practice targeted at the problem area they can use a self-assessment tool to check their own work. Blandford and Lloyd (1987) used this approach very effectively: children checked their own work using a card that asked questions like 'Have you left a finger space between your words?' and/or 'Are your small letters all the same size?' The children's

_____

- -

_____

Figure 12.4 Double-lined paper for positioning ascenders/descenders.

handwriting improved measurably and immediately as a result of this simple device.

Most children with handwriting difficulties appear to benefit from using lined paper for all their work (Pasternicki 1986); those with problems in letter sizing or positioning ascenders and descenders may need to use old-fashioned double-lined paper for a while, until they sort out where each letter sits in relation to the others (see Figure 12.4).

Confusion of b/d (and less commonly, b/p and u/n) is a common problem affecting handwriting. It may lead children to introduce inappropriate upper case B and D in the middle of their work, since they know they can get these the right way round. It also slows them down, and affects the readability of what they write. Many kinds of elaborate schemes, including computer games, have been devised to try to help children with letter reversals, but the most effective intervention is often the simple one of making sure the child can quickly and easily refer to an alphabet frieze on the wall or taped to the desk, and teaching the well-known mnemonic (see Figure 12.5) where the 'b' and 'd' form the end of an imaginary bed, and must point in the right direction in order to 'hold the mattress up'.

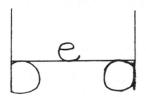

Figure 12.5 b/d mnemonic.

There are many reasons why children develop handwriting difficulties. Inadequate early teaching or inadequate tools are often to blame – for example, when children learning to write have used a visual model (copying what they see on the page) rather than the necessary correct motor model for letter formation, or when they have not been shown how to position paper and pen, or have been given small pencils and paper when their stage of motor development required something on a larger scale.

Some children, however, do have inbuilt motor difficulties, affecting their handwriting development no matter how well they are taught and resourced. For these children, like Suresh in the example below, writing can become such an unpleasant – and even physically painful – chore that the whole of their experience of school is coloured by this one difficulty. Not infrequently, they develop such a dislike of the whole business of writing that they more or less down tools and rarely manage more than a few scrappy, stilted lines of written work. The teacher then concludes that they are either lazy or not very bright, and a downward spiral of motivation and behaviour begins.

Suresh was 7: a lively, articulate little boy who read well and impressed his teacher with his mature sense of humour and wide general knowledge. His written work, however, was barely legible. He could not concentrate for long on anything, but least of all on writing. When his teacher talked to him about the problem, he said: 'I just don't like writing. It's boring. I hate it when we have to copy stuff'. A psychological assessment showed that there was a large discrepancy – of three to four years – between the level at which Suresh was able to reason logically and express himself orally, and his skills in copying shapes with pencil and paper or with coloured bricks. He would often copy shapes in strange ways.

⌐ for example, copied as ⊓ ∫

When asked to describe what Suresh was like as a small child, his mother said he talked very clearly early on, but he was late in learning to walk. He seemed to find learning all motor skills difficult – catching and kicking a ball, hopping, doing anything to a rhythm. He was a messy eater, always seemed to have his clothes on askew or back to front, and infuriated the family with his tendency to drop things or knock them over or bump into them. When he started school he used both his right and left hand for writing; now he was clearly right-handed.

It was agreed at the meeting between his mother, teacher and psychologist that his motor and spatial difficulties were probably causing him much frustration at school, and that though he needed to work on his handwriting he also, paradoxically, needed much of the pressure taken *off* writing, so that he could get out of what his teacher described as his current 'nosedive in motivation'. Suresh and his teacher struck a bargain. For about half of all classroom recording she would reduce the writing load by having him use word processing on the computer, dictate his work to her, or work with a partner who would be happy to act as scribe for their joint ideas. For the remainder of recording tasks, Suresh would set himself a target for the amount of writing he would do; if he consistently reached his targets his mother would do something special with him at home – read him an extra story, or do some maths with him, both of which he very much liked (and with three younger brothers and sisters rarely got much of). Suresh would also spend a few minutes each day on 'Hand for Spelling' sheets and cursive writing patterns, and help the Reception teacher supervise a group of children in her class who were just learning how to form their letters.

This proved particularly motivating for Suresh: his own handwriting soon improved considerably. Initially, he set himself very low targets

---

Box 12.1 Checklist for coordination difficulties

- Difficulties in learning to do buttons, fastenings, shoelaces, a tie
- Awkward or messy eater
- Immature drawings
- Handwriting problems
- Delayed or impaired speech
- Difficulties in balancing, climbing, throwing, catching, skipping, learning to ride a bicycle
- Tendency to bump into things, drop things, trip up
- Difficulty in organizing personal possessions and organizing self for learning
- Easily distracted
- Difficulties in laying out work on a page
- Difficulties with tasks involving spatial skills such as maps, plans, diagrams, coordinates, telling the time, measurement, shape work, design technology
- Difficulty in locating information on busy pages
- Difficulty in finding way around

---

for independent writing in class, but over the weeks, as he produced successful dictated and partner work that was read out to the whole class, he began to increase the amount he was willing to write, until after one term he was managing a page or more at a time.

Suresh's pattern of motor coordination and spatial difficulties, sometimes called developmental dyspraxia (see Box 12.1) is by no means uncommon. Surveys (Gubbay 1975; Portwood 1999) have indicated that between 2 and 5 per cent of children in mainstream schools have significant motor problems of this type. The difficulties can span gross motor coordination, balance, fine manipulative control, spatial and body awareness, visual perception, speech articulation, attention and concentration. The picture presented is of a child who is awkward, uncoordinated, accident prone, disorganized, annoyingly messy and immature in self-help skills such as dressing and eating, and – if their difficulties have gone unrecognized so that people have been impatient and angry with them for their awkwardness – low in self-esteem and lacking in friends. Some (Henderson and Hall 1982) are academically successful, with only minor handwriting difficulties and some slight difficulties in social integration. Others, however, have widespread academic difficulties, with maths (because of its spatial aspects) as well as written recording showing up as areas of particular concern.

Research has shown that children with coordination problems do not, on the whole, 'grow out of them' as they get older (Losse *et al.* 1991). As teenagers, children who were identified as having coordination difficulties in the primary school were considered by their teachers to be less academically competent than a control group, sat fewer public examinations, had more behaviour problems, were bullied more often and continued to show problems of coordination and personal organization.

Many of these long-term problems are preventable, given appropriate early intervention and support in school – intervention and support that goes beyond the handwriting problem alone. Specific coaching in motor skills, on a programme taking only 20 minutes a day and delivered by the child's parents or a teaching assistant, has been shown to have significant effects within a few weeks (Portwood 1999). In the classroom, helpful strategies include:

- Looking at seating: making sure the child is able to sit right back in their chair, with knees at right angles and feet flat on the floor – using a box or large book under the child's feet if necessary.
- Using a portable sloping writing board (from LDA), which gives the child's arm more stability.
- Using triangular and thick-barrelled pencils and pens, and (for older children) smooth-flowing rollerball pens.
- Sticking Dycem (an adhesive material) onto one side of the child's ruler so that it stays in one place without the child having to hold it down when drawing lines; anchoring the paper the child is writing on with Dycem, non-slip mats or repositional glue sticks.
- In art, using stiff non-absorbent paper and loop-handled or two-handed scissors.
- Helping the child to get organized by putting everything they need for each lesson in a separate folder, and providing checklists of equipment they have to bring to school on each day of the week, to use at home each night.
- Keeping copying and redrafting to a minimum.
- Helping the child locate when working from the board, overhead transparency or enlarged text by using different colours to write or highlight each line.
- Pairing the child with a more coordinated friend for work involving fine motor skills – using scissors, making models, using equipment in science and technology.
- Providing pre-prepared layouts (such as charts or graphs) on which the child can record information.
- Using window markers in different sizes to highlight the area of a busy page that the child needs to work from or on.
- Enlarging parts of busy pages on a photocopy, then spacing them out in the child's book.
- Teaching the child to talk themselves through visual and spatial tasks – for example, learning a verbal model like 'start at the top, down, round' for letter formation, or translating visual maths calculations into oral problem form (5×20 into 'I had five lots of twenty pence').
- Compartmentalizing the child's workspace, and if possible seating the child away from distractions; making sure there is plenty of space on the child's right (if right-handed) so as to avoid knocking into a neighbour when working.
- Using alternatives to traditional written recording.
- Providing opportunities for the child to succeed and maintain self-esteem.
- Protecting the child from too public a display of coordination difficulties – for example, at sports day.

Curriculum access for children with spelling and handwriting difficulties

Children who find the secretarial aspects of writing difficult have always been at a great disadvantage in school. They are asked to spend long periods doing something they feel bad at. They may be judged by their busy teachers as less competent in many areas of the curriculum than they really are, because they do not succeed in recording what they know and understand.

In these circumstances it becomes very important for all teachers to know about the many ways in which full written recording can be bypassed, in order to enable children to demonstrate, order and reflect on their learning. Such bypass strategies, applied to subjects other than the specific spelling and presentation attainment targets within English, are perfectly legitimate. Some teachers, and many parents, may need reassurance on this point. They may feel that if children are not required to write all the time – in science, history or whatever – then they will never improve their presentation skills because they will not be getting enough practice. If, this argument goes, they are using a word processor with a spellcheck, or dictating to a scribe, or filling in a cloze sheet the teacher has prepared, then they are somehow getting off lightly, and not learning what they should. The answer to this is that if we try to do everything at once we are likely to overload children. They will find it hard to practise correct spelling, handwriting and punctuation when they are also struggling to think of what to say and how to say it when writing up a scientific investigation, say, or a historical account. There is a place for practising the secretarial skills, but not when the child is having to do all these things at the same time. Literacy lessons are the time to focus on secretarial skills; when the child is working on science or history, it is the science and history we want them to *learn*, and anything that gets in the way of the child with special needs accessing those subjects is best either bypassed or modified.

Curriculum access strategies for children with writing difficulties fall into two groups. First, there are the strategies in which the child is not asked to write at all, but to use alternative means of recording. Second, there are strategies that involve *supported* or *scaffolded* writing in one form or another.

Let us first look at the idea of total writing bypass. If the child is not to be asked to write at all, they can instead:

- Do detailed drawings or diagrams.
- Make audio or video tape recordings.
- Use sorting boards and sorting tasks of all kinds.
- Match labels to pictures or objects.
- Sequence pictures.
- Match sentences to pictures.
- Dictate work to a scribe (parent, peer, helper or teacher), or to a tape recorder to be scribed later.
- Work with a partner or small group, where better writers do the recording but the child can contribute their ideas.

Supported or scaffolded writing is often easier to manage than total bypass. Here the child can:

- Be provided with pre-prepared cloze sheets (filling in missing words). These sheets may be written by the teacher, or be made by photocopying text and then blanking out some words. Or the child's own work that they have dictated to a scribe can have words deleted. The words to go in the spaces can be provided in a box for the child to choose from: how many words, and whether they are put at the end of a long piece of text, or the end of a paragraph or sentence, will depend on the degree of support the child needs.
- Be provided with sentences to cut out, sequence and illustrate, or with halves of sentences ('tops and tails') to fit together.
- Be provided with paragraphs to sequence.
- Fill in speech and 'think' bubbles on prepared sheets.
- Fill in information on prepared tables, charts and matrices.
- Colour and label a drawing or diagram – affixing cut-out labels, or drawing lines to match words with the bits they refer to, as in matching descriptive words to the features and clothing of a character from a descriptive passage the children have listened to.
- Write using a magic line – a line the approximate length of a word the child does not yet know how to write, with parent, helper or teacher filling in the missing words or parts of words later.
- Be provided with word banks, key word lists, 'have a go' pads and glossaries of subject vocabulary for easy reference. One useful idea is a word bank about a particular topic, laminated or sealed in a plastic wallet, which acts as a placemat for the child for the duration of that topic. The word bank is in the form of a grid, referenced with colours along one axis and numbers along the other. The teacher can direct a child to a particular word when needed, by calling out a colour and a number.
- Be provided with a range of dictionaries – subject dictionaries, like those from Questions Publishing which use words from the National Curriculum, and dictionaries specially written for children with spelling difficulties, such as the *ACE Spelling Dictionary* from LDA, or the *Pergamon Dictionary of Perfect Spelling* from Nelson.
- Use a small portable electronic spellchecker on which the child can enter the word they need 'just as it sounds' and be given several alternative correct spellings to choose from.
- Use word-processing software.

Of all these strategies, word processing is probably the most powerful in supporting children with writing difficulties. Using word processing means that the business of editing and producing a published version of an initial draft takes minutes rather than hours. Children are more willing to 'have a go', and write adventurously, because mistakes can so easily be rectified. Davidson (1988), for example, found that the work of a group of children with specific learning difficulties showed a much broader vocabulary and variety of sentence structure, as well as being more technically accurate, when they were using a computer than when they were writing by hand. Word processing also takes the effort out of writing for children who find it difficult to control a pencil and form letters. It means that the child can produce work that always looks good; the problems of handwriting and setting out are overcome. It means that spelling (and, increasingly, grammar) can be checked quickly and easily, in an emotionally neutral way.

Using word processing also means that varying degrees of support can be built into the writing process. At the earliest stages of writing proficiency, children can use concept keyboard overlays that contain important words they will need for their writing, plus lower-case letters, a full stop and a magic line: such overlays will enable them to record their ideas quickly, before they forget what they want to say. Editing will also be quick and easy; they can then print the work out for display, to take home, or to keep in a portfolio or topic folder. They can also use the printout as a basis for cloze exercises, or for making cloze exercises for one another.

At a slightly more advanced level, software such as *Clicker Plus* (from Crick software and available, like other software mentioned in this chapter, in the REM catalogue), acts like a concept keyboard on the screen: the teacher can display a list of core words for the particular writing topic, or a personal dictionary for each child, from which the child selects using a mouse. Words not on the screen are typed in letter by letter in the normal way. *Find Out and Write About*, from Crick, has photographs, differentiated reading levels and lots of practical activities to support non-fiction writing.

Another form of supported writing uses predictive word processors, such as *Predictability* or (for older children) *textHELP*. These predict, on the basis of the first one or two letters typed in, what the word the child intends to use might be, and offer choices: a single keyboard stroke then enters the word in full. Software like this is particularly helpful for children with motor difficulties who find many keystrokes laborious, and for children with severe spelling difficulties. It can also help with punctuation – some software, for example, automatically puts a capital letter after each full stop. Even greater support is provided by voice-operated software, where the child simply dictates text, which then appears on the screen: although the early versions have proved problematic, particularly for younger children, it is improving all the time and is undoubtedly the way of the future for all writers – not just those with SEN.

For the moment, most children do well with simple word-processing programs with a built-in spellchecker. Such spellcheckers can be very useful for poor spellers – if, that is, they can read well enough to recognize the 'correct' spelling from among the several alternatives the spellchecker will suggest. Children with reading difficulties as well as spelling difficulties may do better using a word processor with a speech-output device such as *Talking Pendown*, *Inclusive Writer* and *Talking Textease*, so that they can hear what they have written, keep track of where they are up to and pick up at least some of their more gross spelling errors.

The next example illustrates the successful use of word processing, alongside other alternatives to traditional full written recording. Here a support teacher, working with two Year 4 boys with specific learning difficulties/ dyslexia, was asked to work on improving the boys' written language skills, in the context of class work on the ancient Egyptians:

Mark and Paul both had very noticeable spelling problems and had little confidence in their own writing ability. They could read adequately but not with great range or fluency. Both contributed well to class discussion, but rarely got more than a few scrappy lines down on paper. Their support teacher decided that the main target in her work with them should be re-establishing their confidence, by helping

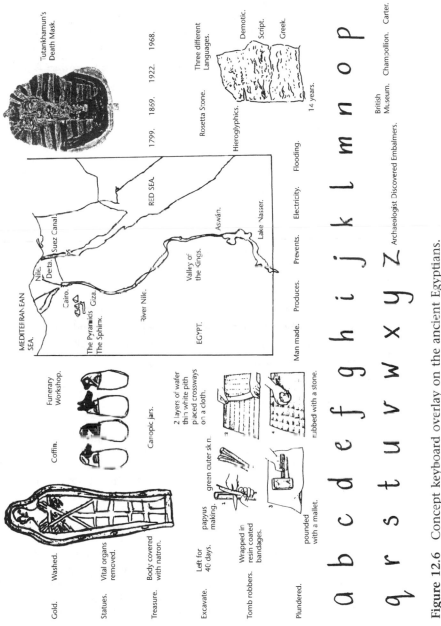

Figure 12.6 Concept keyboard overlay on the ancient Egyptians.

Making a mummy

Cut up the strips. Put them in order to tell how papyrus is made. Draw a picture to go with each sentence.

The dead body was washed, and the vital

Then the body was

It was left for

Finally, it was wrapped

forty days

organs removed

covered with natron

in bandages coated in resin

Figure 12.7   Sentence sequencing worksheet.

Cut up the strips. Put them in order to tell how papyrus is made. Draw a picture to go with each strip.

This was cut into wafer-thin strips, and placed crossways on a cloth.

Finally, a stone was used, like we use sandpaper today, to rub the papyrus smooth.

Its green outer skin was removed, to show the white pith underneath.

First the papyrus was gathered from the banks of the river Nile.

before being pounded to a pulp with a mallet.

Figure 12.8   A tops and tails worksheet.

them to produce high quality work for their subject folders. With her help, they brainstormed the words they would need for their writing about the ancient Egyptians, and made an illustrated concept keyboard overlay (see Figure 12.6). The teacher wrote the alphabet sequentially at the bottom of the overlay, rather than in QWERTY form, to provide extra practice in alphabetical order.

Since sequencing events was difficult for both boys, they needed some extra work on certain aspects of the topic – the making of papyrus and the process of mummification – before being able to write about them. The teacher prepared a sentence sequencing worksheet (see Figure 12.7), and a tops and tails worksheet (see Figure 12.8) for them. They went on to use the prepared keyboard overlay to draft their own piece (see Figure 12.9). The teacher edited the first printout with them, using this opportunity to do some work on 'ou' and 'oo' sounds. The boys revised the piece on the screen, then went on to write in the same manner about the discovery of Tutankhamun's tomb, the Rosetta Stone, the geography of the Nile Delta and the

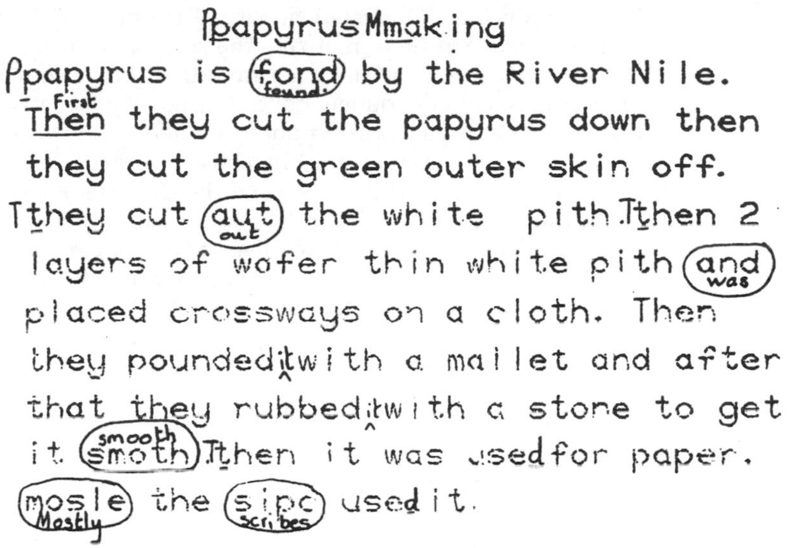

Ppapyrus Mmaking

Ppapyrus is (fond) by the River Nile.
First
Then they cut the papyrus down then
they cut the green outer skin off.
Tthey cut (aut) the white pith.Tthen 2
layers of wafer thin white pith (and)
was
placed crossways on a cloth. Then
they pounded;twith a mallet and after
that they rubbed;twith a stone to get
it (smoth)Tthen it was used for paper.
smooth
(mosle) the (sipc) used it.
Mostly scribes

Figure 12.9 Drafting from a prepared keyboard overlay.

Egyptian gods. They were extremely proud of their final folder of work; their class teacher was surprised at the quality of the language they had used, and the way they had organized their ideas.

Generating ideas and structuring written work

Mark and Paul knew what they wanted to say in their writing, and had the spoken vocabulary in which to express their ideas – though this only really became clear when they were provided with appropriate support with the mechanical aspects of spelling and handwriting. Theirs is a common pattern, even if one that is not always readily apparent to the busy teacher. They do not, however, form the only group of children with difficulties in written recording. There are other children, who may or may not have good mechanical skills, but struggle to generate ideas for written work, to find the right words and to order what they have to say.

These are children who are not, unlike those with specific difficulties in the mechanical aspects of writing, able to improve greatly on the quantity and quality of their work when given the opportunity to dictate pieces to an adult rather than write them by hand. Support for them needs to take the form of careful preparation; before the writing actually begins they will need thorough familiarization with the genre in which they are being asked to write – for example, by listening to taped texts. For some children, who have become very reluctant writers, it may be best to start with genres and writing tasks that are closest to the child's own spoken language – for example, e-mails, faxes, postcards; these can be contextualized, as in writing a postcard from Little Red Riding Hood to her grandmother. The child should be guided through several rehearsals of an idea, story or account at a practical 'doing' level well before they put pen to paper. For example, a child who is to be asked to produce an illustrated booklet retelling a traditional story might need first to take part in dramatizing the story in a small group, to sequence pictures from the story, to tell the story bit by bit around the group and to recount it to a parent or younger child. A child who is to write a description of a character might need to answer questions about the character put by a partner, or sort statements about the character into true or false, or do a series of drawings and use these to describe what the character is like to a small group. A child who has to make up an adventure story might work with visually exciting computer material that stimulates paired or group discussion and leads to ideas for writing a story via an adventure game series-of-choices format.

After preparation comes planning: here the NLS structure of shared and guided writing is proving a great support to children who have difficulties in ordering their thoughts for writing. If they are also supplied with a structure for planning their work, and the teacher or another helper is able to spend a few minutes with them sorting out their plan, they are often then able to write a first draft independently, instead of coming up constantly for help and advice on what to put next.

The structure supplied to children for planning their writing can vary. It may be a sheet folded into small squares, so that they can draw a picture in each, as in a cartoon strip; the writing task will then be to write a sentence or

Figure 12.10 Story planner.

paragraph about each picture in the series. Or it may be a series of prompt questions, like those in Figure 12.10. It may be a writing frame, with formats for different genres such as the 'discussion genre', in which arguments are developed for and against particular viewpoints, or for different types of writing such as a book review, a letter, a character description or the outline of a design. The pack of writing frames available from the Reading and Language Information Centre provides a comprehensive resource. Or it may be a table with headings that ask the child to note the type of story (for example, adventure), the time and setting, a description of each main character, ideas for the plot and ending and so on.

Mind maps are another useful generic tool for planning writing. They work best for children who think and learn visually, in pictures rather than in words. In a mind map, the child writes or draws a key word, representing the subject of the map, in the centre of the page. They then draw coloured branch-lines from the central image, one for each of the key categories of information or main ideas which will make up the final piece of writing.

Planning tools like these work well with writing on the word processor. The child's plan provides the vocabulary for a concept keyboard overlay or personal on-screen dictionary; the vocabulary can then be used and reused for multiple versions and drafts. Commercial software, like *I Can Write* from Resource, is also available, with writing frameworks for a wide range of genres.

Further support may be needed at the time of drafting for children who – even with a prepared plan – find it hard to keep track of where they have got to. These are often children with short-term memory difficulties who cannot hold a long sentence in mind for long enough to get each part down. It can be helpful to have them use their planner to tape-record what they want to say, then play it back a phrase or sentence at a time as they write it.

Conclusion

Writing is a public activity, in a way that reading, for example, may not be: what the child commits to paper is open to the scrutiny not only of the teacher but also of other children. Writing is also permanent: whether the product is good or bad, it does not disappear. Because of this, it is an area where failure is particularly damaging to the child's self-esteem.

We do now have the tools to make sure that this loss of self-esteem is avoided, and that all children are enabled to produce writing that they can feel proud of. What is needed now are whole-school systems that will give teachers the confidence, in time, to make full use of these available tools – for example, word banks and on-screen word lists for schemes of work across the school, readily available spellcheckers and cloze sheets and story planners, adult support deployed to help children plan their writing or scribe for them.

In this chapter we have looked at the strategies for supporting the writing process that might be built into such a whole-school plan, and at the equally vital systems used across the school to remediate children's difficulties in the basic skill areas of handwriting, spelling and presentation.

It is now time to turn from special needs in the 'tool' language skills that children use across the curriculum to needs in another 'tool' area, where difficulties can also have wide-ranging effects – the area of mathematics.

Special needs in maths

Introduction

The NNS has from the start provided primary teachers with excellent models of how to match task to learner. The framework itself outlines the critical teaching objectives for each year group, from which it is possible to match the needs of children across the whole range of mathematical ability. Teachers can readily plan for differentiation during whole-class oral work, during written work or homework. In most cases, this will be via setting objectives linked to the main class objective for *groups* of children. In other cases, it may be appropriate to support children who are very much 'out of step' with their peers with an individualized programme (still linked to the class topic) in the main part of the lesson.

Providing appropriate support of this kind rests on fine-grained assessment of teaching needs, in order to pinpoint where in particular the child has not succeeded in grasping essential foundation concepts (the small steps approach), and of any underlying reasons for the mathematical difficulties. In this chapter we will look at how such an assessment can lead to individualized action planning: first of all planning to circumvent identified difficulties – for example, in sequencing, handling abstractions, or handling linguistic or spatial information – and then, later in the chapter, planning ways of tackling some of the most common stumbling blocks children encounter along the path of their mathematical development.

Assessment

Assessment of mathematical difficulties can take place through:

- Observing children at work – for example, to note patterns of concentration (or lack of it), how often they ask for help, how they go about selecting the approaches and materials to use for practical tasks, what mathematical language they use and whether they are able to make generalizations and predictions.

- Miscue analysis – looking at the kind of errors the child makes in written calculation in order to understand their thinking.
- Using informal assessment materials designed to check children's understanding of particular framework objectives, such as the QCA assessment units: most of the published maths schemes also now include assessment activities and copymasters. A good example is the Collins *Primary Maths* materials, which include a teacher/pupil review to assess termly progress – useful as a way of involving the child in monitoring and target setting.
- Using an informal interview to probe the child's understanding by asking *how* they arrived at certain conclusions, or as a quick check of the concepts they have mastered. One such interview format is described in Derek Haylock's very helpful book *Teaching Mathematics to Low Attainers* (1991); this allows the teacher to assess, in the space of 15 minutes or so, what the child understands of time, money, measurement, place value, calculation and calculator use.
- Using published tests – for example, the QCA optional tests for Years 3, 4 and 5, the Basic Number Screening and Diagnostic Tests from Hodder & Stoughton or those from NFER-Nelson's extensive range. These include the age-standardized 'Maths 6–11' series, and the 'Maths Workout' series for children who require more detailed follow-up assessment.

A combination of these assessment methods will make it possible for the teacher to do two things. First, they should be able to plot precisely the learning objectives for the child: to develop action plans that state, for example, that Michael needs to learn to make up 10p in different ways using 1p, 2p and 5p coins, or order numbers within 100. Second, the teacher should be able, through the assessment process, to gather information on where things might be going wrong for the child in maths, so that teaching styles and approaches – the 'how' of teaching, rather than just the 'what' – can be modified accordingly.

Common reasons for mathematical difficulties

Children with specific learning difficulties and maths

Some children have difficulty with maths merely because of the way in which tasks are presented. Clement (1980), for example, found that a quarter of 12-year-olds' errors in written maths tasks arose from difficulties in reading accuracy or comprehension. The NNS has gone a long way to overcome this difficulty, with its emphasis on oral maths and investigational problem-solving activities. Teachers need only remember to pair and group children carefully so as to ensure that peer support is available where literacy demands are involved in the task.

Children with reading and spelling difficulties may, however, have reasons for experiencing problems with maths that go deeper than mere text readability. Numbers, like letters and words, are abstract symbols to which the child has to attach meanings; like letters, they have to be written the right way round; as with words, the symbols have to be remembered in a particular order – whether counting to 10, or to 100, or learning a multiplication table. Not surprisingly, in view of these similarities in cognitive demands, two-thirds of children with specific learning difficulties/dyslexia also have problems in basic numeracy (Joffe 1981). They may have a good understanding of mathematical ideas – may know, for example, what process or operation to apply in relation to a problem, and be good at making generalizations and predictions – but fall down on basic calculation. Typically, they will take longer than other children to learn the written form of numbers, to attach reliable meaning to mathematical symbols such as < and >, + and –, × and ÷, and to master sequences such as counting, days of the week, months of the year and times tables. They may never develop an automatic knowledge of number facts – although the NNS emphasis on teaching flexible routes to calculation has proved very helpful here, with children benefiting from being taught, for example, how to use doubles and near doubles to work out additions. They may show directional difficulties, putting figures in the wrong order (15 for 51, for example), or taking top from bottom instead of bottom from top when doing column subtraction.

Children with difficulties like these need a slower pace to their mathematical learning only in some areas – generally the strands of calculations, numbers and the number system. In other areas, what they need are strategies that will enable them to bypass their problems in arithmetical calculation in order to access the work on solving problems, measures, shape and space or handling data. The provision of number lines or a ruler clearly marked to at least 20 for counting on and back, for example, will help overcome the problem of not knowing number facts; multiplication grids and a tables matrix will help with the problem of poor memory for tables; a calculator (for older children) will assist with problems of direction and sequence in work with large numbers. The *Interactive Calculator*, from Inclusive Technology, is particularly useful for dyslexic learners; it combines clear visual presentation with auditory feedback, and comes with a 'guess' button to encourage estimation.

It will also be helpful to pupils with specific learning difficulties if the teacher encourages them always to make good use of approximation and checking strategies before doing any kind of calculation, so that they can apply their often good logical ability as a check on the accuracy of their answers. To overcome the problem of left–right sequencing, they need to be made very sure, conceptually, of the way that numbers in certain positions represent hundreds, tens and ones, using colour-coded place value cards reinforced with matching colour-coded pens – where, for example, hundreds are red, tens blue and units green. To help with the problem of attaching names to symbols, it may be a good idea to have the child accumulate a pack of cards, with symbols such as + on the front, and their meanings (such as add, and, plus, total, sum of, increase by) on the reverse, so that parents or a peer helper can run through them on a regular basis to aid recall. Children can also use software such as Sherston's *Maths Keywords* number and calculations program, which has colour-coded icons and a spoken help text.

Finally, with these children it may be necessary to tackle short-term sequential memory problems. Many numerical operations require the ability to hold in mind a series of steps. A problem such as 75p + 39p may involve the child in working out that 70 add 30 is £1, 9p and 5p equal 14p, so the total is £1.14. Some children simply cannot remember where they are in complex multi-step operations like these. They will need to make use of paper and pencil notes and jottings for much longer than many of their peers. When introducing a new topic, the teacher should make sure that the examples they give to start with use 'easy' numbers, so that the child can focus on the new skill rather than struggle with the content. It will be essential to recognize and acknowledge these children's preferred oral/mental methods of calculation: while the teacher will want the child to play a full part in any session and hear others' methods, their own repertoire of methods may have to be acquired more gradually and systematically to take account of the short-term memory problems. Either for their informal jottings methods or later for standard paper and pencil methods they may – if they can read well enough – require the support of an *aide-mémoire*: for example, a Post-it for each operation, setting out the steps in a worked example, and attached to the inside cover of their maths books. For decomposition, the *aide-mémoire* might look like this:

1 Round up and estimate 2 Partition both numbers into T and U 3 Adjust the numbers so that the 9 can be subtracted 4 Perform both subtractions 5 Recombine to get the answer 6 Check answer is close to estimate	$54 - 29 =$ $54 - \quad = 50 + 4 = 40 + 14$ $29 \qquad 20 + 9 = 20 + \quad 9$ — ———— $\qquad\qquad 20 + \quad 5 = 25$

Thinking in the abstract

Some children with mathematical difficulties have problems that are very different from those of children with specific learning difficulties. These children may be very good at learning things by rote, but find it hard to understand what they are doing. They may cope well with straightforward calculation, but be unable to work out whether addition, subtraction, multiplication or division is called for in a given problem – what to do, for example, with things like 'How much less does Mark have than Ben?', or 'How many teams of 5 children will there be in a class of 30?'

For these children it is the abstract, symbolic nature of maths which causes problems. Other aspects of school experience – such as reading or writing – also involve symbols, but usually the symbols have a fairly straightforward relationship with what is symbolized. In maths, it is different: the numeral '1' may sometimes stand for one, but sometimes – if it is in a different place – for ten, or a hundred, or a thousand; a 5p coin, the teacher says, is somehow 'the same as' two 2p pieces and one 1p piece; the symbol '–' stands for 'take away', 'minus', 'decrease', 'count back' and 'the difference between'. The more abstract the concept, the more displaced from what the child can see and hear and touch, the harder it will be to grasp: place value, coin equivalence and patterns such as the relatedness of addition and subtraction, multiplication and division, are frequent stumbling blocks for children with mathematical difficulties of this kind.

The solution for them is to avoid at all costs presenting them with disembedded mathematical tasks, devoid of the real-life and concrete context in which the child may in fact function very effectively. If the Ben in the problem given above is Mark's little brother, and is given 40p to Mark's 30p by their dad, Mark will in all probability be acutely aware of the 10p gap, even if he could not cope with the same problem posed in less personal terms; if the children have to organize their own teams of five ahead of time for a PE lesson, and get out a football for each team, they are likely to have no difficulty in understanding that the required operation is division. Wherever possible the teacher should base work on 'real' numbers in children's lives: car number-plates, house numbers, mobile phone numbers and football league tables are some examples.

Using everyday situations involving the children themselves and their immediate environment, choosing concrete rather than abstract instructions ('Use three dice and find different ways of scoring 12' instead of 'Explore different ways of adding numbers to make 12'), substituting meaningful materials for those with less meaning (using, for example, 1p and 10p coins rather than an abacus to teach place value), turning abstract language into concrete ('one per cent' into 'one in a hundred', for example) and using real objects that can be handled before encountering the same experiences with pictures and diagrams, are all essential principles in teaching children who find it hard to deal with abstractions.

If real-life experience cannot easily be achieved in the classroom, then story and role-play can help to fill the gap. Diane Montgomery (1990), in her book on teaching children with learning difficulties, gives a vivid example: in some work on measurement, one teacher asked pupils to find out who in the class had the largest and smallest hands, without using any words or sounds to communicate. The two pupils with the smallest hands were chosen to role-play the staff serving in a pretend shop; the three pupils with the largest hands were chosen to play customers buying cloth. The rest of the class watched the ensuing argument about whose hand spans should be used to measure the cloth – leaving them able to articulate very clearly the need for standard units of measurement: an abstraction had become real.

As well as work which will translate abstract into concrete, strategies will also be needed to help with the common problem of not knowing which mathematical operation to apply to everyday problems. Research has given us some insights into why this occurs, and what might help. Krutetskii (1976), for example, found that many of the problems of less able children in dealing with verbally phrased questions stem from their inability to pick out essential from non-essential features, or to pay attention to more than one relevant feature at a time.

Simply giving them extra practice does not seem to help; they need a supportive structure, or scaffolding, which can slowly be withdrawn as they become more familiar with the process of turning problems into operations. To begin with, they may need to be taught a list of key words to look out for – for example, words like altogether/total/increase/more, less/fewer/decrease/difference between, heavier/lighter/longer/shorter/older than. They can have the keywords highlighted by the teacher, or practise highlighting them for each other in a range of verbal problems. It is useful to use and stick to a colour code – with all words and symbols which relate to subtraction (where 'the answer is smaller') in one colour, those which mean addition in another, those which mean multiplication in a third, and so on.

Enabling children to use calculators regularly when solving verbal problems is another strategy that is helpful to older children with special needs. It takes the focus off how to go about adding, dividing or whatever, and places it on what the teacher actually wants the child to learn – choosing the relevant operation, or key press. Children can over-learn particular formats using calculator sentences (Haylock 1991): here the teacher writes a sentence in the particular format that is being practised (for example the addition operation in the format 'If the price of £– is increased by £–, the new price will be £–', or '– m is – shorter than – m'). Blank spaces about the size of a calculator are left for the missing numbers. Children work in pairs, turning over cards from two 0–10 packs and placing them in the spaces ('If the price of £10 is increased by £5, the new price will be £☐ ', '25m is 5m shorter than ☐ '). They work out the problem on a calculator and display the calculator with its answer showing, in the empty answer box, before copying the whole sentence into their books.

A particular way of tapping into the child's common sense understanding of real-life experience is to offer graded problems, which start with small numbers within the pupils' grasp (Haylock 1991). A child may be able to cope easily with a problem in the form 'Mark has 2p. The book costs 5p. Mark needs – p more', but have no idea how to deal with a problem such as 'Mark has 52p. The book costs 93p. Mark needs – p more'. The teacher, however, can help by building in a series of intermediate graded problems: 'Mark has 3p. The book costs 6p . . . Mark has 12p. The book costs 15p . . . Mark has 14p. The book costs 24p . . .' and so on, modelling the use of an empty number line to show that the process is the same, whatever the size of the numbers involved.

Making up their own verbal problems for 'sums' is a popular activity, that will also help children make the links between words and figures. It can be enriched if the children work together, and are given the challenge of tape-recording as many 'stories' as they can, set in an ongoing context such as a topic the class are studying, or a story they are reading, for a given calculation.

A final need for children with mathematical difficulties in handling abstractions will be to have help in 'closing in' open-ended mathematical tasks. If it is a real life task, like organizing a refreshments stall at a fête, or planning how to spend PTA money on improving the school environment, children with learning difficulties need the teacher there with them at the planning stage; once they have, with help, listed the questions that need to be answered, they will be able to carry on with relatively little support. If it is an investigation, for example, explaining what happens when you add pairs of odd and even numbers, they may benefit from being taught, over time and with many repetitions, a flow chart structure that turns the open-ended task into a series of more manageable steps: 'start with one example → make up some more examples → decide what is the same about them → write down your idea → use it to predict some more examples → if it doesn't always work, try another idea'.

Spatial difficulties

So far we have looked at the mathematical needs of children with specific learning difficulties, who have problems with written numbers and with sequencing, and at the needs of children with more general learning difficulties, for whom abstractions and open-ended tasks are the problem. There is another group of children who may have particular teaching needs of a different kind, like Gemma in this example:

> Gemma, though a lively little girl with good language skills, seemed to have a complete block when it came to maths. In Key Stage 1 her numbers were poorly formed and often reversed, and she struggled with maths tasks involving pictures. Later on, her work was always messy and all over the page; she could not make sense of 100 squares and needed to handle apparatus to do the simplest calculations; her parents spent many long and unsuccessful hours trying to teach her how to tell the time. She had great trouble with graphs and charts of all kinds. But it was her performance in work on shape and space that finally gave the clue to her difficulties; teacher assessment persistently showed her failing throughout in this area – for example, in following directional instructions in PE, working with symmetry, constructing nets for shapes, understanding angles and using coordinates. Gemma clearly had major difficulty in perceiving the spatial relationships between objects, or between her own body and the world around her.

For children with spatial difficulties like Gemma's – often children who also present mild motor coordination problems – maths can present apparently insurmountable obstacles. The difficulties will go well beyond the obvious shape and space areas to work in many aspects of number. Early on, these children may be slow to acquire any concept of number at all – the threeness of three, the fourness of four – or to handle simple operations of addition and subtraction, because they lose track of groups of objects or pictures they are trying to count. For them, numbers can shift and alter in a way that makes it difficult to attach symbols reliably to the spatial layouts with which they are presented. Later on, they will be confused by the spatial element that runs through more complex number operations: by the fact, for example, that some numbers (1, 2, 3, 4, etc.) increase in value from left to right, whereas others (in the concept of place value) increase in value from right to left; or by the significance of the way numbers are oriented in space and relative to one another – the differences between the meaning of figures and symbols in these calculations, for example, are entirely spatial:

$$
\begin{array}{cccc}
14 & 41 & 14 & 14 \\
+6 & +6 & \times6 & +9 \\
\hline
\rule{0pt}{1.2em} & & & \\
\end{array}
$$

Spatial skills are also critical in the ability to create and refer at will to a mental map of the number system – the map that places 5 before 6, and after 4, or 90 as ten steps back from 100. Without this mental map, children cannot juggle with numbers, work things out in their heads or check the accuracy of their calculations against an estimate; they have to rely on apparatus and working things out on paper to set rules.

Fortunately, if the teacher is aware that the child has spatial problems (something that is usually fairly obvious from their handwriting and drawings),

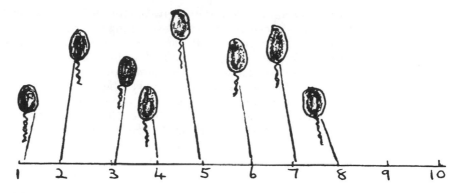

Figure 13.1 Method to circumvent difficulties in counting arrangements.

there is much that can be done to provide appropriate differentiation and support. Early difficulties in counting arrangements can be circumvented if the child is taught to physically move objects from one side of a ruler placed vertically down the table to the other while counting, and later to cross out pictures one by one, or map them into a number line, as in Figure 13.1. Number squares which have alternate rows shaded or coloured will help them to keep track of where they are and read off numbers efficiently. Number cards can have a small hole punched in the top right-hand corner so that these children do not get confused about which way up or round the numerals should go. They should use a number line (for example, the colour-coded *Rainbow Rules* from www.sweetcounter.co.uk) as much as possible when working with addition and subtraction, since they will find counting on and back easier than manipulating counters or fingers. To introduce them to this, they can physically 'walk' a large floor number-line (3 + 2 as 'start at 3, move on 2 steps'), later moving a small toy person along a smaller line, and finally just using their finger. For older children, resources from the BBC CD-ROM *Numeracy in the Classroom*, such as 100 squares for the numbers 1–1000 which can be printed off and stuck together, are useful in helping them understand how the number system fits together. They will need to use a pocket number line, or (even more unobtrusive) a long clearly-marked ruler, for many calculations. Empty number lines may cause problems; they are worth persisting with, however, as it is through activities such as showing where a given number would fit on an empty line (perhaps to begin with immediately after looking at a filled-in line) that these children can slowly build up the mental map which other children carry so easily in their mind's eye.

To help with writing and recognizing numbers, the young child will need ready reference to a card or frieze showing numerals to 10, with a red dot for the starting point of each numeral and an arrow for the direction of pencil movement. Many children with spatial difficulties will benefit from using squared paper when they get to paper and pencil calculations; this enables them to line up numbers next to and under one another, and leads to clearer, neater work. It may be necessary, too, to highlight mathematical signs in different colours (+ always red, for example, and × always blue), to prevent spatial confusion. Confusion between the difficult 'greater than' and 'less than' symbols can be tackled by explaining that the smaller gap between the two lines always points to the smaller of the two numbers being compared. Prepared formats for graphs and tables will help with recording; there is useful software (for example, *Access Maths* from the ACE centre, and the *Maths Books* available from REM) which makes the physical aspects of drawing and recording much easier for pupils with coordination and spatial difficulties.

Other tips include teaching a simple left–right mnemonic (forefinger and thumb on the *left* hand form an L-shape), using a watch or clock face which has the 'past' and 'to' halves highlighted in different colours, laying rulers along coordinates when plotting or reading them, and teaching the child to put visual or spatial information into verbal form: 5×20, for example, becoming 'five lots of twenty', or $20 \div 5$ becoming 'twenty sweets shared between five children'.

Problems with mathematical language

Maths places heavy demands on children's linguistic understanding. For many children, not knowing the meaning of terms such as 'shorter', 'wide', 'same', 'different', 'more than', 'less than', 'few', 'many together', 'as many as', 'each' or 'either' can prevent them from understanding instructions or sharing a mathematical dialogue with others. Sometimes, too, many different words have to be learned for the same concepts – for example, 'equals', 'makes', 'comes to', 'is the same as' for the '=' sign. At another level, children can be held back by the grammatical complexity and sentence length of problems they are asked to tackle: things like 'How many more cats are there than dogs?' or 'What number between 25 and 30 cannot be divided exactly by 2 or 3?'

Difficulties in understanding the language of maths may be due to lack of preschool experience in hearing and using mathematical talk, or to specific language delays and disorders of the kind we looked at in Chapter 10. Either way, the result is the same. Unless the teacher uses the NNS mathematical vocabulary checklists to explore the words the child may not understand, and checks regularly for understanding of complex instructions, the child will be stuck and the teacher will not know how to help.

If teachers are aware of difficulties for the child in responding to mathematical language, they can plan specific work to remedy the gaps. Small-group discussion with the teacher around 'Big Books' from the NNS's booklist, or such resources as LDA's *Talk About Mathematics* photo cards may be enough for some children. Others may need daily practice with a parent or helper on particular vocabulary (a 'word for the week'): work with dad's ties or mum's belts to identify the *widest*, for example, or choosing the group or picture that has the *most* in a variety of situations at home or at school.

Mnemonics will be useful: children can remember, for example, that 'columns go up and down, because columns hold up the roof in buildings'.

For older children there should be mathematical dictionaries and a simple glossary in every classroom, specifying all the possible meanings of mathematical symbols, and the real-life meaning of commonly misunderstood words:

difference   the result of subtracting one number from another
equivalent   equal in value to

factor   a number which will divide exactly into another
fractions   parts of a whole

The teacher may also need to simplify instructions and explanations, rewriting them in shorter steps and in an active rather than a passive voice: the 'What number between 25 and 30 . . .' problem above, for example, becoming:

You are looking for a number between 25 and 30
You cannot divide this number exactly by 2 or 3
What is the number?

The need for over-learning

As we have seen many times in this book a common difficulty for children with special needs is that teaching can expose them to a new concept or idea, but then moves on before they have had a chance to become really fluent and automatic in the new skill. In maths, where learning is often sequential, and one concept or skill builds on earlier ones, this is particularly damaging. It means that maths failure tends to be cumulative; it breeds frustration and irritation in teachers and parents who do not understand why a child seems to have got something one minute, but then forgotten it a few days or weeks later.

Some of the solutions to problems like these were outlined in earlier chapters: building in extra practice (often timed, in order to increase fluency) well beyond the point where the child appears to have grasped the idea, and frequent reviews of earlier learning – in a ratio, some argue, of one-third review to every two-thirds of time spent on new learning. Ideas for over-learning include:

- Investigations, in which pairs or groups of children get repeated practice in a particular skill in the context of a more open-ended task. For example, an investigation like this gives repeated practice in subtraction of two-digit numbers:

    Take two sets of cards numbered 0 to 9. Turn over a pair, and
    write down the number – for example, 71. Reverse the pair and
    write down the number – for example, 17. Now find the difference,
    71 – 17. Repeat with more pairs in order to find out which pairs
    give the biggest difference, and which the smallest difference.

- Games to play in school. Board games and games with number cards provide an enjoyable way of practising a wide range of skills. Many publishers offer packs of number cards with accompanying activities – for example, *20 Activities for KS1 and 2* from Active Maths. Other attractive, inexpensive games are available from BEAM, NES Arnold and Collins.
- Games to play at home. Many traditional board games played at home, like Ludo and Snakes and Ladders, support children's learning of basic mathematical concepts. Some schools (Harrison 1989) have built on this through 'Paired Maths' schemes, where a stock of games, coded according to the predominant mathematical skill or concept involved, and with an

accompanying card to highlight the kinds of mathematical language the game could bring out, are loaned for home use: parents borrow a game or two each week, and record how play went in a home–school book. The Basic Skills Agency is an excellent source of ideas for home-based activities: their *Count and Figure it Out Together* materials include leaflets for parents/carers and a number of ready-to-use game boards. Active Maths are another useful publisher: their *Homework* packs contain booklets outlining key objectives, along with games and suitable equipment in zipped bags.

- Puzzles, such as the crosswords from BEAM's *Number Calculations*, or picture puzzles (Haylock 1991) made by pupils for one another – for dot-to-dot puzzles, for example, pupils place a sheet of tracing paper over an outline drawing and mark significant points with dots; they then write a series of sums or questions under the dot outline, and write the answers to the exercises, in order, next to the dots, so that their partner can answer the questions and join up the corresponding dots to make the picture.

- Calculator marking – another Derek Haylock idea – where older pupils work in pairs using a calculator to check each other's answers. Instead of written pages of exercises, they can deal each other numbers (to be added, multiplied or whatever it is they need to practise) from packs of cards.

- Daily challenge sheets, with a set number of problems to be completed: the pupils record their own speed and error rate, and plot these on a weekly or monthly chart. A useful ready-made resource for this is *Spot On*, by Ruth Rowley.

- Using computers at home. Arcade-type drill and practice games may not be the best use of limited school computer time, but can be a motivating way of providing extra practice at home. Popular software includes *Fun School* which includes time, money and database use as well as practice in basic number skills, and *Maths Blaster*, covering four rule work and fractions with built in self-assessment and record keeping – both are available from REM.

- Using computers at school. The infant age range is well covered by software that practises one-to-one correspondence, counting, ordering and number recognition: Sherston's *Number Train*, *123* and *Tizzy's Toy Box* are good examples. White Space's versatile *Number Shark* remains one of the most popular suites, suitable for Key Stages 1–3, because the level of difficulty can be preset by the teacher or by the child. Children with mathematical difficulties can work on this without damage to their self-esteem; they can be seen playing the same games as their peers, but within their number range. Other popular software for over-learning includes Smile Mathematics' *Microsmile* packs and Collins' *Rapid Maths*.

Motivation, anxiety and dependency

Mathematical difficulties can arise from the interaction of the way in which maths is taught and children's individual characteristics: forgetfulness, spatial confusion, inability to cope with abstractions. Equally, however, difficulties in maths can arise not from cognitive patterns like these but from the way the child *feels* about themselves in relation to maths.

Many writers have commented on the extent to which maths arouses complex emotions in children and adults – perhaps because more than any other subject it is open to absolute failure (not just the relative judgements which teachers make about a piece of writing, a drawing or a model, but absolute judgements of answers as right or wrong). Common reactions to the possibility of failure of this kind include anxiety and panic, overdependence on the teacher for help in getting everything correct, or avoidance in the form of poor concentration and motivation. It is important that investigation of children's special needs in maths include watching them at work, and asking them how they feel about their work, in order to assess whether any of these behavioural patterns may be contributing to the problems they experience.

Anxiety about maths makes children lose their common sense, grasp at straws for answers and follow set rules and patterns whether or not they are appropriate to the situation. Children who are anxious need, first of all, active encouragement from their teachers to make 'mistakes'. They need to be told, at regular intervals, that if they always got everything right and knew everything there was to know then their teacher would be out of a job, and the school closed. They will benefit from oral and mental starter activities like 'Show Me', where pupils hold number fans, place value cards or number generators up so that only the teacher can see them, and where they can, if they need to, have a quick confidence-building peep at what others are doing before deciding on their answer. They should have opportunities to work in pairs during whole-class teaching, so that they can discuss their ideas before they present their answer: this will avoid the feeling of being 'on the spot' which makes some anxious children freeze when asked a question. They also need plenty of exposure to paired or group investigations that do not have one right answer (or through which they can see that the same outcome can be reached by several equally valid methods), to work that they check themselves with a calculator, or to the emotionally neutral feedback provided by a computer. They need to be helped to make connections between the real world they know and can handle (sharing sweets among friends, giving the right coins in a shop) and the often unreal world of school maths.

Children who are overdependent on the teacher also need these kinds of anxiety-reducing strategy, coupled with challenges to make up their own problems for other children, to take part in maths games in small groups, or help younger children with their maths work. They may need to be set targets for certain amounts of work to be completed within a set period, reinforced regularly with praise or points for tackling new tasks independently, or given time with the teacher to explain how they went about tackling particular problems as a reward *after* they have completed them rather than during the process.

Maths is very vulnerable to the effects of poor concentration. This can be induced by inappropriate teaching methods, such as expecting a child to plough through solitary activities in close proximity to their best friends, or to work through a series of disembedded tasks that have no obvious relationship with reality. Cross-curricular links will help to motivate pupils: Active Maths' materials on the Romans, Greeks and Egyptians have proved very successful here.

It may be necessary, for children who do not concentrate, to use some of the strategies for increasing concentration suggested in Chapter 8, but not until the teacher has first observed the child's concentration in other situations:

using mathematical software on the computer, perhaps, or playing maths games, or engaging in the kinds of highly active learning involved in the best Numeracy Hours. Even better, find the child a real task to do and watch them concentrate – as with the boy described by Derek Haylock, who was given the job of buying the right amount of orange squash for refreshments at a football tournament, and on discovering that he could use repeated addition to find out how many bottles of squash, each providing 26 drinks, were required for 90 children each needing 6 drinks, said to his teacher in excitement: 'You can use adding for this, miss. I reckon that's why we learn it, so we can use it for things'.

Common problem areas

Conservation and early number concepts

Many young children, who appear to be competent in counting groups and attaching written numerals to them, begin to fail when they move on to work on simple addition and subtraction. The reason is often that they have no concept of the stability of numbers attached to groups. If they are shown two lines of counters, and count them to see that they are equal, and then see one line spread out so that it now looks longer than the other, they are likely to say that the longer line now has more counters. If they count a line of objects, then see it spread out and are asked 'How many now?', they will count again rather than know that the number remains unchanged.

In these circumstances, where numbers are seen as shifting things attached to perceptual appearances rather than permanent qualities, what can something like 4 + 2 really mean? If the child has not achieved number conservation, it will be necessary to go back a stage and offer activities that will help them to separate the real meaning of numbers from surface appearances:

- Playing number dominoes – joining cards that have the same number of dots, in different perceptual patterns. BEAM sell giant dominoes, which are particularly popular. Variations include a game from Active Maths where children have to count the spots on dice and match to the number of spots on ladybirds.
- Dropping a number of small objects (e.g. buttons) and drawing all the different patterns made.
- Colouring on squared paper all the patterns of a given number that the child can think of.
- Playing a game like *Ele Flips* from NES Arnold, which encourages children to develop a notion of number not affected by position.
- Using software such as the *Conserve* game in the *Number Shark* suite.
- Provoking what is called 'conservation conflict' – having the child make a line to match another, rearranging one to make it longer (or shorter), while simultaneously removing (or adding) one item, and then asking whether the two lines have the same number.
- Using meaningful materials that have real value to the child (e.g. money or sweets) and posing the question, 'Which line would you rather have now?' as an alternative to 'Which has more?'

Once conservation is established, the child can be helped to see the meaning and usefulness of numerals, using Martin Hughes' (1986) suggestions for games to play with young children:

- Assembling tins with 0–3 bricks in them for the children to see; putting lids on them, shuffling them around and asking the child to pick, for example, 'The tin with three bricks in it'; suggesting the child uses magnetic numerals to help them remember how many bricks were in each tin.
- Adding bricks to a tin and introducing the '+' symbol: 'One brick, then another, so 1 + 1 goes on the lid; how many altogether? Now close your eyes . . . the lid says 1 + 2; how many have I put in now?'
- Playing a simple board game (where the child moves a counter along a row of squares to reach 'home'), first with a traditional dice marked with dots, then with two dice with dots, then with one dice that has numerals on labels stuck over the relevant number of dots (3 over ∴), then with two dice, one of which has numerals and the other dots.
- Having the child order magnetic (or peg-on) numbers and then count them (so as to see that the last numeral in the series equals the total number); covering some with your hand, for example, 1, 2 and 3, and asking the child to guess how many are hidden.

Addition and subtraction facts

To be seen to be counting on your fingers, or worse still using apparatus when everyone else is doing clever things in their heads, is a source of embarrassment to many children; yet a lack of rapid recall of number facts is a common mathematical difficulty. Endless practice with addition and subtraction sums is not the answer. Investigations and games can do the same job in a much more interesting way; here is a selection of ideas:

- Clock arithmetic (Womack 1988). There are several forms of this game, based on the card game clock patience. The game 'Seven-up' requires 35 cards on which are written all the addition facts that use the numbers 0–7. The child shuffles the cards and deals them face down around the 'clock' in positions 1–7 as shown below: two cards at position one, three at position two, four at position three and so on.

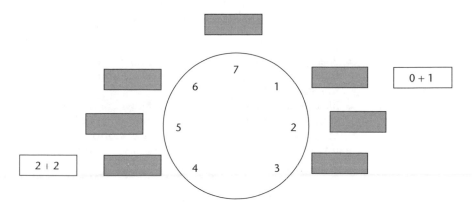

The child turns up the last card dealt to position 7, works out the addition, places the card next to the position corresponding to the answer (for example, a card saying 2 + 2 at position 4), and turns the top card in that pile over. The game continues until the child places a card next to a position that has no unturned cards left; occasionally, and this is the point that makes the child want to continue playing the game, all the cards get turned over and successfully placed.

In 'Nine-up', all the subtraction facts involving two-digit numbers less than 20 with answers 1–9 (45 of them) are practised. There are now nine positions around the clock; this time one card is dealt to position 1, two to position 2, three to position 3 and so on.

- The game of WAR (Henderson 1989). This uses an ordinary pack of cards; face cards are worth 10 and an ace worth 1. The pack is dealt out to two or more players. All the players in turn put down two cards from the top of their pile, and either add them (in one version of the game), or subtract them (in another). Whoever in that round has the highest value collects all the cards. When two players have equal highest, then it is WAR. Each player lines up their soldiers – five cards face down – and turns over two more from their main pile. Whoever now has the higher sum wins all 14 cards. Other games involving regular playing cards are described in Fran Mosley's *Cards on the Table*, from BEAM; the game 'Avoid Ten' (where children have to make sure none of the pairs of cards they play total 10) is particularly motivating.

- Games with two dice – board games, or games with number cards, for example a game where number cards 2–10 are laid out face up on the table in lines of three. The child rolls both dice, adds up the throw and turns over the corresponding card (a 4 card for 2 + 2, for example). The next child does the same; the person who succeeds in turning over the third card in a line scores a point. Then all the cards are turned face up again and the game continues until one player reaches a score of 5 points.

- The 'One to Twenty' game (Haylock 1991). Two 1–10 card packs, with 10s, 11s and 12s added, are used to produce a pair of numbers to be added. Each player has a strip of card marked off in 20 sequentially numbered squares, and 20 counters to place on the squares. The aim of the game is to cover as many numbers on the strip as possible. The child is dealt their cards, totals them and places counters on the strip in any combination of numbers that make up this total. A player who cannot make up the total is out. *Bingo*, from Active Maths, is based on the same idea. The commercially available game *Shut the Box* uses a similar principle for number bonds 0–10.

- Board games such as *Race Track* from Active Maths; NES Arnold's *Number Spinners*; computer games such as 'Numberline', 'Rods' and 'Crocs' in *Number Shark*.

- Making up star sums – for example, where the numbers in horizontal and vertical lines total the same (given) number, or '*Stringalings*' (BEAM's strings of linked addition and subtraction operations).

- Investigating number puzzles like '*Crossover Magic*' (also from BEAM) where opposite pairs of numbers mysteriously add to the same total, or completing magic squares where, for example, rows, columns and diagonals add to a constant number.

- Games with skittles, ringboards or darts where pairs of numbers have to be added.
- The password game: a particular number fact (e.g. 8 + 6 = 14) becomes the 'password' for the day; the children have to say the password in order to enter or leave the classroom, use certain equipment, etc.

Understanding the relationship between addition and subtraction, and solving missing number equations

All primary teachers are very familiar with the difficulties of children who can do straightforward addition and subtraction, but do not know where to start when faced with problems like 8 + ☐ = 12, or 'There were 12 buttons in this box but now there are only 8; how many were taken out?'

For younger children, talk around number stories (like Kingscourt's Mathslink Big Book, *A Week Away*) is the best way to develop understanding. Another good practical activity from Mathslink uses a photocopiable folder fact card, which allows children to fold over and unfold numbers to enact addition and subtraction stories within any given number to 10, using the language of 'How many more will make . . . ?', and 'How many left . . . ?'

For older children, games with number cards can help – for example, this game where two number cards and the matching total number of counters are placed in a box: one child takes out one of the cards but does not show it to the other child, who has to guess what it says by finding the difference between the number of counters in the box and the number on the remaining card. This provides a concrete model of the relationship between addition and subtraction. Other ways of showing the relationship include number lines and apparatus such as trays for interlocking cubes where the action of breaking off three from a strip of seven to leave four can be subsequently seen as 4 add 3 making 7. Derek Haylock's (1991) recommendation of short periods of daily class work for helping children see this relationship (and other relationships, such as that between multiplication and division) lends itself well to the oral and mental starter of the daily maths lesson: the teacher writes an addition fact (such as 8 + 4 = 12) on the board and asks as many questions as possible based on this fact: 'What is eight add four, what is twelve take away four, what number is four more than eight, what is the difference between twelve and four, how many more than eight is twelve, what number must I take from twelve to leave eight, I am eight and my sister is twelve, so how much older is she?' and so on. Making up their own number stories and questions for each other based around a particular number fact is the next step.

Coin recognition and equivalence, making up amounts

Understanding money – recognizing coins, making up amounts, adding amounts and working out change – can be difficult for some children with learning difficulties because of the abstract nature of the relationship between coins and their value. On the other hand, because of the relevance of money to important everyday experiences, learning how to handle it can prove a concrete way into number operations in general: for this reason it is worth spending quite a lot of time making sure that essential money concepts have been grasped.

Coin recognition activities include games with dice that have 1p, 2p, 5p and so on marked on their sides. The children take turns to throw the dice and pick up the relevant toy (or real) coins to cover a space on a lotto board or a picture (like a 'money man' or 'money cat') made out of coins of various values.

For work on coin equivalence, exchange games are very useful. Up to four players plus a banker play a game where the winner, for example, is the first to get ten 5p pieces (or 2p, or 10p or whatever). Each player in turn takes a card from a face-down pile of 0–10 number cards; the banker pays them their winnings in 1p pieces. When they have five they ask the banker to exchange them. A class shop and bank can provide similar experiences of exchange in a role-play context.

For making up amounts, an obvious game is a small group one where one player is banker, and children have a supply of coins and draw cards for items and their prices. This can be played at many levels; if there is an additional 1–9 card pack the children will need to work out the cost, for example, of five pens at 11p each. There are many commercially available packs on these lines – for example, Learning Materials Ltd's *Money Street*. None is a substitute for the 'real' experience with money, through suggestions for things parents can do at home and in the shops, and through classroom work such as investigating best buys, running a tuck shop, going down to the dinner hall each morning with a support assistant to look at the day's menu and work out the coins needed for what you want to eat, budgeting for a class trip or planning how to spend money on a project to improve the school environment. For children with special needs, however, money games (and software such as *Number Shark*'s 'Coin Change' or, for older pupils, *Lifeskills: Time and Money* from REM) do provide the element of extra structured practice that provides for consolidation and over-learning.

Times tables

The emphasis on knowledge of multiplication facts in the NNS can present problems for children with special needs, since some (notably those with specific learning difficulties/dyslexia) find learning times tables almost impossible. Some simple teaching tips can, however, go a long way towards making them able at least to get by in this area.

An excellent starting point is the *Times Tables* CD-ROM (available from iansyst), a resource which explains to children (and learners of all ages) ways in which they can minimize the number of facts they have to learn, and demonstrates strategies for learning those that are essential.

It is important that the full potential of NNS mental maths work is used to make clear to children that the task of learning tables can be reduced to manageable proportions. Most children learn their five and ten times tables easily; if the principle of reversibility is explained, there are only 21 multiplication facts left to be learned (see Box 13.1). These can be represented on cards, with a number, such as 27, on one side and the relevant facts ($3 \times 9 = 27$, $9 \times 3 = 27$, $27 \div 9 = 3$, $27 \div 3 = 9$) on the other, and used for daily practice with a peer or at home. Teaching the patterns in tables will also be

---

Box 13.1   21 table facts

$3 \times 3 = 9$	$6 \times 6 = 36$
$4 \times 3 = 12$	$7 \times 6 = 42$
$6 \times 3 = 18$	$8 \times 6 = 48$
$7 \times 3 = 21$	$9 \times 6 = 54$
$8 \times 3 = 24$	$7 \times 7 = 49$
$9 \times 3 = 27$	$8 \times 7 = 56$
$4 \times 4 = 16$	$9 \times 7 = 63$
$6 \times 4 = 24$	$8 \times 8 = 64$
$7 \times 4 = 28$	$9 \times 8 = 72$
$8 \times 4 = 32$	$9 \times 9 = 81$
$9 \times 4 = 36$	

---

helpful: that when the figures in the answers to the three times table are added ($4 \times 3 = 12$ and $1 + 2 = 3$, $5 \times 3 = 15$ and $1 + 5 = 6$, and so on) there is a recurring pattern of 3, 6, 9 throughout the table, and that the figures in the answers to the nine times table always total 9. Or, for the larger multiplication facts, children can be taught how to use lower tables they do know and double the answers – for example, if they do not know 7×8, they can use double 7×4 instead.

Other useful strategies include teaching the child that the five times table can be thought of as half of the ten times table, the two times table as doubling, the four times table as double the two times table, the three times table as adding the one to the two times table ($3 \times 8 = 2 \times 8 + 1 \times 8$), the six times table as adding the one to the five times table ($6 \times 8 = 5 \times 8 + 1 \times 8$), the seven times table as adding the two to the five times table ($7 \times 8 = 5 \times 8 + 2 \times 8$), and the nine times table as the ten times table minus the one times table.

The difficult nine times table can alternatively be easily mastered by a finger maths method. Here the child holds up both hands and starts from the left hand. They fold down the thumb for one times nine: this shows nine fingers left (the answer nine). For two times nine, the child folds down the left index finger, leaving the left thumb standing up; that represents the ten in the answer, with the remaining fingers standing up representing the eight. For three times nine, the middle finger of the left hand is folded down: the thumb and index finger each represent tens, making twenty, with the remaining fingers standing up representing the seven in the answer 27 and so on, right through the table to ten times nine.

Almost all the games and activities described in the section on addition and subtraction facts can be used to reinforce multiplication as well – for example, the clock patience 'Nine-up' game can be played with 45 cards containing the multiplication facts from $1 \times ? = 1$ through $1 \times ? = 2$ and $2 \times ? = 4$ up to $9 \times ? = 81$. Useful computer software includes *Mathsblaster*, and *Smudge – Times Tables in Space* (both from REM), Sherston's *Mental Maths Olympics* and *Table Aliens*, *Megamaths Tables* from Longman Logotron. From the BBC, *Tables with Dynamo* provides a useful video and activity books for practice at home.

Differentiation and participation

So far we have looked at particular 'sticking points' for some children's mathematical learning, and at the particular activities they may need in order to overcome them. This does not mean, however, that they need to spend large amounts of time doing something different from what the main body of the class are doing. On the contrary, the structure of the daily maths lesson has made possible a level of participation and inclusion for children with mathematical difficulties which was never possible in the days when children worked individually and alone through endless pages of maths schemes, as this example shows:

> Jordan, a Statemented Year 6 pupil with global difficulties in cognition and learning was observed by a specialist support teacher in the course of a Year 5/6 mixed age-group maths lesson. During the oral/mental starter his teacher put a series of questions to him which he was able to answer relatively easily. This gave him the confidence to have a go (sometimes successfully) at other questions. He listened well to vocabulary and concepts technically beyond his grasp. In the main part of the lesson he participated well with a peer partner on tasks which could be undertaken at a range of ability levels. The support teacher was surprised at times at the amount he had learned; he was later able to explain to her concepts that she would have thought far too difficult for him, even though she had worked with him for some time and knew him well. Her feeling was that he was benefiting hugely from moving away from what he had previously experienced ('flogging to death' basic number facts which he had not successfully learned or been able to use, while all the time missing out on what other pupils were covering). At last he was able to experience a broad and balanced exposure to the maths curriculum, enjoying the variety and feeling himself to be a learner like his peers.

Conclusion

Jordan's learning difficulties were significant; he experienced many of the problems in thinking in the abstract, understanding mathematical language and retention of new concepts which we have examined in depth in this chapter. Nevertheless, he successfully took part in the learning experiences of other children in the mainstream, in line with the developments in inclusive practice which are rapidly becoming the norm rather than the exception in our primary schools.

Such inclusion required planning across the whole curriculum, with maths as just one aspect. It also required a high degree of teamwork between Jordan's teacher and the other people (children and adults) who played a part in supporting him. It is to this kind of planning and teamwork that we fittingly turn in the last chapter of this book: a chapter that brings us full circle from the consideration of what needs to be 'special' for some children's learning, to what needs to be shared.

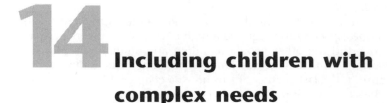

14 Including children with complex needs

Introduction

So far, this book has looked mainly at how teachers can support children with 'high incidence' SEN: that is, children with a broad range of learning and behaviour difficulties. These children are to be found in every classroom; every teacher will want to have a good grasp of the inclusive teaching strategies which enable their needs to be met.

But what about children with 'low incidence' needs – those less commonly occurring learning difficulties which teachers will meet from time to time in their classrooms, such as sensory impairment, autistic spectrum disorder, physical impairment and so on?

In this chapter we will look at issues around the increasing inclusion of children with complex needs like these within mainstream schools, and at the systems which will ensure effective support.

Why include?

Increased inclusion within mainstream schools has become a cornerstone of national strategy (DfEE 1998). Recent legislation has strengthened the rights of parents to ask for an inclusive placement for their child, giving 'a clear signal that a mainstream place should only be refused in the small minority of cases where it cannot be demonstrated that the interests of all children cannot be safeguarded' (DfES 2001a).

Many teachers, however, remain sceptical about inclusion. Croll and Moses (2000), for example, found that a third of primary teachers and over a half of headteachers thought that more children should go to special schools; less than one-tenth thought fewer children should be attending special schools.

On the other hand, the same study produced some interesting results when the same questions about inclusion were asked in a slightly different way. When they were asked about children with SEN currently in their own classes, teachers overwhelmingly felt that the mainstream class was the right placement. They frequently emphasized the social benefits to the child of being in a mainstream class, and the fact that the child was happy there.

How can we reconcile these apparently contradictory findings? On the one hand, when 'thinking in the abstract' about inclusion, teachers feel that the more favourable teacher–pupil ratios, the specialist knowledge and the other facilities which they assume to be available in special schools provide the right conditions for children to make progress; on the other hand, when they have experienced working with children who have complex needs in their own classrooms, they tend to feel that the children should stay there.

This apparent paradox in fact fits in well with the conclusions from research (Sebba and Sachdev 1997) that the experience of inclusive education appears to have a positive effect on teacher, pupil and parent attitudes, shifting the focus away from the child's perceived disability onto the child as a person.

The arguments for 'giving inclusion a go' in this way are compelling. First, there is the human rights issue – that children should have equal rights to membership of the same groups as everyone else, irrespective of disability. Second, there is the consistent failure to find evidence (Sebba and Sachdev 1997; Crowther *et al.* 1999) that the assumed benefits of education in special schools (in terms of greater educational attainment or improved self-esteem) can in fact be demonstrated. Third, there are the very clear benefits for children of going to school with other children from their neighbourhood, summed up by this parent: 'She's never going to be a doctor or whatever . . . if she gets a job that's good; if she doesn't that's life – but she can't do without friends. All children like to be liked and need to be with their peers. That's why I want her to go to her local school with the children she's grown up with' (NLS 2000).

Children and young people – whatever their impairment or approach to learning – have a part to play in society in adult life. They can more easily play that part if they have not been cut off from the mainstream early on; society will only begin to change to take account of the needs of disabled people if we can break down the barriers of ignorance and prejudice by educating children together right from the start.

How is inclusion different from integration?

Many teachers interpret 'inclusion' as a simple statement about where children are educated: in mainstream as opposed to special schools. Current thinking tends, however, to adopt broader definitions, based on ideas about building capacity in mainstream schools:

> Inclusive education describes the process by which a school attempts to respond to all the children as individuals by reconsidering and restructuring its curricular provision and allocating resources to enhance equality of opportunity. Through this process, the school builds its capacity to accept all children from the local community and, in so doing, reduces the need to exclude children.
>
> (Sebba and Sachdev 1997)

This definition highlights the difference between inclusion and integration. Many schools 'integrate' disabled children by bringing them onto their premises – but on the school's terms. The pupil can stay if they can benefit from what is already on offer; the school does not in this case expect to change to accommodate and support diverse needs.

Inclusive education, by comparison, seeks to adapt systems and structures to meet needs. Adaptations to the school curriculum, to buildings, to attitudes and values, to language, images and role models are some of the changes required if we are to move from integration to real inclusion.

Tools are available to help schools make these changes: notably the *Index for Inclusion* (Booth *et al.* 2000), from the Centre for Studies in Inclusive Education. This is a self-evaluation tool which allows a school to look at its work under three headings: inclusive policies, inclusive cultures and inclusive practices.

Making it work

Whole-school planning on these lines will form the best possible backdrop to the inclusion of individual children with complex needs. Then, for these children, schools need to ask themselves how to make inclusion work effectively – given the evidence (Zigler and Hodapp 1986) that individualized teaching programmes are effective but relatively uncommon in mainstream schools, and given the continuing risk that children with special needs in inclusive placements can be stigmatized and rejected by their peers.

The answer to the challenge of individualizing teaching lies, for the most part, in the school's existing arrangements for differentiating the curriculum to meet the needs of *all* their children. As HMI observed (1990), in some classes 'the fact that a child has a Statement of special educational needs was almost incidental, as the general classwork was carefully matched to children's abilities'. In others, inappropriate work for all but 'average' children in the class meant that a child with very special needs would clearly stand out and fail to achieve. Once again, we are back to the idea of the whole-school policy: of access for staff to consultation with a trained special needs coordinator and outside agencies, of decent action planning for individuals, of differentiated schemes of work and the availability of teaching resources that have been gathered and developed to meet a range of needs within these planned schemes.

As for reducing stigmatization and peer rejection, there is a great deal that can be done (and is, in many schools), to promote in children, as well as adults, an acceptance of one another's differences and a commitment to inclusion rather than exclusion for those we perceive as different from ourselves. Circle time and class work in personal and social education can help children think about the effects of name-calling, in groups and out groups and friendship patterns in their class and school. Curricular work (in science, in the humanities and through literature) can help children gain insight into the experience of others who may not see, or hear, or understand, or be able to use their bodies as they do (Rieser and Mason 1990). On this can be built an understanding of the ways in which as individuals and as a society we can either choose to 'enable' or 'disable' people with learning difficulties or physical and sensory impairment.

Schools also need to plan how they will encourage social interaction between a particular child with very special needs and his or her peers. Schemes here have been many and imaginative. Children with hearing impairment and Down's syndrome have, for example, had their social standing raised by being asked to teach a sign language to others. Children with learning difficulties have been taught new games which they then introduce to a selected group in the playground. Peer partners for learning have been appointed and buddy systems set up outside the classroom. Socially isolated children have been given a key role or key piece of information in small-group problem solving work, so that they are actively involved from the start rather than marginalized by other group members.

In the most imaginative projects of all, schools have adopted a model that originated in Canada (Shaw 1990), where planned strategies are used to prepare peers for the integration of new students into their mainstream classes, and to make sure that things are going well socially as well as academically after the move. In one of these strategies, called 'Circle of Friends', a teacher visits the class and briefly describes the new student who is about to be integrated. The teacher helps the children to map, for themselves, the circles that represent the important people in their lives. In the first and smallest circle go the people closest to them – family, best friends, those with whom they can be at ease and those whom they can trust. In the second circle are people they really like, and see a lot of, but who aren't quite close enough to go in the inner circle. In the third go people they do things with from time to time – people in clubs they belong to, people in their street, people in their class. The last circle is for people who are paid to be in their lives and do things for them, like their doctor or dentist. The teacher then introduces an imaginary person, with a disability, who is the same age as the children in the class. In this person's circles there are parents and perhaps a brother in the centre, but nothing in the other circles except for circle four, which is full of people: doctors, physiotherapists, social workers and so on. The students talk about how they would feel if their circles looked like this. Finally, the teacher again mentions the student who is coming to join them, asks the children why they think they did the activity on circles of friends, and promises to return in a few weeks 'to see what's happening'. This experience alone is usually enough to prompt children in the class to set up their own circle of friends for the new student – to telephone the student before they arrive, for example, and to plan ways of including them in their activities out of school as well as in.

In a second strategy, 'Making Action Plans', a team is set up which includes the student with a disability or learning difficulty, family members and the professionals who work with the child. Importantly, members of the student's circle of friends in their class are also included, because they can contribute a unique perception of the social processes that go on in the class, and the student's social needs. The team meet regularly, first to listen to the parents' hopes and fears for the child's future, and build a shared picture of the student's strengths, personality and needs; later to plan the details of how the student will spend their time in school. Achieving real social integration is a goal that is given a high priority throughout the planning process – as high a priority as progress in academic areas.

Building the class teacher's confidence: working in partnership

Understandably, many class teachers lack confidence in their ability to develop inclusive classrooms, because they feel they are dealing with very special needs that lie outside their previous experience and knowledge base. This feeling can be prevented if they are aware that a detailed knowledge of the child's particular disability is not actually required of them at all. They need *some* background knowledge, but no more than can be obtained from some basic reading provided by the SENCO or a member of the central support services. Beyond this, their main professional requirement is to know how to make effective use of specialist consultancy, and how to coordinate their own work with that of others. They need to be able to:

- work with a specialist (either from within the school or from an outside agency) to identify appropriate learning objectives (in both academic and social areas) for the child;
- develop a termly action plan that will specify who is going to do what (parents, classroom assistants, support teachers, the class teacher) in helping the pupil meet these objectives;
- work with the specialist to identify any particular teaching approaches or styles which may be effective, and make sure that appropriate access strategies are in place to circumvent impairments and enable the child to take part in the curriculum and the full life of the school;
- work with the specialist on differentiating the overall class schemes of work and methods of assessment, in the light of the identified teaching styles/access strategies; build this into lesson plans;
- provide any classroom assistants or other helpers, in the light of the negotiated action plan, with a clear description of their roles and responsibilities in relation to those of the class teacher;
- seek regular feedback from the child that the support which is in place is working from their point of view, and that of their parents/carers.

The next example will illustrate how one teacher, initially very concerned about how he would cope with a child with complex needs in his classroom, succeeded in using his existing skills in special needs work as a whole to coordinate a highly effective programme for a child with a visual impairment:

Alison's Statement said that she was a sociable but rather anxious little girl, with particular strengths in oral language skills. She was partially sighted, but able to use print with the help of magnification. Her support was to come from five hours a week of teaching assistant time, plus fortnightly visits from a teacher from the service for sensory impairment. In addition, she was to be supplied with her own computer, with a specially adapted keyboard and software to enable her to produce large-print text, and with a range of magnifying devices.

Mrs Potter, Alison's special needs assistant, was one of the school's own part-time ancillaries, who had been keen to take on the extra hours attached to the Statement. She had no experience of work of this kind, however, and went to the class teacher to voice her concerns. He arranged a meeting between himself, the visiting specialist teacher and the ancillary, at which it was agreed that Mrs Potter should spend some time visiting the LEA's unit for primary visually impaired children, and enrol on a specialist course run by the Royal National Institute for the Blind for learning support assistants. The visiting teacher also promised to bring some literature on Alison's particular visual problem for Mrs Potter and the teacher to read. Together, the three looked at the reports which had been compiled for Alison's Statement and identified some targets they felt they should work on – at least to start with. These included building Alison's confidence by planning ways for her to make a valuable contribution in small group work in speaking and listening, increasing the vocabulary of high frequency words she could spell correctly and ensuring full curriculum access – particularly in practical subjects like science and technology, where she had tended to hang back in the past.

Mrs Potter's support time, it was agreed, would be partly spent on preparing materials for Alison – copying, enlarging and spacing worksheets in particular. For the remainder of the time, however, she would come into class for science and technology lessons to support Alison directly. The class teacher would, at the start of the week, meet her in assembly time to review any difficulties and outline the practical work that the class would be doing in the week ahead. Mrs Potter's role might sometimes be to give hands-on assistance, but more often would focus on praising Alison for having a try herself, once Mrs Potter had set the scene for her and provided her with large-size or tactile materials.

The visiting teacher felt that her role would be observing in the classroom, so as to feed back to the class teacher any information that would help him plan work for Alison. For example, after one visit she advised him that it would help if he always read out anything he put up on the blackboard as he wrote, and made sure the board was really clean so as to provide a good contrast. Another time she was able to suggest and bring in some electronic measuring devices for Alison to use instead of the regular scales, thermometers and tape measures available in the classroom.

The class teacher also asked the visiting teacher to look at his planning at the start of each term, and make written comments on areas where he would have to take special care to make sure that Alison could participate fully. He requested help, in the spring term, in picking out from all the reading he had to do on the forthcoming SATs the adaptations that were allowed for visually impaired children. Finally, it was agreed that the visiting teacher would be responsible for training Alison and her parents in the use of her low-vision aids and specialist technology, and sorting out any hitches that arose in this area.

Complex needs: sensory impairment

Vision impairment

As we have seen from the example of Alison, schools can expect to draw on the advice of a qualified teacher of the visually impaired when working with children who are partially sighted or educationally blind. Such teachers will work with the school to plan specialist learning that the child will need – for example, the teaching of Braille, touch-typing skills, independence skills, orientation and mobility training. In addition, the teacher will advise on how to overcome the most difficult challenge faced by visually impaired pupils – accessing large amounts of written information. Often this will be through the provision of specialist computer technology, and adapted large print or CD-ROM texts.

The class teacher's main role is to understand the constraints on the child in terms of speed of information processing – particularly in whole-class teaching – and the frustrations this can lead to if not carefully managed. The teacher will need to remember that much of their classroom communication – facial expression, gesture, all the information on the classroom walls – may be lost on the visually impaired child. The teacher will, therefore, need to learn to give a verbal commentary to replace the missing visual information, and take into account the fact that many words and concepts rely on vision for full understanding (how do you know what an elephant is if you have never seen one?).

Specific access strategies will include:

- advance planning so that the child's support team (LSA and visiting teacher) can modify texts ahead of time;
- pre-tutoring before a lesson, so as to explain concepts that rely on vision for understanding;
- positioning – seating the child so that the light source is behind them, and making sure that the teacher never stands in front of a window where the glare will make it very hard for the child to see;
- using the child's name first to alert them to questions;
- ensuring that the teacher speaks at the same time as writing – for example, on the blackboard or on an overhead transparency;
- organizing the child's equipment (pencils, pens, etc.) so that it is easily located and stays in one place – on a tray, for example;
- maintaining good, clear contrast for all written work – bold print on non-glossy paper;
- using speech-supported word processing and speech access on computers.

Hearing impairment

For children with hearing impairment, specialist support from a qualified teacher of the deaf should be available. The class teacher needs to understand the particular nature of the child's hearing impairment. This might be an ability to hear sound only at high volume, or equally it might be a selective hearing loss affecting only certain frequencies, so that vowels are picked up but not consonants. Some children will benefit from hearing aids; others

– particularly those with losses affecting high frequencies – will not. Even where they are used, aids do not provide a child with instant normal hearing; the amplified sound tends to be distorted, and the aid amplifies background noise as well as speech. Understanding will always be greater when the child can use context to help predict what others might be saying: communication which comes 'out of the blue' without prior context-setting presents the child with real problems.

Whatever the type of loss, the child will tire quickly in listening situations: they have to concentrate much harder than other children on making sense of classroom communication, whether this be through hearing aids, lip-reading or signing, and may not be able to keep this up for long.

Access requirements for children with a hearing impairment include:

- planning the best possible listening conditions for the child: avoiding seats near the classroom door or any other 'heavy traffic' area, and avoiding where possible background distractions such as noisy heaters and buzzing lights;
- checking regularly that any hearing aids are working properly, and remembering that aids only really function effectively over a 2–3 metre distance;
- positioning: again ensuring that the light is on the teacher's face, the blackboard or shared text, with the light source behind the pupil rather than in front;
- facing the pupil so that they can make maximum use of lip-reading – making sure other children also face the child when speaking or that the teacher repeats back what they have said;
- speaking clearly at normal volume and avoiding exaggerated 'mouthing', as this interferes with the normal rhythm and information of speech;
- taking care to set a context before speaking ('Now we are going to talk about . . .') and avoiding any unsignalled changes of topic;
- saying the child's name before asking a question;
- questioning the child after some other pupils have been called on first, so that they have experienced a model of what is required;
- making maximum use of visual cues – real objects, pictures, writing down words and instructions as well as saying them – when teaching;
- checking for understanding of instructions – for example, by asking the child to explain what they have to do;
- if working alongside a British Sign Language interpreter, checking that the speed of delivery is matched to the interpreter's requirements;
- being aware that some children with hearing impairment may miss grammatical word endings like -s, -ed and -ing.

Complex needs: physical impairment

In many ways teachers find it easier to 'include' children with physical impairments than they do those who have difficulties in cognition and learning or emotional, social and behavioural needs. On the face of it, the issues can seem straightforward: the child simply needs adaptations like ramps or handrails, or the provision of extra adult support, in order to be able to cope with the same curriculum as their peers.

In reality, the issues are often more complex than this. Children with movement problems (for example, those with cerebral palsy) often have additional difficulties in perception, memory and maintaining attention, which it is important for teachers to understand. They may find it very hard to screen out irrelevant information, and appear easily distracted, they may have problems in recalling information unless it is experienced practically and visually as well as verbally, they may struggle with spatial information and find it hard to make sense of 'busy' text and diagrams, they will certainly experience greater fatigue than other children – not only because of the constant effort of managing movement, but also because of a shortened concentration span.

Access strategies need to take into account these potential difficulties, as well as the more obvious physical needs. They may include:

- colour-coded rails around the school;
- making sure that corridors and cloakrooms are not cluttered with things that will get in the child's way;
- organizing the classroom so that there are uncluttered routes for the child to use;
- organizing the child's table space so that the equipment they need is to hand and will not roll away – for example, by using Dycem;
- making sure the child has plenty of space – for example, sitting at the end of a table rather than in the middle;
- creating a workstation for the child which is as far as possible distraction free – for example, by the use of screens;
- checking seating carefully: the child should be able to sit so that their feet are flat on the floor, with the lower back firmly against the back of the seat – a chair with arms is often helpful;
- using concrete aids (pictures and objects) to reinforce abstract concepts;
- using mind-mapping and mnemonics to aid recall;
- building in rest periods;
- minimizing written recording, using predictive word processing, dictation to a peer or support assistant, writing frames and 'fill-in-the-blanks' sheets;
- making text and worksheets less 'busy': uncluttered layout, using different colours to make things clearer (for example, the separate syllables in a word), using a cardboard overlay frame to limit vision to one part of the page at a time.

Complex needs: cognition and learning

All teachers have in their classes children with a broad range of learning difficulties. An increasing number, however, are now succeeding in meeting the needs of children whose particular learning difficulties are more complex – children who might once have attended special schools for children with moderate or severe learning difficulties.

Every child like this has unique needs; there is no single prescription that will work for all. Nevertheless, common features include:

- the need to have abstract concepts made concrete and real;
- the need for support in comprehending and using complex language – which may include the use of a signing system such as Makaton;

- the need for repetition and reinforcement of new learning;
- the need to have new learning broken down into small, manageable steps;
- the need to have specific practice in generalizing new learning from one situation to another;
- the need to have information presented in ways which hold the attention, as one would with any 'developmentally young' child;
- the need, at the same time, for appropriate self-esteem and dignity to be maintained through age-appropriate materials and social contacts – not, for example, keeping a child back to work in a year group several years younger or using books with illustrations and subject matter appropriate for a 4- or 5-year-old when a child is 10 or 11.

Getting the learning objectives right for these children will involve differentiated modelling and questioning within whole-class work, so as to address objectives (in literacy and maths, for example) which link to the shared class focus but come from earlier stages in the relevant teaching framework. Along with this there will need to be supplementary teaching, specifically targeted at the objectives for the particular child. There may be an increased emphasis, in the chosen objectives, on key skills communication, application of number, information technology, working with others, problem solving. There may also be an increased focus (QCA 2001b) on learning objectives relating to personal, social and daily living skills – like money, time, learning to read the words the child will need to respond to in the everyday environment.

Access strategies in the classroom will aim to increase the range of supports available to the child by providing various forms of scaffolding for the child's learning. The child may, for example, need to prepare for story writing by orally retelling a story, dramatic re-enactment, or sequencing a series of pictures or pages first. The child can use software where words are supported by picture symbols, or where a limited choice of words and/or pictures allow them to construct short pieces of writing by choosing particular items from the menu. In maths, real objects (like coins) will go on being needed when other children have moved on to abstract forms of representation.

Peer support offers another form of scaffolding. In one classroom, the teacher always arranges for the child with severe learning difficulties to do more complex tasks towards the end of the week, when they have learned from watching other groups tackle them and report back. In others, the teacher organizes a circle of friends to whom the child can go for help if they get stuck.

Children with Down's syndrome form a sub-group of those with complex learning difficulties, whose needs are increasingly (and with great success) being met in mainstream schools. A recent study (Buckley 2001), for example, found significantly greater academic achievement and expressive language skills in children with Down's syndrome who were educated in mainstream than in a matched comparison group who attended special schools.

Children with Down's syndrome commonly share a particular pattern of strengths and weaknesses, which needs to be taken into account when planning inclusive teaching strategies. Many have poor muscle tone and loose joints, causing difficulties in both fine and gross motor coordination. Sensitive approaches to practical lessons and PE, plus specific practice in motor skills will be needed, along with approaches which minimize written recording.

Speech articulation may also be affected: many children may still be reliant on a signing system such as Makaton; adults should always speak and sign simultaneously, and take care not to minimize language demands too much – finishing sentences for the child, for example, or asking questions that require only a yes/no answer. Instead, they should prompt more complex language by using forced choice ('Do you want to go on the computer first, or finish making your model?') and actively teaching the use of grammatical structures and new vocabulary.

Because many children with Down's syndrome are visual learners and have strengths in word reading, reading can be used as a tool to develop spoken language – practising reading sentence strips which have on them the connecting words like 'and', 'to', 'the', which they may miss out in speech, for example.

Reading needs to be taught visually, building up a sight vocabulary using a whole-word approach. Phonics may be difficult for these children, because of their difficulties in phonological awareness and the articulation of speech sounds; nevertheless, they should be given the opportunity to learn simple phoneme–grapheme correspondences, one step at a time and with plenty of practice.

Maths can be the most difficult area of all because of the complex and abstract language involved. Again, visual approaches work best – all the concrete representations of abstract operations suggested in the NNS framework, plus repeated teaching of the meaning of mathematical vocabulary, using a flashcard approach.

Because of difficulties in short-term memory, spoken instructions are hard for children with Down's syndrome to remember and act on. Visual prompts – like a planner showing the sequence of events in each day – are helpful. To improve memory skills, the child can also be taught to repeat back instructions out loud and then to rehearse them 'in their heads' as they get on with the task.

Complex needs: communication and interaction

In Chapter 9 we focused on the needs of children with speech and language difficulties – one aspect of special needs in communication and interaction. Here, we take a brief look at another, increasingly common, aspect of communication and interaction – children with autistic spectrum disorder (ASD).

ASD is an umbrella term for a number of disorders, of varying severity, that include autism and Asperger's syndrome. At one end of the spectrum children may have severe learning difficulties, virtually no social contacts, no speech and highly stereotyped, repetitive behaviour; at the other, children may have average or above average intelligence, speak fluently and show behaviours that appear to others no more than occasionally 'odd'. All manifestations of autism, however, share the same key characteristics:

- *Difficulties with social relationships.* Children with ASD find it hard to read the social signals that most of us take for granted – that tell us, for example, whether others want us to come near or stay away, talk or stop talking, fight or make friends. They lack basic awareness of how others are feeling; they cannot easily put themselves in another's place or understand how others are likely to respond.

- *Difficulties with communication*. Even if they learn to speak, these children will have difficulties in sustaining meaningful conversation. They may also fail to understand metaphor, sarcasm or hidden meanings in language – responding literally to the instruction, 'You'll have to pull up your socks', looking anxiously at the sky for falling objects if someone says 'It's raining cats and dogs', saying 'Yes' and putting the phone down if someone rings home and says 'Is your mother in?'
- *Difficulties with imagination*. Children with ASD may never play 'pretend' games, or be able to respond to narrative fiction; their thinking tends to be rigid and they often develop rituals, routines and obsessive topics for play or conversation.

If these impairments are not properly understood, the child with ASD can develop highly challenging behaviour, and make little progress in learning. Many of these secondary effects are, however, preventable if parents and teachers develop an understanding of the child's confused world, and are able to take simple steps to help them make sense of everyday life.

The teacher with an ASD child in the class must have access to a specialist who can advise on these simple steps. They might include:

- explaining metaphors, jokes and idiom;
- being precise with language – saying 'We are going outside now' not 'Shall we go outside?';
- providing visual timetables so the child can see, at any point in the day, exactly what is going to happen next;
- preparing the child carefully for any changes in routine;
- avoiding the unexpected – as an example, when asking questions during whole-class teaching, telling the child that they will have to answer questions number one and number five;
- using illustrated task cards in a consistent format to show the steps in the task and what to do when finished;
- avoiding open-ended work in favour of structures such as cloze procedure, multiple choice answers or use of writing frames;
- structuring play and lunchtimes with tasks like helping in the library or taking part in an organized club.

The child's peers will need a simple explanation of the nature of autism if they are to support them appropriately. Here the class teacher can help with a planned programme of personal and social education (Gross 1994) which promotes understanding and tolerance; thereafter, buddy systems and circles of friends can be as effective in ASD as they are for any of the other needs we have looked at in this chapter.

The future

In many countries, all children with SEN attend mainstream schools. In the UK, a number of LEAs are now close to this position. A steady stream of books (Booth *et al.* 1991; Thomas *et al.* 1998) has provided us with compelling examples of successful inclusive practice across the country.

In some ways, however, despite the inclusive thinking of central government, it appears to be becoming harder for schools to include children with difficulties. The competitive ethos engendered by league tables and the ever-present threat of a failed inspection if standards for the majority do not rise, understandably make some schools wary of taking on new demands.

In these circumstances, will it be possible in the future for schools to maintain a commitment to inclusion, and to the idea of neighbourhood schools that serve the *whole* of their local community? Will it be possible for governors, parents and staff to resist the pressures to up the school's test results by shipping out those who might lower the tone – still less ship in those who are already educated outside the mainstream system?

The answers remain to be seen. Schools can, however, feel justifiably confident that if they have effective systems for assessment, action planning and differentiation for the 18 per cent of their children who will, at some point in their school career, have some kind of SEN, then they will also be able to work effectively with the more severe, long-term and complex needs of a much smaller group of children.

They may also want to reflect on the evidence that schools can and do raise their test results while including more pupils with disabilities (Flack 1996). Every adaptation made to help one child access the curriculum will have spin-offs for half a dozen others who also have difficulties, of a lesser nature, in the same areas. Staff who work hard to make the curriculum more relevant for pupils with disabilities are likely in so doing to provide a stimulating curriculum for all.

They can, moreover, take comfort from the considerable evidence that their capacity to meet special needs of all kinds is a reliable indicator of the health of their organization as a whole. Schools that are good at knowing when their system is not working well for an individual child with difficulties in learning, and adjusting the system accordingly, are the same schools that can adapt their system to the needs of the very able, to those who are interested as well as those who seem uninterested, to those who are going through a spurt in learning and those who are going through a slower patch, and to those who can feel neglected because they are neither the best nor the worst.

It is schools like this that parents want for their children. Ultimately, they will choose schools where the teachers seem to know – and care – what makes their individual child tick, and get the best from them as a result, rather than those who work to some mythical idea of the norm.

Conclusion

This book has been about the ways in which schools can develop the responsiveness to individuality that parents value. It has been about teachers acquiring confidence in their own very real skills, and very real power to have an intimate and far-reaching positive effect on the achievement and self-worth of every child they teach.

The outcomes of such confidence will work for *all* children; meeting special needs and meeting ordinary needs do not, as we have seen, have to be mutually exclusive. But for the children at the margins of our society, the outcome of such confidence will be especially welcome. It means that they will meet teachers who do not have to pass them on to others, who do not have to feel anxious about their ability to cope with everyday problems of behaviour and learning.

And it means, perhaps, that all children with SEN can rely on meeting teachers who will say: 'The buck stops here, with me. And in this school, with the support I get, and the resources I can call on, I can do a good job for every single child in my class. I can do it. I know that I can'.

Resources and addresses

Chapter 3
Source materials for small steps within the national curriculum

Assessment for the National Literacy Framework, Learning Development Aids (LDA).
Profiles of Development – Avec Designs Ltd., PO Box 1384, Bristol BS 41 9DF.
SNIPP – Northumberland County Council Education Department, Psychological Services, Tyne House, Hepscott Park, Morpeth, Northumberland NE61 6NF.
Supporting the Target Setting Process, QCA, DfEE Publications.

Chapter 7

ACE (Advisory Centre for Education), Unit 1b Aberdeen Studios, 22–24 Highbury Grove, London N5 2EA.
GAMZ, 25 Albert Park Road, Malvern, Worcestershire, WR14 1HW.
Hodder Wayland, Hodder Children's Books, 338 Euston Road, London NW1 3BH.
Incentive Plus, PO Box 5220, Great Horwood, Milton Keynes, MK17 OYN.
Kirklees Psychology Service, Oastler Centre, 103 New Street, Huddersfield HD1 2UA.
Lucky Duck Publishing, 3 Thorndale Mews, Clifton, Bristol BS8 2HX.
Learning Materials Ltd, Dixon Street, Wolverhampton WV2 2BX.
LDA, Duke Street, Wisbech, Cambridgeshire PE13 2AE.
NASEN (National Association for Special Educational Needs), NASEN House, 4/5 Amber Business Village, Amber Close, Amington, Tamworth, Staffs B77 4RP.
Questions Publishing, Leonard House, 321 Bradford Street, Digbeth, Birmingham B5 6ET.
REM, Great Western House, Langport, Somerset TA10 9YU.
SEMERC, Granada Television, Quay Street, Manchester M60 9EA.
Sherston Software, Swan Barton, Sherston, Malmesbury, Wiltshire SN16 0LH.
Taskmaster Ltd, Morris Road, Leicester LE2 6BR.
Watts Publishing, 96 Leonard Street, London EC2 4RH.

Chapter 10

Acceleread AccerelWrite – iANSYST, The White House, 72 Fen Road, Cambridge CB4 1UN.
Mastering Memory – CALSC, PO Box 621, Sutton, Surrey SM1 22S.

Chapter 11

Alpha to Omega, available from LDA.

Direct Instruction Programmes, Science Research Associates, McGraw-Hill, Shoppenhangers Road, Maidenhead, Berkshire SL6 2LQ.

Multisensory Teaching System for Reading, Manchester Metropolitan University, Didsbury School of Education, 799 Wilmslow Road, Manchester M20 2RR.

NASEN Enterprises, NASEN House, 4/5 Amber Business Village, Amber Close, Amington, Tamworth, Staffs B77 4RP.

Phonographix, PO Box 52, Harpenden, Herts AL5 2ZX.

Quicktionary Pen, from iANSYST, The White House, 72 Fen Road, Cambridge CB4 1UN.

Software suppliers:

Granada/SEMERC, Quay Street, Manchester M60 9EA.

iANSYST, as above

Inclusive Technology, Saddleworth Business Centre, Delph, Oldham OL3 5DF.

REM, Great Western House, Langport, Somerset, TA10 9YU.

THRASS, available from Collins Educational.

Toe by Toe, Keda Cowling, 8 Green Lane, Baildon, West Yorkshire BD17 5HL.

Units of Sound, Dyslexia Institute, 133 Gresham Road, Staines, Middlesex TW18 2AJ.

Chapter 12

I Can Write, from Resource, 51 High Street, Kegworth, Derby DE74 2DA.

Mnemonic Spelling System, from Senter, FREEPOST NT2550, Whitley Bay NE26 1BR.

Spelling Made Easy, by Violet Brand, from Egon Publishers, Royston Road, Baldock, Herts SG7 6NW.

The Wizard's SpellingToolbox, from Barnstormer Publishing, Middle Barn, King's Lane, Gurney Slade, Somerset.

Teaching and Learning Spellings, from The Helen Arkell Dyslexia Centre, Frensham, Farnham, Surrey GU10 3BW.

Chapter 13

Spot On, by Ruth Rowley, available from the Staffordshire Special Educational Needs Support Service.

References

Aardema, V. (1997) *Bringing the Rain to Kapiti Plain*. London: Macmillan.

Adams, M. (1990) *Beginning to Read*. Boston, MA: MIT Press.

Ainscow, M. (1991) Effective schools for all: an alternative approach to special needs in education, in M. Ainscow (ed.) *Effective Schools For All*. London: David Fulton.

Aram, D. and Nation, J. (1980) Preschool language disorders and subsequent language and academic difficulties, *Journal of Communication Disorders*, 13.

Arora, T. and Bamford, J. (1989) *Paired Maths*. Kirklees: Kirklees Psychological Service.

Bale, K. (1999) Managing to cope: special needs in a large primary school, in J. Davies, P. Garner and J. Lee (eds) *Managing Special Needs in Mainstream Schools*. London: David Fulton.

Balshaw, M. (1999) *Help in the Classroom*. London: David Fulton.

Bennett, N. (1991) Cooperative learning in classrooms, *Journal of Child Psychology and Psychiatry*, 32, 4.

Bennett, N., Desforges, C., Cockburn, A. and Wilkinson, B. (1984) *The Quality of Pupil Learning Experiences*. London: Lawrence Erlbaum.

Berger, A. and Gross, J. (eds) (1999) *Teaching the Literacy Hour in an Inclusive Classroom*. London: David Fulton.

Blandford, B. and Lloyd, J. (1987) Effects of a self-instructional practice procedure on handwriting, *Journal of Learning Disabilities*, 20: 342–6.

Blatchford, P., Burke, J., Farquahar, C. *et al.* (1989) Teacher expectations in the infant school, *British Journal of Educational Psychology*, 59: 1.

Bonathan, M., Edwards, G. and Leadbetter, J. (2000) *Success for Everyone*. Birmingham: Birmingham City Council.

Booth, T., Swann, S., Masterton, M. and Potts, P. (eds) (1991) *Curricula for Diversity in Education*. London: Routledge.

Booth, T., Ainscow, M., Black-Hawkins, K., Vaughan, M. and Shaw, L. (2000) *Index for Inclusion*. Bristol: Centre for Studies in Inclusive Education.

Bowers, T., Dee, L. and West, M. (1998) The Code in action, *Support for Learning*, 13(3): 99–105.

Bristol City Council (2000) *The Bristol Early Years Screening Schedule for EBD*. Bristol: Bristol City Council.

British Psychological Society (1999) *Dyslexia, Literacy and Psychological Assessment*. Leicester: British Psychological Society.

Brooks, G. (1998) *What Works for Slow Readers*. Slough: NFER.

Brooks, P. and Weeks, S. (1999) *Individual Styles in Learning to Read and to Spell*. London: DfEE publications.

Brown, C., Topping, K., Henington, C. and Skinner, C. (1999) Peer monitoring of learning behaviour, *Educational Psychology in Practice*, 15(3).

Brown, E., Frederickson, N., Iyadurai, S., Jackson, M. and Kynan, S. (1998) Differences between children with specific learning difficulties (SpLD) and moderate learning difficulties, *Education and Child Psychology*, 15(4): 18–33.

Bryant, P. and Bradley, L. (1985) *Children's Reading Difficulties*. Oxford: Blackwell.

Buckley, S. (2001) *The Education of Individuals with Down's Syndrome: a Review of Educational Provision and Outcomes in the UK*. Portsmouth: The Down's Syndrome Educational Trust.

Byron, D. (1991) Direct instruction in Avon's schools, *Direct Instruction Scene*, September.

Canter, L. and Canter, M. (1976) *Assertive Discipline*. Santa Monica, CA: Lee Canter Associates.

Charlton, T. (1998) Enhancing school effectiveness through using peer support, *Support for Learning*, 13(2).

Clark, A. and Warlberg, H. (1968) The influence of massive rewards on reading achievement in potential school dropouts, *American Educational Research Journal*, 5(3).

Clay, M. (1979) *Reading: The Patterning of Complex Behaviour*. London: Heinemann.

Clement, M. (1980) Analysing children's errors on written mathematical tasks, *Educational Studies in Mathematics*, 11(1).

Cockcroft, W. (1982) *Mathematics Counts: Report of the Committee of Enquiry into the Teaching of Mathematics*. London: HMSO.

Cook, J. and Cook, R. (1999) *Reading and Spelling Progress Charts*. Lyminster: Lyminster Publications.

Craig, F. (1990) *The Natural Way to Learn: The Apprenticeship Approach to Literacy*. Worcester: The Self Publishing Association.

Croll, P. and Moses, D. (1985) *One in Five*. London: Routledge.

Croll, P. and Moses, M. (2000) Resources, Policies and Educational Practice, in B. Norwich (ed.) *Developments in Additional Resource Allocation to Promote Inclusion*. Tamworth: NASEN.

Crowther, D., Dyson, A., Elliott, J. and Millward, A. (1999) *Costs and Outcomes for Pupils with MLD in Special and Mainstream Schools*. London: DfEE.

Dalton, J. (1997) Dalton's diary, *Times Educational Supplement*, 7 March.

Davidson, P. (1988) Word processing and children with specific learning difficulties, *Support for Learning*, 3(4).

DES (Department of Education and Science) (1981) *Education Act*. London: HMSO.

DfE (Department for Education) (1994) Circular No. 6/94: *The Organization of Special Educational Provision*. London: DfE.

DfEE (Department for Education and Employment) (1996) *Education Act*. London: HMSO.

DfEE (Department for Education and Employment) (1998) *Meeting Special Educational Needs: A Programme of Action*. London: DfEE.

DfEE (Department for Education and Employment) (1999) *English: The National Curriculum for England*. London: DfEE.

DfEE (Department for Education and Employment) (2000) *Working with Teaching Assistants*. London: DfEE.

DfEE (Department for Education and Employment) (2001) *Special Educational Needs in Schools 2001 – Provisional Statistics*. London: DfEE.

DfES (Department for Education and Skills) (2001a) *Special Educational Needs and Disability Act*. London: HMSO.

DfES (Department for Education and Skills) (2001b) *Special Educational Needs Code of Practice*. London: HMSO.

DoH (Department of Health) (1989) *The Children Act*. London: HMSO.

Dring, J. (1989) The impact of a tape-cassette library on reading progress, *Special Children*, November.

Dudley-Marling, C., Snider, V. and Tarver, S. (1982) Locus of control and learning disabilities: a review of research, *Perceptual and Motor Skills*, 54.

Evans, G. (1992) *Child Protection: A Whole Curriculum Approach*. Bristol: Avec Designs.

Faupel, A., Herrick, E. and Sharpe, P. (1998) *Anger Management: A Practical Guide*. London: David Fulton.

Feiler, A. and Webster, A. (1998) Success and failure in early literacy: teachers' predictions and subsequent intervention, *British Journal of Special Education*, 25(4): 189–95.

Flack, M. (1996) The usual suspects, *Special Children*, 97: 11–13.

Fox, G. (1999) *A Handbook for Learning Support Assistants*. London: David Fulton.

Fry, E. (1972) *Reading Instruction in Classroom and Clinic*. New York: McGraw-Hill.

Galton, M., Simon, B. and Croll, P. (1980) *Inside the Primary Classroom*. London: Routledge.

Gathercole, S. and Pickering, S. (2001) Working memory deficits in children with special educational needs, *British Journal of Special Education*, 28(2).

Goleman, D. (1996) *Emotional Intelligence*. London: Bloomsbury.

Good, T. and Brophy, J. (1977) *Educational Psychology: A Realistic Approach*. London: Holt, Rinehart & Winston.

Goodman, R. (1997) The strengths and difficulties questionnaire: a research note, *Journal of Child Psychology and Psychiatry*, 38.

Gordon, T. (1974) *Teacher Effectiveness Training*. New York: David McKay.

Goswami, U. and Bryant, P. (1990) *Phonological Skills and Learning to Read*. London: Lawrence Erlbaum.

Gross, J. (1994) Asperger syndrome: a label worth having, *Educational Psychology in Practice*, 10(2): 104–10.

Gross, J. (1996) Working with parents, *Special Children*, 93.

Gross, J. (2000) Paper promises? Making the Code work for you, *Support for Learning*, 15, 3.

Gross, J., George, J. and Hunt, M. (2000) *The National Literacy Strategy Framework: A Special Needs Resource Pack*. Wisbech: LDA.

Gubbay, S. (1975) *The Clumsy Child – A Study of Developmental Apraxic and Agnosic Ataxia*. London: W. B. Saunders.

Gurney, P. (1988) *Self Esteem in Children with Special Educational Needs*. London: Routledge.

Hanson, D. (1991) Assessment: the window on learning, in *Differentiating the Secondary Curriculum*. Trowbridge: Wiltshire County Council.

Haring, N., Lovitt, T., Eaton, M. and Hansen, C. (1978) *The Fourth R: Research in the Classroom*. Columbus, OH: Merrill.

Harrison, P. (1989) Numbers game, *Times Educational Supplement*, 17 February.

Haylock, D. (1991) *Teaching Mathematics to Low Attainers 8–12*. London: Paul Chapman Publishing.

Henderson, A. (1989) Multisensory maths, *Special Children*, 34.

Henderson, S. and Hall, D. (1982) Concomitants of clumsiness in young schoolchildren, *Developmental Medicine and Child Neurology*, 24.

Hersov, L. and Berger, M. (1980) *Language and Language Disorders in Childhood*. Oxford: Pergamon Press.

Hickey, K. (1992) *The Hickey Multisensory Language Course*, 2nd edn. London, Whurr Publishers.

HMI (Her Majesty's Inspectorate of Schools) (1990) *Education Observed: Special Needs Issues*. London: HMSO.

Horner, E. (1990) Working with peers, *Special Children*, November.

Hornsby, B. and Farrer, M. (1990) Some effects of a dyslexia-centred teaching programme, in P. Pumfrey and C. Elliott (eds) *Children's Difficulties in Reading, Spelling and Writing*. Basingstoke: Falmer Press.

Hughes, M. (1986) *Children and Number: Difficulties in Learning Mathematics*. Oxford: Basil Blackwell.

Hunt, M. and George, J. (1999) Developing your own structured programme, in A. Berger and J. Gross (eds) *Teaching the Literacy Hour in an Inclusive Classroom*. London: David Fulton.

Hurry, J. (2000) *Intervention Strategies to Support Pupils with Difficulties in Key Stage 1*. London: QCA.

Ireson, J., Evans, P., Redmond, P. and Wedell, K. (1989) *Pathways to Progress*. London: University of London Institute of Education.

James, J., Charlton, T., Leo, E. and Indoe, D. (1991) A peer to listen, *Support for Learning*, 6(4).

Jewell, T. (1986) Involving parents and teachers in individual education programmes, *Educational Psychology in Practice*, July.

Joffe, L. (1981) Quoted in *Mathematical Difficulties and Dyslexia*. Reading: British Dyslexia Association.

Johnson, D. and Johnson, R. (1987) *Learning Together and Alone: Cooperation, Competition and Individualisation*, 2nd edn. New Jersey: Prentice Hall.

Joyce, B., Murphy, C., Showers, B. and Murphy, J. (1991) School renewal as cultural change, in M. Ainscow (ed.) *Effective Schools For All*. London: David Fulton.

Juel, C. (1988) Learning to read and write: a longitudinal study of fifty-four children from first through fourth grade, *Journal of Educational Psychology*, 80: 437–47.

Kavale, K. and Forness, S. (1985) *The Science of Learning Disabilities*. Windsor: NFER.

Keogh, B. (1982) Children's temperament and teachers' decisions, in CIBA Foundation Symposium 89, *Temperamental Differences in Infants and Young Children*. London: Pitman.

Klein, R. (2000) *Defying Disaffection*. London: Trentham Books.

Krutetskii, V. (1976) *The Psychology of Mathematical Ability in School Children*. Chicago: University of Chicago.

Lawrence, D. (1973) *Improved Reading through Counselling*. London: Ward Lock.

Lawrence, D. (1988) *Enhancing Self Esteem in the Classroom*. London: Paul Chapman Publishing.

Layton, L., Deeny, K. and Upton, G. (1997) *Sound Practice – Phonological Awareness in the Classroom*. London: David Fulton.

Leeves, I. (1990) Now hear this, *Special Children*, April.

Levin, H. and Glass, G. (1986) The political arithmetic of cost-benefit analysis, *Phi Delta Kappa*, 68(1).

Lewis, A. (1995) *Primary Special Needs and the National Curriculum*. London: Routledge.

Lewis, A. (1999) Integrated learning systems and pupils with low attainments in reading, *British Journal of Special Education*, 26(3).

Lewis, A. and Norwich, B. (2000) Mapping a SEN pedagogy. Monograph, University of Exeter, University of Warwick.

Lewis, M., Wray, D. and Rospigliosi, P. (1994) Making reading for information more accessible for children with learning difficulties, *Support for Learning*, 9(4).

Limbrick, E., McNaughton, S. and Glynn, T. (1985) Reading gains for underachieving tutors and tutees in a cross-age tutoring programme, *Journal of Child Psychology and Psychiatry*, 26(6).

Long, M. (1988) Goodbye behaviour units, hello support services: home–school support for pupils with behaviour difficulties in mainstream schools, *Educational Psychology in Practice*, 4(1).

Long, R. (2000) *Developing Self Esteem through Positive Entrapment for Pupils with EBD*. Tamworth: NASEN.

Lorenz, S. (1999) *Effective In-class Support*. London: David Fulton.

Losse, A., Henderson, S., Elliman, D. *et al.* (1991) Clumsiness in children – do they grow out of it? *Developmental Medicine and Child Neurology*, 33.

Lunzer, E. and Gardner, K. (eds) (1979) *The Effective Use of Reading*. London: Heinemann.

Maher, C. (1984) Handicapped adolescents as cross-age tutors, *Exceptional Children*, 51(1).

Maines, B. and Robinson, G. (1989a) *Bag of Tricks*. Bristol: Lame Duck Publishing.

Maines, B. and Robinson, G. (1989b) *B/G Steem: A Self Esteem Scale*. Bristol: Lame Duck Publishing.

McNamara, S. and Moreton, G. (1997) *Understanding Differentiation*. London: David Fulton.

McPake, J., Harlen, W., Powney, J. and Davidson, J. (1999) *Teachers' and Pupils' Days in the Primary Classroom*. Edinburgh: Scottish Council for Research in Education.

MENCAP (1999) *On a Wing and a Prayer*. London: MENCAP.

Merrett, F. and Wheldall, K. (1987) Natural rates of teacher approval and disapproval in British primary and middle school classrooms, *British Journal of Educational Psychology*, 57.

Merrett, J. and Merrett, F. (1992) Classroom management for project work: an application of correspondence training, *Educational Studies*, 18(1).

Miller, A., Jewell, T., Booth, S. and Robson, D. (1985) Delivering educational programmes to slow learners, *Educational Psychology in Practice*, 1(3).

Montgomery, D. (1990) *Children with Learning Difficulties*. London: Cassell.

Moran, H., Smith, K., Meads, J. and Beck, M. (1996) Let's try that word again in a new way, *British Journal of Special Education*, 23(4).

Moses, D. (1982) Special educational needs: the relationship between teacher assessment, test scores and classroom behaviour, *British Educational Research Journal*, 8(2).

Mosley, J. (1992) Value added pacts, *Special Children*, March.

Mosley, J. (1993) *Turn Your School Around*. Wisbech: LDA.

Moss, G. (1992) The right to teach, *Special Children*, 58.

NCC (National Curriculum Council) (1989) *A Curriculum For All*. York: NCC.

Newton, C. and Wilson, D. (1996) Circles of friends, *Educational Psychology in Practice*, 11(4).

NLS (National Literacy Strategy) (2000) *Supporting Pupils with Special Educational Needs in the Literacy Hour*. London: DfEE.

Norman, K. (1990) *Teaching, Talking and Learning*. York: NCC.

Ofsted (1997) *The Implementation of the Code of Practice for Pupils with Special Educational Needs*. London: Ofsted.

Ofsted (1999) *The SEN Code of Practice: Three Years On*. London: Ofsted.

Ofsted (2000) *Inspecting subjects 3–11: Guidance for Inspectors and Schools*. London: Ofsted.

Ofsted (2001) *Evaluating Educational Inclusion*. London: Ofsted.

Oxley, L. and Topping, K. (1988) Cued spelling, in K. Topping, J. Scoble and L. Oxley (eds) *The Cued Spelling Training Pack*. Huddersfield: Kirklees Paired Reading Project.

Pasternicki, J. (1986) Teaching handwriting: the resolution of an issue, *Support for Learning*, 1: 37–41.

Pearsall, E. and Wollen, E. (1991) *Differentiating the Secondary Curriculum – DARTS: Directed Activities Related to Text*. Trowbridge: Wiltshire County Council.

Pearson, S. (2000) The relationship between school culture and IEPs, *British Journal of Special Education*, 27(3).

Phillips, D. (1989) Teachers' attitudes to pupils with learning difficulties, in A. Ramasut (ed.) *Whole School Approaches to Special Needs*. Lewes: Falmer Press.

Portwood, M. (1999) *Developmental Dyspraxia: A Manual for Parents and Teachers*. London: David Fulton.

QCA (Qualifications and Curriculum Authority) (2001a) *Supporting the Target Setting Process*. London: DfEE.

QCA (Qualifications and Curriculum Authority) (2001b) *Planning, Teaching and Assessing the Curriculum for Pupils with Learning Difficulties*. London: DfEE.

Rathbone (2001) *Could Do Better*. Manchester: Rathbone.

Reason, R. and Boote, R. (1995) *Helping Children with Reading and Writing*. London: Routledge.

Reeves, G. and Berger, A. (1999) Reviewing your policy, in *SEN Coordinators' File*. London: pfp publishing.

Rieser, R. and Mason, M. (eds) (1990) *Disability Equality in the Classroom*. London: ILEA (now published by Disability Equality in Education).

Robinson, G. and Maines, B. (1997) *Crying for Help: The No-Blame Approach to Bullying*. Bristol: Lucky Duck.

Safran, S. and Safran, J. (1985) Classroom context and teachers' perceptions of problem behaviours, *Journal of Educational Psychology*, 77(1).

Sawyer, C. and Knight, E. (1991) A fast method for calculating text readability levels, *Support for Learning*, 6(2).

Sebba, J. and Sachdev, D. (1997) *What Works in Inclusive Education*. Ilford: Barnardo's.

Share, D. (1995) Phonological recoding and self teaching, *Cognition*, 55: 151–218.

Shaw, L. (1990) *Each Belongs: Integrated Education in Canada*. London: Centre for Studies on Integration in Education.

Shaw, L. (2001) *Learning Supporters and Inclusion*. Bristol: Centre for Studies on Inclusive Education.

Sheridan, M. and Peckham, C. (1975) Follow up at 11 years of children who had marked speech defects at 7 years, *Child Care and Health Development*, 113.

Slavin, R.E. (1996) *Education for All*. Lisse: Swets & Zeitlinger.

Snowling, M., Bishop, D. and Stothard, S. (2000) Is pre-school language impairment a risk factor for dyslexia in adolescence? *Journal of Child Psychology and Psychiatry*, 41(5): 587–600.

Solity, J.E. (1991) Special needs: a discriminatory concept? *Educational Psychology in Practice*, 7(1): 12–19.

Solity, J.E., Deavers, R., Kerfoot, S., Crane, G. and Cannon, K. (2000) The early reading research: the impact of instructional psychology, *Educational Psychology In Practice*, 16(2).

Somerville, D. and Leach, D. (1988) Direct or indirect instruction? An evaluation of three types of intervention programmes for assisting students with specific reading difficulties, *Educational Research*, 30(1).

Stacey, H. and Robinson, P. (1997) *Let's Mediate*. Bristol: Lucky Duck.

Swing, S. and Peterson, P. (1982) The relationship of student ability and small group interaction to student achievement, *American Educational Research Journal*, 19(2).

Teacher Training Agency (1999) *National Special Educational Needs Specialist Standards*. London: TTA.

Thacker, J. (1983) *Steps to Success*. Windsor: NFER.

Thomas, G. (1992) *Effective Classroom Teamwork*. London: Routledge.

Thomas, G. and Tarr, J. (1996) *The Monitoring and Evaluation of Schools' SEN Policies: A Report of a Research Project Conducted for the DfEE*. London: DfEE.

Thomas, G., Walker, D. and Webb, J. (1998) *The Making of the Inclusive School*. London: Routledge.

Thompson, P. (1992) Raising reading standards: the reader-leader scheme, *Support for Learning*, 7(2).

Thomson, M. (1989) Evaluating teaching programmes for children with specific learning difficulties, in P. Pumfrey and C. Elliott (eds) *Children's Difficulties in Reading, Spelling and Writing*. Basingstoke: Falmer Press.

Thomson, M. (1991) The teaching of spelling using techniques of simultaneous oral spelling and visual inspection, in M. Snowling and M. Thomson (eds) *Dyslexia: Integrating Theory and Practice*. London: Whurr Publishers.

Topping, K. (1987) Children as teachers, *Special Children*, October.

Topping, K. and Ehly, S. (1998) *Peer Assisted Learning*. London: Lawrence Erlbaum.

Topping, K. and Lindsay, G. (1992) Paired reading: a review of the literature, *Research Papers in Education*, 7(3).

Topping, K. and Wolfendale, S. (eds) (1985) *Parental Involvement in Children's Reading*. London: Croom Helm.

Veit, D., Scruggs, T. and Mastropieri, M. (1986) Extended mnemonic instruction with learning disabled students, *Journal of Educational Psychology*, 78(4).

Ward, B. and Houghton, J. (1991) *Good Grief 2*. Salford: TACADE.

Waterhouse, P. (1990) *Classroom Management*. London: Network Educational Press.

Wells, G. (1981) *Learning through Interaction*. Cambridge: Cambridge University Press.

Westmacott, E. and Cameron, R. (1981) *Behaviour Can Change*. London: Globe Education.

Westwood, P. (1982) Strategies for improving social interaction of handicapped children in regular classes, *Australian Journal of Remedial Education*, 16(1).

Wheldall, K. (1988) The forgotten A in behaviour analysis: the importance of ecological variables in classroom management, with particular reference to seating arrangements, in G. Thomas and A. Feiler (eds) *Planning for Special Needs*. Oxford: Blackwell.

Wheldall, K. and Merrett, F. (1984) *Positive Teaching: The Behavioural Approach*. London: Unwin Education.

Womack, D. (1988) *Special Needs in Ordinary Schools: Developing Mathematical and Scientific Thinking in Young Children*. London: Cassell.

Wood, D. (1986) *Teaching and Talking with Deaf Children*. London: John Wiley & Sons.

Wooster, A. and Leech, N. (1982) Improving reading and self-concept through communication and social skills training, *British Journal of Guidance and Counselling*, 10(1).

Wragg, E., Bennett, S. and Carre, C. (1989) Primary teachers and the National Curriculum, *Research Papers in Education*, 4: 17–46.

Young, P. and Tyre, C. (1983) *Dyslexia or Illiteracy? Realizing the Right to Read*. Milton Keynes: Open University Press.

Zigler, E. and Hodapp, R. (1986) *Understanding Mental Retardation*. Cambridge: Cambridge University Press.

Author index

Subject index

schemes of work, 108
school
 inclusion and performance of, 243–4
 management, 17
 role and responsibilities, 10–11
 screening checklist for identification
  of special needs, 54–5, 56
 whole-school policies, *see* whole-
  school policies
School Action, 8
School Action Plus, 8
school governors, 9–10
school improvement programmes, 3–4
school inspection, 14–15
school refusal, 142
science, 110–11
screening instruments, 53–4
seating in classroom, 133
segmentation, 176
self-assessment, 66–7, 199–200
self-confidence, 55
self-esteem, 29, 30, 67, 91
 and behaviour, 120
 building, 145–51
 exploring child's self-concept, 59,
  60
 and reading, 183–5
self-monitoring, 125, 126, 132
SENCO, 8–9, 69
sensory impairment, 238–9
 see also hearing impairment; visual
  impairment
sentence sequencing worksheet, 208
sequencing, 175, 214–15
short-term memory problems, 130–1,
 167–8, 214–15
'Show Me', 223
sight vocabulary, 174, 175
simultaneous oral spelling, 195
small steps, 36–9
 anxiety, 141–2
 assessment and, 56, 58, 61–2, 66,
  156–8, 174–5
social control, 55
social difficulties, 74, 75
social interaction, *see* relationships
social model of disability, 4, 5
software, 112, 183, 196, 206, 222
spatial difficulties, 200–3, 217–20
special educational needs, 2–6
 assessment, *see* assessment
 Code of Practice, 8, 10, 13, 65, 71, 93
 identification, 22, 52–4, 154–8
Special Educational Needs and Disability
 Act, 14

Special Educational Needs and Disability
 Tribunal, 12
Special Needs Individualized Programme
 Planning (SNIPP), 39
special needs summary card, 81, 82–3
special schools, 232, 233
 support services, 106–7
specialist consultancy support, 236–7,
 238
specific learning difficulties/dyslexia, 53,
 180, 185
 indicators, 185, 186
 and maths, 213–15
speech, 152–71
 children with Down's syndrome, 242
 difficulties, 163–4
 expressive language, 159–62
 identification and assessment of
  special needs, 154–8
 reluctance to talk, 162–3
 see also oracy
speech and language therapist, 164
spellcheckers, 205, 206
spelling, 97, 194–7
 materials in resource base, 109–10
St Agnes Primary School, 166
staff questionnaire, 28
staffing, 23
standardized tests, 58, 65, 213
Statements, 11, 12–13
 review, 79, 80
step-parents, 141
stigmatization, 234–5
storytelling, 161–2
strategies
 action planning, 74–5, 76–7, 78
 behaviour, 120–1
structured multisensory approaches, 65,
 181, 197
structuring written work, 209–11
study skills, 54–5, 110
subjective teacher assessments, 53
subtraction, 225–7
success/exit criteria, 81
support, 69, 84–113
 ICT, 111–12
 in-class vs withdrawal, 104–5
 levels of, 84, 85
 outside agencies, 106–7
 parental involvement, 93–9
 peer tutoring, 91–3, 146, 196
 resource base, 107–11
 small amounts of teaching time,
  86–91
 teaching assistants, 100–2

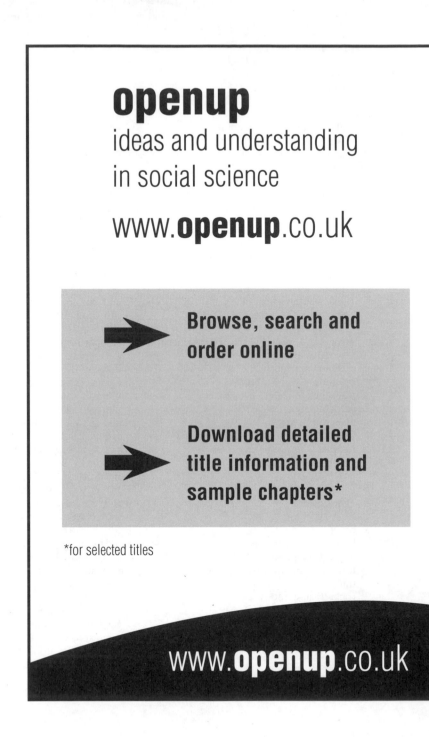